PURE SOLDIERS

OR

SINISTER LEGION

SOL
LITTMAN

PURE SOLDIERS

OR

SINISTER LEGION

THE UKRAINIAN
14TH WAFFEN-SS DIVISION

BLACK
ROSE
BOOKS

MONTRÉAL/NEW YORK/LONDON

Black Rose Books No. GG319

National Library of Canada Cataloguing in Publication Data
Littman, Sol, 1920-
Pure soldiers or sinister legion : the Ukrainian 14th Waffen-SS Division / Sol Littman
Includes bibliographical references and index.
Hardcover ISBN: 1-55164-219-0 (bound) Paperback ISBN: 1-55164-218-2 (pbk.)

1. Waffen-SS. Grenadier-Division, 14--History. 2. Ukraïns'ka natsional'na armiia.
Ukraïns'ka dyviziia "Halychyna"--History. 3. World War, 1939-1945--Regimental
histories--Germany. 4. World War, 1939-1945--Regimental histories--Ukraine.
5. World War, 1939-1945--Campaigns--Eastern Front. I. Title.

D757.85.L58 2003   940.54'1343   C2002-904813-3

*We wish to thank the State Archives in Kiev for providing photographs from captured German
newsreels. Every effort has been made to secure permission for materials reproduced herein.*

Cover design: Associés libres

BLACK ROSE BOOKS

C.P. 1258	2250 Military Road	99 Wallis Road
Succ. Place du Parc	Tonawanda, NY	London, E9 5LN
Montréal, H2X 4A7	14150	England
Canada	USA	UK

To order books:

In Canada: (phone) 1-800-565-9523 (fax) 1-800-221-9985
email: utpbooks@utpress.utoronto.ca

In United States: (phone) 1-800-283-3572 (fax) 1-651-917-6406

In the UK & Europe: (phone) London 44 (0)20 8986-4854 (fax) 44 (0)20 8533-5821
email: order@centralbooks.com

Our Web Site address: http://www.web.net/blackrosebooks

A publication of the Institute of Policy Alternatives of Montréal (IPAM)

Printed in Canada

The Canada Council | Le Conseil des Arts
for the Arts | du Canada

CONTENTS

dedicated to

the 40,000 Canadians of Ukrainian descent who served in the ranks of Canada's armed forces in World War II

the 4.5 million Ukrainians who served in the Red Army

the 1.4 million Ukrainian prisoners-of-war that perished in brutal Nazi prison camps

the 7 million inhabitants of Ukraine deliberately massacred by the Nazis during the Second World War

the 20 million Soviet citizens overall who died of hunger, cold, and sickness as a result of Nazi brutality

ACKNOWLEDGMENTS

SOME YEARS AGO, WHILE ATTENDING A UKRAINIAN/JEWISH CONFERENCE at McMaster University, I mentioned to Professor Michael Marrus of the University of Toronto that my interest had been piqued by documents in Canada's National Archives indicating that some two thousand members of a Ukrainian military unit that had fought on the German side had succeeded in gaining entry to Canada in the early 1950s. "Do you know of anyone doing work on this specific topic?" I asked Marrus. He replied that he knew of no one currently researching this topic and suggested that I undertake it. My first expression of thanks must, therefore, go to Professor Marrus for launching me on this task.

My second goes to English journalist Tom Bower, author of a series of incisive books and television documentaries such as *Blind Eye to Murder*, based largely on archival documents. I wish to thank him for his generosity in sharing research sources along with the beer and sandwiches we consumed in his London kitchen.

Next, I must acknowledge the advice and inspiration offered by British historian and social activist, Dr. Gerald Fleming, Emeritus Reader in German at the University of Surrey and author of the decisive work on the "Hitler Order," *Hitler and the Final Solution*.

My acquaintance with the late Lord Thomas Brimelow was one of those fortunate coincidences that sometimes happen in the course of a tough research project. A United Kingdom Labour peer who was active in the Refugee Division of the Northern Department* during the period in which the Foreign Office was debating the fate of the Ukrainian Waffen-SS Division, Brimelow wrote lengthy letters to me and provided me with archival documents from his own files. His familiarity with the major actors in the Foreign Office in the years between 1945 and 1950 was invaluable.

I was also fortunate to encounter American historian Bradley F. Smith, author of *Reaching Judgment at Nuremberg*, in the cafeteria of the London Public Record Office. Smith, who devoted himself to research in the intelligence field in recent years, showed an immediate interest. He scoffed at the idea that members of the Ukrainian Waffen-SS had been screened prior to their arrival in Canada. He pointed out that by 1950, Britain had no staff and no instrument capable of screening such a large body of men.

I thank the numerous curators of the State Archives in Kiev and Lviv, Yad Vashem in Jerusalem, the London Public Record Office, the Imperial War Museum, the Wiener Library, the Polish Library in London, the National Archives in Washington, D.C., and the

---

* The Foreign Office List for 1947 describes the Northern Department as having responsibility for Czechoslovakia, Denmark, Estonia, Finland, Iceland, Latvia, Lithuania, Norway, Poland, the Soviet Union and Sweden.

Archives of the Canadian Jewish Congress for their unstinting assistance. I must add a special word of thanks to archivist Rodney Young of the National Archives of Canada for his patience in leading me through the labyrinth of Immigration Department files.

Myron Momryk, curator of Social and Cultural Archives at the National Archives in Ottawa, has repeatedly gone well beyond the call of duty in acquainting me with significant files. On all occasions he and his colleague, Lawrence Tapper, have demonstrated the highest degree of professionalism.

The late Sybil Milton, formerly of the U.S. National Holocaust Memorial Museum in Washington, D.C. shared her encyclopedic knowledge of archival sources with me and was gracious enough to review my translation of Himmler's speech to the officers of the Ukrainian Division.

John Loftus and Mark Aarons, authors of numerous books exploring crucial sidebars to World War II history, were generous in sharing their vast knowledge of previously secret material stored in American archives. I am especially grateful to them for providing me with a copy of Friedrich Buchardt's little known but invaluable "The Treatment of the Russian Problem During the Time of the National-Socialist Regime in Germany."

Shulamit Zhabinskaya, the Vilnius-born, Yiddish, Russian, and Polish-speaking librarian at Montreal's Jewish Public Library has been enormously helpful in suggesting Yiddish sources and translating several Russian and Polish documents I brought back from Vilnius and Lviv. Similarly, Alexander Schnerer, a former resident of Kiev, has cheerfully lent his services as a translator of Ukrainian materials. Oscar and Danuka Abene were kind enough to translate a batch of Polish documents and Lotta Borister assisted me with the text of several key paragraphs of an academic German volume.

On my visits to Lviv I was assisted by several people who, given the changing circumstances in Ukraine, prefer that I not mention them by name. I thank them, nevertheless, for their help in translating and explaining numerous documents, chiefly copies of Ukrainian newspapers published during the German occupation.

I also owe a debt of gratitude to two Polish scholars, Professor Tadeusz Piotrowski of the University of New Hampshire, author of *Poland's Holocaust,* and Professor Wiktor Poliszczuk, author of an important monograph, *Legal and Political Assessment of the OUN and UPA,* who have shared their work with me.

My deepest thanks also to Professors John Crow and John Garard of the University of Arizona and Professor Shmuel Spector of Yad Vashem for their helpful criticism and advice. And finally, I wish to express my heartfelt thanks to Rabbis Marvin Hier and Abraham Cooper of the Simon Wiesenthal Center in Los Angeles for their support over the many years we worked together.

INTRODUCTION

BETWEEN 1950 AND 1955, SOME TWO THOUSAND VETERANS of a notorious German-led, Ukrainian Waffen-SS Division took ship from English ports to take up residence in Canada. They departed from Liverpool and Southampton on immigrant ships named *Asconia, Columbia, Neptunia* and *Scythia*. On the ship's passenger lists, some claimed to be Polish citizens, others claimed to be stateless, but the majority described themselves unequivocally as Ukrainians.

The Division, was informally known as the "Halychyna Division," the "Galician Division" and the "Ukrainian Division." However, its official designation, applied when the military formation was first formed in the spring of 1943, was the *14. Freiwilligen- Grenadier Division der SS (galizische Nr. 1)*. In the two years of active service that followed, the Division's name underwent several changes, finally emerging as the First Ukrainian Division of the Ukrainian Army.

Those unfamiliar with the Ukrainian Division's history are bound to wonder how it happened that a military formation that had fought hard on the German side, was granted shelter in England after the war, and how it happened that three years later the bulk of its 16,000 members managed to emigrate to Canada, the United States, Argentina, Australia and New Zealand. They might also wonder how it happened that those who debarked in Halifax, Quebec and Montreal came with the full consent of the Canadian government despite immigration regulations in force at the time that forbade entry to all who served in any branch of the SS, including the Waffen-SS.[1]

The arrival of the Ukrainian Waffen-SS veterans precipitated an acrimonious dispute that has continued to the present day, resulting in numerous articles, several books,[2] a recent television documentary,[3] and web sites. While their advent was a cause for celebration by a sizeable segment of the Ukrainian-Canadian community, it was a cause for despair for a smaller, left-wing, pro-Soviet faction that bitterly opposed their admission.[4]

Another sizeable portion of the Canadian-Ukrainian community, consisting largely of its earliest, most fully assimilated settlers in Canada was cautious in its acceptance of these latest immigrants. In particular, the pioneer settlers feared that the newcomer's radical nationalist ideology might upset established relationships within the community and harm the community's hard-won acceptance by the Canadian government. Ukrainian-Canadian leadership worked hard during the war years to persuade their fellow Canadians of their undivided support of the Allied war effort. The post-war introduction of Ukrainian Displaced Persons (DPs) who had collaborated with the enemy in one way or another threatened to bring down the house of cards, especially if the new arrivals openly espoused totalitarian ideas.

Paul Robert Magocsi, who occupies the Chair of Ukrainian Studies at the University of Toronto, distinguishes between "two kinds of Ukrainian-Canadians," those who see themselves as Canadians of Ukrainian background and those who regard themselves as Ukrainians first and foremost, who happen to be living in Canada.[5] The presence of two thousand Ukrainian Waffen-SS veterans swelled the ranks of those who saw themselves as Ukrainians currently living in Canada and increased the uneasiness of those who regarded themselves as Canadians of Ukrainian background.[6]

Canada's Jewish community was extremely exorcised over the admission of the Halychyna Division veterans. Its central organization, the Canadian Jewish Congress (CJC) fought a brief but futile battle to persuade the Canadian government to deny entry.

At issue was the nature of the Division and its war record. Were they "pure soldiers" as many of their supporters contend or were they, to use Goldhagen's phrase, among Hitler's willing executioners?[7] Elements of the British press referred to the Division as a "sinister legion" and called its members "monsters." Polish historians characterized them as "bloody cutthroats" and the Soviet delegate to the newly-formed United Nations denounced them as traitors and demanded their return to the Soviet Union. The Division was reputed to be riddled with war criminals who had engaged in the mass murder of thousands of innocent civilians.

On the other hand, a well-organized body of Division supporters continued to insist there was nothing "monster-like" or "cutthroat" about the young men who had volunteered to serve in its ranks. They declared them exceptional soldiers who obeyed the international rules of war to the extent possible, given the horrors of the conflict on the Eastern Front. They described them as the most politically aware, patriotic and idealistic of Ukraine's youth, eager to serve as the vanguard of a free and independent Ukraine. They praise them for being dedicated soldiers who took up arms to free their land from Ukraine's "most terrible enemy—Bolshevism." As such, they claim, the soldiers of the Division harbored no hatred for Jews, guarded no concentration camps, and committed no crimes against humanity.[8]

In their eyes, the Waffen-SS was a prime combat organization entirely separate from the ill-reputed *Allgemeine-SS* which began as Hitler's bodyguards and developed into the ruthless organization responsible for the extermination of Europe's Jews.[9] Therefore, service in the Galician ranks of the Waffen-SS brought high honour rather than abysmal shame.

Wasyl Veryha, a Division veteran and author of several books and numerous articles on its history, insists that the 14. Waffen-SS Division was only incidentally an SS formation, that its placement in the ranks of *Reichsführer* Heinrich Himmler's legions was a su-perficial matter of military nomenclature without meaning or significance. He makes much of the fact that "unlike the other SS units, the Galicia [Division} would have its own chaplains to feed the spiritual needs of its soldiers" and would carry its own emblem con-sisting of a "golden lion resting on its haunches with three crowns, one above its head and two beneath its haunches."[10]

A further claim is forwarded—dubious at best—that the nationalist Ukrainian politi-cal leadership exacted an agreement from the German command that "the Division, when organized, would be used only against the Bolsheviks on the Eastern Front" and would never be called on to fight the British, French and American allied forces.[11]

Apologists for the Division claimed that its personnel were repeatedly screened by Soviet and British teams and that no war criminals were found among them. They quote extensively from a once secret 1947 report by D. Haldane Porter of the Refugee Screening Commission in which the British representative states that in his view, the Ukrainians who enlisted in the Division had done so "in the hope of securing a genuinely independ-ent Ukraine" and that they probably were not then and certainly do not now, seem to be at heart pro-German.[12]

Much the same story was offered by British Secretary of State Hector McNeil who, under fire in the House of Commons for transferring the bulk of the Division from a pris-oner-of-war camp in Italy to serve as agricultural workers in England, replied:

> There is no evidence that any of these Ukrainians are 'bloodthirsty cutthroats.'
> Cross sections of them have been screened at various times by Soviet and British
> missions without any war criminals being revealed.[13]

Soviet allegations of the Division's participation in the destruction of countless Polish vil-lages, the clearing of Jewish ghettos and the forced shipment of thousands of Ukrainian youths as slave laborers to Germany, have been repeatedly dismissed by Division publi-cists as outright lies and deliberate misinformation produced by the Communist propa-ganda machine.[14] Canadian Ukrainian Civil Liberties Association spokesman Lubomyr Luciuk, in a 1983 article published in a Ukrainian-Canadian student newspaper attrib-uted the vile rumors which swirled over the Division since the close of World War II to Soviet authorities who "generated a stream of undocumented brochures associating the Division with the Holocaust." Luciuk concludes: "No scholarly work has substantiated these claims."[15]

The Uniate clergy also entered the fray in defence of the Division. Fr. Myron Stasiw of St. Mary's Ukrainian Catholic Church in Toronto, himself a veteran of the Galician Divi-sion, offers no apology for his service in Himmler's army.[16] On the contrary he insists that the Jews were the villains and his fellow Ukrainians the victims. In a passionate homily delivered in 1985 over radio station CHIN, Fr. Stasiw proclaimed:

> The Jews in their hatred for the Ukrainian people go back three hundred years and more, but [the Jews] do not say what caused the Jewish pogroms, that [the Jews] held the keys to the Christian churches and would not allow the [Ukrainian] people to pray. [The Jews] were the tavern keepers who robbed the peasants of their lands for whiskey and made them serfs.[17]

Instead of chasing after Ukrainians accused of war crimes, Fr. Stasiw urged Nazi- hunter Simon Wiesenthal to direct his attention to his own "blood brothers." He denounced "the *Judenrat kapos* who together with the Gestapo and the SS killed and destroyed their fellow Jews."[18]

Division supporters vigorously applauded the 1986 decision of Justice Jules Deschênes, who, after a lengthy investigation into the presence of Nazi war criminals in Canada, decided that:

> Charges of war crimes against members of the Galicia Division have never been substantiated... No case can be made against members of the Galicia Division for revocation of citizenship or deportation since the Canadian authorities were fully aware of the relevant facts in 1950 and admission to Canada was not granted them because of any false representation or fraud or concealment of material circumstances.[19]

Given such sweeping exculpations and such illustrious guarantors it would appear foolhardy if not futile to question the *bona fides* of the Division and its members. Yet, as we shall see, high ranking British civil servants who served under McNeil questioned the Secretary of State's pronouncement and a respected Canadian historian who served as a senior researcher on Deschênes' staff, did not share the learned judge's conclusions.[20]

Despite the passage of time, many issues concerning the Division remain unresolved. To deal with them adequately one must examine the Division's origins and the record of its training, skirmishes, battles and retreats. One must pay particular attention to its participation in anti-partisan actions in which civilians were the deliberate victims of German ruthlessness, as well as the activities of the auxiliary police battalions that comprised the nucleus of the Division's recruits.

Still outstanding is the question of whether the Division—or any part of it—participated in the cruel suppression of the 1944 Polish uprising in Warsaw. One must also determine whether the Division recruits were in fact "volunteers" as indicated by the Division's official designation, or were they drafted or in some way coerced into joining up. How valid is the claim that they were systematically screened for war crimes first by the Russians, then by the British and the Americans? Or was their history fudged for Cold War purposes?

Equally at issue are the ideological convictions held by Division members and their political sponsors. Was the defeat of Bolshevism their prime concern and what was the nature of the state they were determined to erect in the event of Bolshevism's defeat? Was there a significant difference between the Ukrainian "Integral Nationalism" espoused by Ukrainian ideologues and the fascist ideology of Hitler and Mussolini?[21]

A recruiting poster that states: "Join the Battle Against Bolshevism in the ranks of the "Galicia" Division!"

What part did raw anti-Semitism play in the recruitment, training and actions of the Division? To what extent did the Ukrainian Division participate in the persecution and mass murder of Jews in Galicia?

Additionally intriguing is the extent to which the Ukrainian nationalist movement became a pawn in the battle between the SS and the *Abwehr*, between *Reichsführer* Heinrich Himmler and Admiral Wilhelm Canaris, a battle mirrored in the bloody contest for pre-eminence between competing factions of the Organization of Ukrainian Nationalists (OUN) led by Andrei Melnyk and Stefan Bandera.

Finally, what prompted the British authorities to rescue the Ukrainian Waffen-SS Division by moving it repeatedly out of the Soviet's reach in defiance of the Yalta Agreement? What inspired the British to transport some 11,000 Division members to England in 1947, and what induced them to insist on their removal in 1950?

The search for answers to these questions has taken the author to archives in Kiev, Lviv, Warsaw, Ludwigsburg, Paris, Belgrade, Bratislava, Jerusalem, London, New York, Washington and Ottawa over a fifteen year period. It has caused him to read widely the works of Ukrainian, German, American, English, and Jewish historians with varying approaches to the disputed questions.

The research presented numerous difficulties. For one, the Division systematically destroyed the bulk of its records in an effort to obliterate its past. Few of the unit's reports and standing orders remain. Individual soldiers were advised by their British captors to destroy their personnel records in order to obscure their pre-1939 citizenship. Division rosters have disappeared; British archives failed to produce a single file containing the names of the men taken into British custody in the last days of the war. Nor is there any record of the names of the men transported in British ships in 1947 from prisoner-of-war camps in Italy to serve as agricultural workers in England.[22]

Equally frustrating is the absence of any systematic record of the activities of the 14th Volunteer Grenadier Waffen-SS Division (Galicia No. 1) in the U.S. National Archives in Alexandria, Virginia. Ironically, the hallowed National Archives contain extensive files on Albanian, Azerbaijani, Belgian, Bosnian, Moslem, Croatian, Danish, Dutch, Estonian, Flemish, German, Hungarian, Khirghiz, Latvian, Norwegian, Rumanian, Soviet, Tadzhik, Tatar, Turkoman, and Uzbek Waffen-SS units, but there are none available for the Ukrainian Division.[23] Their absence is not fatal, however, since collateral files containing Himmler's reports, speeches and correspondence make numerous references to the Galician Division. But the basic files are gone and no one knows where.

Adding to the difficulty of providing a clear-eyed description of the Division is the fact that most of the existing histories have been written by Ukrainian émigrés who, according to Professor Shmuel Spector of Yad Vashem have been involved to one degree or another in the Ukrainian nationalist movement.[24]

Nevertheless, sufficient material remains and sufficient time has passed to allow the diligent researcher to provide an alternative perspective to that offered by nationalist Ukrainian historians. The author recognizes that much of what he has uncovered will be challenged, denied, minimized and trivialized by apologists for the Division. As a veteran reader of academic journals and reviews, he anticipates that somewhere in the body of the text, they are sure to find a source unattributed, an article overlooked, an author slighted, or an archive unexplored. However, the author feels confident that he has examined the salient issues with sufficient care and gathered more than enough data to support his conclusions. The facts will speak for themselves.

So, read on.

Notes

1. A February 7, 1949 memorandum issued by the Canadian Immigration Commissioner (Mines and Resources, SF-S-I, PT. 1) listed the grounds for rejection of non-German immigrants. Included were "Member of SS or German *Wehrmacht*. Found to bear mark of SS Blood Group." A July 6, 1951 memorandum from the acting director of the Department of Citizenship and Immigration summarizes the conclusions of the July 5 meeting of the Security Panel which stated that "Non-German members of the Waffen-SS found to bear mark of SS Blood Group were to be considered "Not Clear." A further paragraph stated: Non-German members Waffen-SS who voluntarily enlisted subsequent to January 1, 1943, to be considered "Not Clear." (SF-S-I, PT. 2) This policy remained in effect as late as February 2, 1956, according to a memorandum issued by the Deputy Minister of Citizenship and Immigration which called for some modification of the regulation barring members of the S.S., S.D., S.A. and Waffen SS. (SF-S-I, PT.3)

2. Amongst others see: Yuri Boshyk, editor, *Ukraine During World War II: History and its Aftermath* (Edmonton: Canadian Institute of Ukrainian Studies, 1986); Tadeus Piotrowski, *Ukrainian Integral Nationalism* (Toronto: Alliance of Polish Eastern Provinces, 1987); Taras Hunczak, *On the Horns of a Dilemma* (New York: University Press of America, 2000); Michael O. Logusz, *Galicia Division: The Waffen-SS 14th Grenadier Division, 1943-1945* Atglen, PA: Schiffer Military History, 1997) and Julius Hendy, producer, *The SS in Britain*, York Television.

3. *The SS in Britain*, Yorkshire Television, Julius Hendy, Producer.

4. For an excellent sociological map of the pre-war Ukrainian-Canadian community, its conflicts and divisions see: Orest T. Martynowych, *Ukrainians in Canada: The Formative Period, 1891-1924* (Edmonton: Canadian Institute of Ukrainian Studies Press, 1991) 521-526.

5. Paul R. Magocsi, preface to *Canada's Ukrainians: Negotiating an Identity*. See following footnote for complete reference.

6. See: Lubomyr Y. Luciuk, "This Should Never Be Spoken or Quoted Publicly: Canada's Ukrainians and Their Encounter with the DPs," in *Canada's Ukrainians: Negotiating and Identity* (Toronto: University of Toronto Press, 1991).

7. Daniel Jonah Goldhagen, *Hitler's Willing Executioners: Ordinary Germans and the Holocaust* (New York: Knopf, 1996).

8. Wasyl Veryha, "The 'Galicia' Ukrainian Division in Polish and Soviet Literature," *The Ukrainian Quarterly*, Autumn 1980, Vol. XXXVI, No. 3, 252-270.

9. See: Myroslav Yurkevich, "Galician Ukrainians in German Military Formations and in the German Administration," *Ukraine during World War II: History and its aftermath*, Yuri Boshyk (editor) (Edmonton: Canadian Institute of Ukrainian Studies, 1986), 75.

10. Veryha, *supra*.

11. Michael Yaremko, *From Separation to Unity* (Toronto: Shevchenko Scientific Society, 1967), 261.

12. The original report can be found in the London Public Record Office (PRO) under the designation: FO 371/66605/117266. D. Haldane Porter, Refugee Screening Commission Report on Ukrainians in Surrendered Enemy Personnel (SEP), February 21, 1947.

13. London Public Records Office, FO 371/66712, Hector McNeil, letter to Richard Crossman, M.P., July 1947.

14. Lubomyr Luciuk and Myroslav Yurkevich, "The Ukrainian Division 'Galicia' – war criminals in Canada?" *OKO*, September-October, 1983, Vol. V, No. 7.

15. *Ibid*.

16. See: Jock Ferguson, "Ukrainian veterans expect investigation by war crimes study," *The Globe and Mail*, May 6, 1985.

17. Transcript courtesy of "Ukrainian Hour," CHIN Radio, Toronto, 1985.

18. The *Judenrat* was a body of Jewish leaders appointed by the Nazis to transmit the orders of the German occupation authorities to the dwellers in the Jewish ghetto. *Kapos*, some of whom were Jewish, were inmates of concentration camps appointed to carry out the wishes of the camp guards.

19. The Commission of Inquiry on War Criminals was conducted from February 7, 1985 to December 30, 1986. Its findings were presented by Justice Deschênes in *Commission of Inquiry on War Criminals: Report, Part I: Public*, (Ottawa: Canadian Government Publishing Centre, 1986), 261.

20. See: Alti Rodal, "Nazi War Criminals in Canada: The Historical and Policy Setting from the 1940s to the Present," prepared for the Commission of Inquiry on War Criminals, September 1986, 390.

21. John A. Armstrong, *Ukrainian Nationalism*, Third Edition (Englewood, Colo.: Ukrainian Academic Press, 1990), 212-213.

22. Despite repeated visits and persistent correspondence with the directors of the London Public Record Office and the Imperial War Museum, no rosters were located. Nor were the directors able to suggest where they might be found. Chances are that the files containing such records were culled. Although the British were not as compulsive in their record keeping as the Germans in their record keeping, the rosters must have existed at one time since they were needed to provision prisoner-of-war camps, to maintain ships' passenger lists and to keep track of the Ukrainian agricultural workers in their various camps across Britain.

23. See: "Guides to German Records Microfilmed at Alexandria, VA., No. 79. Records of the Waffen-SS, Part II, National Archives and Records Service, General Services Administration, Washington, 1981."

24. Shmuel Spector, "The Attitude of the Ukrainian Diaspora to the Holocaust of Ukrainian Jewry," in *The Historiography of the Holocaust Period* (Jerusalem: Yad Vashem, 1988), 275.

Otto Wächter, Governor of Galicia.

Opera House of Lviv, where recruits form guard of honour before reviewing stand, 18 July, 1943.
Note SS banners, Halychyna lion and swastikas.

Wächter (front row centre) leads the parade to the reviewing stand.

Wächter at podium, Lviv (Lemberg), 18 July, 1943.

Wächter (front row, far right), on reviewing stand.

Recruits on the way to the reviewing stand give Nazi salute and carry Nazi flags.

Recruits march to review by Wächter and then by train to boot-camp. The wording on the banner is "Kreislemberg-land Freiwillige SS Schutz-manndivision Galizien."

Despite the rain, a huge crowd attended the ceremony in Lviv.

Nationalist Ukrainian dignitaries.

Wächter in conversation with veterans of World War I Ukrainian army.

Division church parade, Stanislau, 11 July, 1943.

Uniate Chaplain Vasyl Laba conducts service.

German officers, recruits, and Ukrainian dignitaries at Division church parade, Stanislau, 11 July, 1943.

General Fritz Freitag (front row, third from the left) and his officers, and Ukrainian dignitaries.

Opera House, Lviv, 1990.

Partisan leader David Kruitikov who witnessed the destruction of Huta Pienacka.

Holocaust memorial at gate of Jewish cemetary, Lviv, 1990.

CHAPTER 1

THE DIVISION IS ORGANIZED

THE ESTABLISHMENT OF A UKRAINIAN WAFFEN-SS DIVISION "to satisfy the demand of the Ukrainian population for an active share in the struggle against the Bolsheviks" was first announced over radio Weichsel-Donau on March 24, 1943.[1] The broadcast reported that the Germans had established a Ukrainian war committee in Krakow for the purpose of enlisting a Ukrainian division to fight side-by-side with the Germans for the salvation of Ukrainian freedom, independence and self-determination. On April 22, Radio Weichsel-Donau announced that the Division's insignia, to be worn on the soldiers' sleeves and carried on its battle banners, would be the ancient heraldic symbol of Ukraine's princes, the Lion of Halych. In keeping with the insignia, the division would be named "Galician."

The Division's insignia, the Lion of Halych, was worn on the soldier's sleeve. In the background, behind the soldier, is the 'tryzub' or three-pronged scepter, symbol of the Ukrainian nationalist movement.

A more formal announcement was made at Lviv on May 5 by SS Brigadier Otto Wächter, the German Governor of Galicia "supported by the President of the Ukrainian Aid Committee, Professor Dr. Kubijovyc[2] and one Michael Chronovat, an engineer, chairman of the Ukrainian War Committee." On May 23, the German Transocean Agency stated that 60,000 Galician Ukrainians had already enrolled.[3]

German newsreel film of the period shows the volunteers of the newly formed Halychyna Division passing in review before Governor Wächter in Lviv on July 18, 1943. Still in their civilian clothes, they proudly display their SS and swastika insignia alongside the Halych Lion as they march by in ranks of four on their way to the railway station and thence to boot camp. As they pass the swastika-bedecked reviewing stand, they raise their arms in the stiff-armed Hitler salute. As they swing by, the film's sound track intones: "One more train is leaving the Fatherland with volunteers so that after their training they can join the German army in defending Europe against the world Bolshevist enemy."[4]

In a similar send-off ceremony in Kolomya that same month, the same SS, swastika and Halych Lion banners are prominently displayed. The captured film shows Wächter addressing the recruits. "In joining the ranks of the volunteers you show that you are not indifferent to the struggle now taking place in Europe, but are marching together with others into battle," the Nazi Governor proclaims. "You wish, with arms in hand, to serve the fatherland and the New Europe."[5]

The campaign against "the world Bolshevist enemy" was also seen as a campaign against the Jewish enemy. For example, on May 13, 1943, the newspaper *Lvivski Visti* trumpeted: "To carry a gun is a great honour for the Ukrainian nation." Accompanying the article was a cartoon showing a Jewish moneybag surmounting Uncle Sam and his British donkey.

The following day, *Lvivski Visti*, controlled and edited by Ukrainian nationalists, ran a cartoon showing Stalin, wearing a royal crown, staring into a mirror. The reflected image is that of a heavy-nosed Jew wearing a dollar sign on his sleeve. On May 20, 1943, *Lvivski Visti* reported the appointment of new generals to the Red Army. The article implied that the new generals were all Jews. Illustrating the article was a cartoon showing a gross Jewish figure draped in a Russian general's uniform. The cutline read: "In the name of the newly appointed generals I swear to fight to the last Red Army man."

Articles proclaiming the glories of the Galician Division carried frequent references to "Jew-Bolsheviks." Among them was a *Lvivski Visti* article on May 22, 1943, describing "the struggle against world Judaism." The Jews, the writer claimed, are seeking to dominate the world. Bolshevism is one of many Jewish instruments for gaining power everywhere in the universe.. "We know the cruelty of Bolshevism, the millions of non-Jews murdered by the Cheka, the GPU and the NKVD. The most prominent Jewish executioners are Trilisser, Unschlicht, and Hershel Yagoda—all Jews. These Jewish hangmen killed five million victims... Jews are the same everywhere. Only Hitler can save the world from them, with the assistance of Ukrainians, of course. Jews mustn't win, [Ukrainian] blood must not be shed in vain.[6]

As late as June 13, 1944, *Lvivski Visti* carried a cartoon showing a fat-bellied Jew, a Star of David stickpin prominently displayed on his chest, leading a savage dog bearing Stalin's features on a leash.

Origins of the Freiwilligen Legionen

The SS Halychyna Division, like its Latvian, Estonian and Caucasian Waffen-SS counterparts, had its origin in the locally recruited militias enrolled as support groups by the German-led mobile killing squads known as *Einsatzgruppen*. Highly efficient because of their intimate knowledge of the local terrain and the local population, the *Einsatzgruppen* were responsible for the ruthless murder of close to 1,500,000 Jewish men, women and children on Soviet territory.[7] In turn, these local support groups, variously designated as self-defense units, punitive divisions and police battalions, had their origin in the numerous pro-Nazi and pro-fascist political groups that flourished in pre-World War II Europe.

In France, the members of the *Milice* actively assisted Lyon's Gestapo chief Klaus Barbie in rounding up members of the French *resistance*. The *Milice*, in turn, recruited its members largely from the ranks of the openly fascist *Action Francaise* and the *Cagoule*. In the Netherlands, the militia that patrolled the highways and rounded up Jews was recruited from the ranks of the Dutch National Socialist Party. In Belgium they came from the ranks of the *Rexists*, in Croatia they were members of the *Ustasha*, and in Romania they belonged to the Iron Guard.

The Latvian 15th and 19th Waffen-SS Divisions grew out of the Nazi inspired *Perkonkrust* (Thunder Cross) and *Aizsargi* movements via the "security battalions" led by the infamous General Oskar Dankers and Colonel Voldemar Arajs.[8] In Estonia, the pro-Nazi VABS (The War of Liberation Soldiers' League) and a thoroughly nazified German-Estonian minority, prompted the early organization of the Estonian 20th Division.[9]

As the war progressed, Soviet resistance stiffened and the German army suffered devastating losses. By December 1943, the *Ostheer's* (Army of the East) overall strength was down by more than a million men. In an effort to make up for this mammoth shortage, the Army in the East greatly intensified its recruitment of local, non-German volunteers. The SS combed the prison camps for ideologically sympathetic Soviet POWs and stepped up its appeals to civilians. Ultimately, some 320,000 *Hiwis* or *Hilfswillige* (volunteers) served as drivers, cooks and medical orderlies, replacing German service troops reassigned to combat duty. Another 150,000 men belonging to Soviet national minorities were organized into *Ostlegionen* (eastern legions) in which German officers universally were organized into *Ostlegionen* (eastern legions) in which German officers universally controlled the key command positions.[10] By the end of the war, fully half of the SS divisions consisted mostly of foreigners who fell short of the usual SS racial standards.

In Ukraine—or at least that part of Ukraine centered on Lviv and Stanislaviv which had been part of the pre-World War I Austro-Hungarian Empire—the Organization of Ukrainian Nationalists (OUN) was to become the predominant, pro-German political force. Much of the character of that organization and its adherents was influenced to a remarkably high degree by the tumultuous events and contradictory personalities set loose by the 1917 Russian Revolution and the fratricidal Civil War that followed the Bolshevik takeover.

Notes

1. *The Wiener Bulletin*, Vol. 4, No.5/6. 35.

2. Professor Volodymyr Kubijovyc's name has been given a wide variety of spellings in English. We are using the present spelling because it is close to the one employed by Kubijovyc himself and all the letters are available on our computer.

3. *The Wiener Bulletin*, Vol. 4, No. 5/6. 35

4. Captured German film, Ukrainian State Archive, Kiev.

5. Soundtrack voice-over, captured German film, Ukrainian State Archive. A copy of the film is in the author's possession.

6. *Lvivski Visti*, May 22, 1943

7. Raul Hilberg, *The Destruction of the European Jews* (New York: Harper and Row, 1961) 256.

8. Max Kaufman, "The War Years in Latvia Revisited," in *The Jews in Latvia*, ed. M. Bobe, S. Levenberg, O. Maor, Z. Micaheli (Association of Latvian and Estonian Jews in Israel). Also see, *The Baltic States* (Oxford: Royal Institute of International Affairs, 1943) 54-55.

9. Evald Uustalu, *The History of the Estonian People* (London: Boreas Publishing Company Ltd., 1952) 203-204.

10. Omer Bartov, *Hitler's Army* (Oxford: Oxford University Press, 1991) 44-45.

CHAPTER 2

THE 1917–1920 CIVIL WAR IN UKRAINE

BOTH THE EASTERN AND WESTERN UKRAINE WITNESSED more violence, more destruction and more unvarnished cruelty of man to man than any other part of the Czar's former empire during the civil war that erupted following the Russian Revolution. Its lands repeatedly shredded by German occupation, Bolshevik expansionism, Ukrainian nationalism, peasant anarchism and Polish invasion, Ukraine became a battlefield over which desperate armies fought without respite between the fall of 1917 and the summer of 1920.

In the rich lands that had once been the Russian empire's fertile granary, Reds fought Whites, peasants rebelled against landlords and townsmen, Ukrainians fought Germans, Russians and Poles, while anarchists fought all efforts to impose a state of order upon society. In that brief, three-year period of ultimate turmoil, three different governments—the socialist *Rada*, the monarchist Hetmanate and the nationalist Directory—rapidly succeeded each other. Each was fated to fail or was ignominiously driven out.[1]

Despite the turmoil, York University historian Orest Subtelny discerns two separate, distinct mind-sets that emerged during this period in Ukraine. One was composed of men who generally gave higher priority to radical social reform than national independence. Their geographic centre was Kiev and the land to its east. The other—in western Ukraine—was led by men with an intense nostalgia for the Austro-Hungarian monarchy and a distinctly conservative social outlook. "As a result," he writes, the easterners accused the Galicians of being 'reactionaries' and the latter returned the compliment by calling the former 'near Bolsheviks.' "[2]

Subtelny also points out that Russia actually experienced two revolutions in 1917: The first, called the February Revolution, he describes as more of a collapse than an uprising as people poured into the streets to protest food shortages, the factory workers went on strike and the tsarist troops refused to fire on civilians.[3] "Although bringing tsardom down had been incredibly easy, finding a generally acceptable substitute proved to be incredibly difficult. Two claimants to political authority emerged. One was the Provisional Government…which sought to perform a caretaker role until Russia established some permanent new form of government."[4] The other was the Bolshevik inspired Petrograd Soviet of Workers and Soldiers Deputies.

The second revolution, the Bolshevik-led October Revolution, saw Worker and Soldier Soviets seize towns and factories throughout Russia. In response, White forces organized to recover the factories, estates and privileges Lenin's socialist revolution promised to take from them. Leading czarist generals assembled in the Don Cossack lands to launch a civil war that would claim the lives of millions of men and women in the next three years through battle, executions, hunger and disease.

Within days of learning of the March revolution in Petrograd, Ukrainian moderates and democratic socialists established the Central *Rada* (council) in Kiev. Originally conceived as an extension of the Provisional government, it soon began to take on the character of a national assembly intent on establishing Ukrainian independence. On June 23, 1917, the *Rada* defied the Provisional government and proclaimed a free, independent Ukraine.[5] The Ukrainian Central *Rada* survived for two years. In that time it attracted support from a wide spectrum of followers ranging from liberal moderates to Radical Socialists. Writer and politician Volodymyr Vynnychenko, one of the leaders of the Revolutionary Ukrainian Party (RUP) became head of the Executive Committee and his thirty-five year-old colleague, Symon Petliura, served the infant state as its Minister of War.

Despite their noble intentions, the *Rada's* leadership proved to be hopelessly inept administrators, unable to maintain law and order, supply food to the major cities and keep the railways running. In addition, the regime failed to win the support of the urban workers and the landless peasants who found the Bolshevik slogans more convincing than the *Rada's* promises. The Bolsheviks denounced the Central *Rada* as "enemies of the people" and "traitors to Socialism." Occupied on many fronts, the Bolsheviks withheld their attack on Ukraine until mid-December, 1917. After a hard-fought five-day battle the Red forces poured through the gates of Kiev.

But this was fated to be only the first round. Desperate for recognition and foreign allies, the *Rada* insisted on sending its own delegates to the Brest-Litovsk treaty negotiations and succeeded in persuading the Germans and Austrians that it would be to their advantage to join with Petliura's army to drive the Bolsheviks from Kiev.[6] In return, Ukraine was to deliver massive supplies of grain to feed the Central Powers' hungry cities. Within weeks, the German and Austrian military, true to their promise, drove the Red Army from Ukraine.

The agreement quickly soured, however, when the Germans realized that the young Ukrainian utopians had no more talent for collecting and shipping huge quantities of foodstuffs than they had shown for maintaining law and order and fighting the

Bolsheviks. Concerned primarily with keeping supplies of grain moving, the German generals determined to install a friendlier, more efficient regime.

They chose General Pavlo Skoropadsky, one of the largest and most socially backward landowners in Ukraine, to serve as Hetman (Chief) of the new regime.[7] Everything about the Hetmanate was reactionary, including its title that harked back to the ancient Zaporozhian Cossack states.[8] A former aide-de-camp to Czar Nicholas II, Skoropadsky spoke no Ukrainian yet sought to restore Kiev as the ancient capital of Ukraine.

In effect, Skoropadsky was designated to be a dictator, dedicated to the Old World of imperial privilege the Revolution had swept away.[9] In response to German demands, Skoropadsky shipped vast amounts of grain, leather, hemp and tobacco to the Central Powers without regard for the needs of Ukrainians.

The collapse of the Central Powers and the Armistice of November 11, 1918 shattered the base of Skoropadsky's regime; without German protection his government was doomed. As the Russian general's aristocratic regime tottered, the former *Rada* leadership headed by Petliura and Vynnychenko organized an open rebellion against the Hetmanate. Some of the Hetman's best units deserted Skoropadsky and went over to the Central *Rada*, now renamed the "Directory." Among the regiments that changed sides were the Sich Riflemen commanded by Evhen Konovalets and his chief-of-staff, Andrii Melnyk, both of whom were to play key roles in the Ukrainian nationalist movement in the period between the wars and beyond.

On December 14, 1918, the Germans evacuated Kiev and Skoropadsky decamped with them. That same day, the Directory's forces entered the Ukrainian capital in triumph and announced the reestablishment of the Ukrainian National Republic.

But once again, the Ukrainian Republic was unable to sustain itself. Attacked on one side by Red forces determined to establish Bolshevism and on the other by White armies intent on restoring one indivisible Russia, the Ukrainian state failed to survive the winter of 1919.[10] On the eve of its demise it engaged "in several symbolic demonstrations of sovereignty" including the celebration of the Union of the Ukrainian National Republic with the newly formed West Ukrainian Republic (ZUNR) in Galicia.[11]

The Civil War in Galicia

As the Hapsburg Imperial and Royal Monarchy dissolved in the wake of World War I, its various ethnic components made strenuous bids for independence. Czechoslovakia, Poland and Yugoslavia succeeded in establishing modern, democratic states within boundaries set out in the Treaties of Versailles and Trianon. The same nationalistic strivings inspired the Ukrainians of Galicia.

Prior to the First World War, the old Polish Commonwealth was repeatedly "partitioned" by its German, Russian and Austrian neighbors. In 1772, the Hapsburgs snatched Galicia, a mixed area of Ukrainians and Poles. For the next century it remained an "economically impoverished, socially undeveloped, culturally stagnant and politically weak"[12] eastern outpost of the Kaiser's Austrian-Hungarian empire. Neglected by the Austrians, scorned and discriminated against by Polish-born viceroys, the West Ukrainians developed an ardent political and cultural consciousness of their own.

Before the outbreak of World War I, that consciousness was directed to reinforcing the position of Ukrainians within the Austro-Hungarian Empire in competition with Galicia's Poles. As soon as war came in August 1914, a combination of conservative Galician political parties met in Lviv to form the General Ukrainian Council (ZUR) to serve as a unified liaison with the Hapsburg monarchy. The Council, assuming its best hope for Ukrainian autonomy lay in showing maximum support for the Hapsburg Kaiser against the Romanov Czar, called for volunteers and succeeded in fielding a distinctly Ukrainian, 2500-man military formation called the Ukrainian Legion or the Ukrainian Sich Riflemen (*Ukrainski Sichovi Striltsi*).

But by the Fall of 1918, the Council recognized that the Central Powers had lost the war and the Austro-Hungarian Empire was dissolving rapidly. In response, the Council set out to "make history" by establishing an independent Ukrainian state on Galician territory. On November 1, a contingent of Ukrainian veterans of the Austrian army seized Lviv. The Poles, determined to establish their suzerainty over the territory, drove them out the next day. Unable to establish their capital in Lviv, the Ukrainian-Galician leaders fled to Stanislaviv where they officially proclaimed the West Ukrainian National Republic (*Zakhidno Ukrainska Narodna Respublyka*) on November 13.

The ZUNR survived for nine months, during which it introduced representative government, proclaimed full voting rights for all citizens and guaranteed the cultural and political rights of all minorities. But the Poles would have none of it. The newly resurrected Polish state claimed Galicia as part of its "severed body" and sent its army to reclaim the territory it regarded as its own by historic right. Superior Polish forces pushed back the Galician army until—on July 16,1919—it was forced to cross over into Eastern Ukraine where it joined forces with Petliura's army. Short of supplies, decimated by typhus, and attacked simultaneously by General Denikin's White Army, the Red Army and the Poles, the combined Ukrainian armies disintegrated. Petliura took refuge, first in Poland, then in France. The bulk of the Galician leaders fled to Vienna.

The Ukrainian battle for independence continued for yet one more futile round. In April 1920, Petliura and the last remnants of his forces joined the Poles in a combined attack against the Bolsheviks. Despite early gains by the Poles that brought them within reach of Kiev, Leon Trotsky's Red Army rallied and by November had driven back the Polish forces to the gates of Warsaw. The Ukrainian army was utterly destroyed.

For the Directory, independence was a means to a socialist state without Bolshevik totalitarianism. For the Galicians, independence was both an end in itself and a means of dampening revolutionary fervor. In their cooperation with the Germans and Austrians, in their nostalgia for the Hapsburg Empire and their resistance to social and economic reform, the Galicians stood closer to Skoropadsky than Vynnychenko. In both east and west, opportunism—in the name of the need to survive—became the order of the day. Alliances enthusiastically joined one day were cynically abandoned the next. Today's comrade frequently became tomorrow's enemy.

Despite the military and political defeats that put an end to the 1917-1920 effort to create an independent Ukraine, the dream did not die among the nationalist Ukrainians. The nostalgia for what were seen as days of glory remained strong. The *Sich* riflemen were revered as forerunners of a Ukrainian national army. Independence-minded Ukrainians continued to celebrate the Central *Rada's* 1918 declaration of Ukraine's independence and the 1919 Act of Union between the Ukrainian National Republic and the Western Ukrainian National Republic.[13]

The Anti-Jewish Pogroms

Whatever quarrels existed between nationalists and federalists, Ukrainians and Russians, peasants and aristocrats, hatred of the zhidy, the Jews, was common coinage. In 1905, the Jewish population of the Russian Empire numbered approximately five million. By the Czar' royal decree, Jewish residence was restricted largely to the narrow strip on Russia's western and southern border dubbed "The Pale of Settlement" or "The Pale." Even there, Jews were expressly forbidden from living in major cities without special permission. As a result, they tended to live in thousands of small towns and villages where educational and employment opportunities were severely limited.

As might be expected, the misery and violence inflicted on Jews led to the radicalization of many of their youths. A high proportion was inspired to participate in radical political parties. The most prominent of these radical Jewish groups was the Social Democratic *Bund,* or Brotherhood. Jews were also prominent in the leadership of both the Bolshevik and Menshevik wings of the Social Democratic movement.[14]

Jews suffered discrimination and pogroms throughout the Russian Empire but their experience in Ukraine was particularly bitter. Historian W. Bruce Lincoln describes Ukraine as a land of chronic pogroms dating back to the days when the Cossack legions under Count Bohdan Khmelnitsky butchered two hundred thousand Jews and eradicated seven hundred Jewish settlements in the mid-seventeenth century. Less than a hundred years later, Ukrainian peasants, rebelling against Polish rule, murdered another fifty thousand Jews in Russia's west and southwest corners.

In the years that followed, Jews endured periodic outbreaks of anti-Jewish hatred. As the nineteenth century approached, pogroms became a regular, fearfully anticipated feature of life in the Pale. The assassination of Czar Alexander II in 1881 was followed by especially violent attacks on Jewish communities.[15]

The year 1905 saw violence burst upon the Jews of Bessarabia. The famed Kishinev pogrom took the lives of fifty Jews, injured six hundred and destroyed thirteen hundred shops before the troops were ordered in to end the violence. Two years later, as an accompaniment to the 1905 revolution which followed Russia's loss of its war with Japan, nearly seven hundred pogroms were inflicted on the Jews with more than eight out of ten occurring in Ukraine or adjoining Bessarabia.[16]

Lincoln reports that in 1919, "as the last vestiges of effective government crumbled into uncontrollable violence...the one and a half million Jews of Ukraine became victims of the most vicious anti-Semitic attacks to sweep their land since the days of Khmelnitsky. Between December 1918 and April 1921, more than 1,200 large and small pogroms were inflicted on Ukrainian Jews."[17]

The exact number slain is hard to estimate. Ronald Saunders, author of *Shores of Refuge: A Hundred Years of Jewish Immigration,* claims "at least thirty thousand were murdered instantly, but a great many more died subsequently on account of wounds, so that the final figure may be more than a hundred thousand. It was the worst holocaust the Jewish people had ever known."[18]

The massacres were committed with equal ferocity by Denikin's White forces, the armies of the Directory and the rebellious Atamans (chieftains) of Ukraine who were at odds with the Directory. For the simple-minded, who had long identified Jews as "Christ-killers" and "blood-suckers," there were now the added accusations that they were agents of the Bolsheviks who intended to replace the landlord's yoke with Jewish slavery. For the sophisticated, anti-Semitism became a callously exploitable weapon as the Ukrainian leadership struggled to find a common base of support among the bitterly anti-Semitic factions in Ukraine. "All across the Ukraine," Lincoln comments, "anti-Semitism poisoned the minds of men. Officers of high principles, good education and deeply ingrained personal scruples began to rob, rape and murder as a matter of course... Then, as the Reds began to challenge the Volunteer Army more effectively...the pogroms turned into orgies of mass butchery."[19]

Only the Bolsheviks condemned anti-Semitism and shot pogromists; only in Bolshevik-held territories were Jews safe from mass murder. Small wonder then that Jews were reluctant to volunteer their services to either of the two Ukrainian Republics.

Small wonder that they frequently preferred the Bolshevik's iron rule to the blandishments of shaky Ukrainian states.

What Ukrainian governments might have eventually become, what measure of democracy and freedom they might have sustained is an historical unknown since both collapsed early under the attacks of the Soviets and the Poles. In the view of some nationalist Ukrainians, they were beacons of freedom, culture and tolerance that provided protection for minorities and reserved cabinet positions for representatives of the Jews. In Jewish eyes, they were weak, temporary structures that—whatever their intention—could not impose order on their wildly undisciplined and deeply prejudiced troops and thereby failed abysmally in protecting the lives and property of their Jewish citizens.

Petliura included a Ministry of Jewish Affairs in his Directory Cabinet and issued orders warning his army that the death sentence would overtake the perpetrators of pogroms. Nevertheless, considerable question remains whether he and his officers did enough to prevent and punish pogroms. Even more doubt remains whether he and his government maintained sufficient control over his followers to prevent their outbreak.[20]

Indeed, the pogroms intensified as the short-lived Ukrainian state suffered defeat after defeat at the hands of the Communists. In an article in *The Ukrainian Quarterly*, Ukrainian scholar Stefan T. Possony points out that "the more decisive these defeats were, the more often the beaten [Petliura] troops had to carry out evacuation of territories which they had occupied, the more cruelly the defeated and irritated troops began to revenge their setbacks and hardships on the peaceful Jewish population, and the more often they began to treat the Jews as Communists."[21]

Petliura did not fare well in exile. Assailed on all sides by the numerous, fractious Ukrainian political organizations, the former general was far from a popular figure in the Ukrainian Diaspora. However, on May 25, 1926, Petliura was assassinated on a Paris side street by young Samuel Schwartzbard as an act of revenge for the pogroms committed by Petliura's troops. His assassination immediately transformed Petliura "from one of the most reviled of Ukrainian statesmen to a national martyr and hero."[22]

Petliura came to be seen as a national hero by a wide spectrum of Ukrainian political opinion, from extreme nationalist to democratic liberal. He was portrayed as "the Great Patriot and Indefatigable Fighter to realize the ideal of Ukrainian statehood"[23] and his killing was interpreted as an attack on the whole Ukrainian people.[24] "At the same time, Petliura's death was assigned mystical overtones and the Ukrainian cause transformed into a well-nigh religious matter."[25]

But for the Jews, who held him responsible for many of the 1918-1921 pogroms, he was the personification of evil. In the years 1918 and 1919 alone, the Jews of eighty-seven

Ukrainian towns were victimized by Petliura's soldiers. Chief among them were Berdychev, Cherkasy, Kiev, Mogiliev, Vynnitsa and Zhytomyr.

No Jewish tears were shed when Petliura was assassinated.

Notes

1. W. Bruce Lincoln, *Red Victory: A History of the Russian Civil War* (New York: Simon and Schuster, 1989), 302.

2. Orest Subtelny, *Ukraine: A History* (Toronto: University of Toronto Press, 1989), 373.

3. Subtelny, 344.

4. *Ibid.* 345.

5. Lincoln, *Red Victory*, 305

6. Subtelny, *Ukraine*, 353-353.

7. "Hetman" is a Cossack term. The Cossacks, largely runaway serfs and frontier-style adventurers, settled on the southern steppes in the 16th century. They called their chiefs "Hetman" and the separate states they formed "Hetmanates."

8. The Zaporozhian Cossacks were one of the major Cossack bands.

9. Lincoln, *Red Victory*, 308.

10. Petr Wrangel, *Memoirs of General Wrangel* (London: Williams and Norgate, 1929), 120.

11. Subtelny, *Ukraine*, 361-362.

12. *Ibid.* 307.

13. Anonymous, "Imperialism and Independence," *The Ukrainian Weekly*, January 27, 1991.

14. Martin McCauley, *Octoberists to Bolsheviks: Imperial Russia 1905-1918* (London: Edward Arnold Publishers, 1984), 208.

15. Lincoln, *op. cit.*, 317.

16. Lincoln, *Ibid.* Lincoln makes reference to: I. Cnernikover, *Antisemitizm I pogromy ne Ukraine 1917-1918* (Berlin: k istorii ukrainsko-evreiskikh otnoshenii, 1923); Elias Heifetz, *The Slaughter of Jews in Ukraine in 1919* (New York: 1921) and Maurice Paleologue, *An Ambassador's Memoirs*, 3 volumes (New York: Henry Holt & Co.., n.d.).

17. Lincoln, 319.

18. Ronald Saunders, *Shores of Refuge: A Hundred Years of Jewish Immigration* (New York: Henry Holt & Co. 1988), 358.

19. Lincoln, 322-323.

20. Stefan T. Possony, "The Ukrainian-Jewish Problem: A Historical Retrospect," *The Ukrainian Quarterly*, Vol. XXXI, No.2, Summer 1975, 146.

21. Saul S. Friedman, *Pogromchik: The Assassination of Simon Petlura*, (New York: Hart Publishing Company, 1976), 219.

22. Alexander J. Motyl, *The Turn to the Right: The Ideological Origins and Developments of Ukrainian Nationalism 1919-1929* (New York: Columbia University Press, 1980), 49.

23. *Ibid.*

24. *Ibid.*

25. *Ibid.*

CHAPTER 3

THE ORGANIZATION OF UKRAINIAN NATIONALISTS (OUN)

IN THE INTER-WAR YEARS, THE EASTERN AND WESTERN UKRAINIAN nationalists confronted different enemies. On Soviet territory, the Ukrainian peasantry was embittered by the forced collectivization of their farms and the grim famine that followed in 1932-1933. On Polish territory, the Galician Ukrainians faced the all-out efforts of the Polish government to "Polonize" the area by making Polish the dominant language in Ukrainian schools, excluding Ukrainian students from Lviv University, and encouraging large scale colonization by Polish settlers. Subtelny reports that "despite the fact that Galicia was one of the most over-populated agricultural regions in Europe, the Polish settlers received large allotments of the best land as well as generous financial subsidies. Those who chose not to work on the land obtained privileged positions as village policemen, postal and railroad employees or petty officials."[1]

The more radical nationalist elements fought back through assassination, sabotage and terror tactics, particularly the burning of crops on Polish estates. In response, the Polish government launched a massive and frequently brutal pacification campaign. In the summer of 1930, large police and cavalry units descended on the Ukrainian countryside to impose order. This conflict gave birth to a number of Ukrainian nationalist organizations and political parties. The Organization of Ukrainian Nationalists (OUN) emerged as the most militant and determined of them all.

Formally founded at the First Great Congress of Ukrainian Nationalists convened in Vienna in January 1928 under the leadership of Ievhen Konovalets, it drew for its early membership on an array of exiled Galician army officers and veterans of the various armies that fought to defend the short-lived Ukrainian states. Aware that the aging veterans could not provide the numbers and dynamism necessary to sever Galicia from Poland and emancipate the Soviet Ukraine, Konovalets drew the impassioned youth into his movement. Historian John A. Armstrong comments: "Through its appeal to the frustrated youth living under Polish rule and through its attraction for many of the embittered émigrés from the East Ukraine, the new movement rapidly attained considerable strength."[2]

The nationalist youth movement, SUNM (*Soiuz Ukrains'koi Nationaaiistychnoi Molodi*), invented its own set of ten commandments (Decalogue) to guide its members:

1. Attain a Ukrainian state or die in the battle for it.

2. Do not allow anyone to defame the glory or honour of Your Nation.

3. Remember the great days of our efforts.

4. Be proud that you are an heir of the struggle for the glory of Volodymyr's Trident.

5. Avenge the death of the Great Knights.

6. Do not speak of the cause with whomever possible, but only with whomever necessary.

7. Do not hesitate to commit the greatest crime, if the good of the Cause demands it.

8. Regard the enemies of Your Nation with hate and perfidy.

9. Neither requests, nor threats, nor torture, nor death can compel you to betray a secret.

10. Aspire to expand the strength, riches, and size of the Ukrainian State even by means of enslaving foreigners.[3]

Alexander J. Motyl in his monograph on the Ukrainian nationalist movement, comments that the SUNM Decalogue, with its emphasis on deeds and lack of ideology, resembled the esoteric instructions of a mystical sect in which the world of reason, logic and doubt are abandoned.[4] In the union of SUNM and Konovalets' veterans' organization (UNVO), the Decalogue became the credo for all of the OUN with each member required to memorize the ten propositions as they were published originally in the underground newspaper *Surma*.[5]

The OUN—like the Croatian Ustasha and the Romanian Iron Guard—held a mystic belief in the necessity of violence to achieve national emancipation.[6] German historian Hans Höhne describes the OUN as: "Anti-parliamentary and hostile to the Western democracies, the movement planned to use brute force to break open what is referred to as 'Greater Russian imperialism's prison of nations.' "[7]

The eminent American historian David Dallin—son of the equally eminent Alexander Dallin—described the OUN as "A violently nationalistic, conspiratorial and terroristic group (which) had as its goal the unification of all Ukrainian areas and the establishment of a united Ukraine as an independent and sovereign power."[8] While Konovalets and Melnyk sought to lead the movement from abroad, a new, younger breed of OUN leaders arose in the cities of Ukraine to challenge the older leaders for preeminence. Militant and fanatical, they carried out thousands of anti-Polish acts of violence against Polish officials, school superintendents, writers, post offices and government agencies.

In 1930, the OUN launched a widespread program of murder, violence and arson throughout Eastern Galicia, with a view to demoralizing the Polish administration and inviting international sympathy for their cause.[9] In 1931, they assassinated Tadeusz Holowko, a highly respected advocate of Polish-Ukrainian compromise; in 1932, they killed the Polish police commissioner in Lviv. In 1934, OUN terrorist Matsekov, operating under specific orders from Bandera, fatally ambushed Interior Minister Bronislaw Pieracki as he went to lunch at his favorite restaurant. Polish-American sociologist Tadeusz Piotrowski concludes that these acts of terror were intended to provoke the Polish authorities to retaliation in keeping with the OUN maxims: "Blood is needed; we will provide a sea of blood."[10]

Pavel Sudoplatov, the former director of the KGB's Administration for Special Tasks who infiltrated the Ukrainian nationalist movement so thoroughly that he became a confidant of Konovalets,[11] writes in his memoirs that Pieracki's assassination came to him as a complete surprise:

> ...the assassination of the Polish minister General Bronislaw Pieracki...by Matsekov was undertaken contrary to the order of Konovalets and was carried out on the command of Bandera, his rival. Bandera had wanted to seize control of the organization by capitalizing on the natural enmity of Ukrainians against Pieracki, who was responsible for repression of the Ukrainian minority in Poland. Konovalets told me that the Germans and Poles had just signed a treaty of friendship and the Germans, for the time being, were in no way interested in acts against the Poles. The Germans were so outraged by the assassination that they turned over Bandera and his followers to the Poles, but the assassin Matsekov managed to escape.[12]

Bandera was sentenced to hang, but the *Abwehr* preferred not to destroy the terrorist organization that was receiving their support and put pressure on the Polish government to reduce his sentence to a prison term.[13]

The OUN's terror campaign did not meet with general approval. It was forcefully condemned by Count Andrii Sheptytsky, the revered Metropolitan of the Ukrainian Greek Catholic (Uniate) Church in his message to the OUN: "If you want to kill everyone who is against your activities, you will have to kill all professors, all pedagogues who work for the good of Ukrainian youth, all parents of the Ukrainian children, all teachers, all headmasters, all politicians, all involved in social activities."[14]

The Ukrainian Galicians were not the only victims of Poland's efforts to reconstitute themselves. Encouraged by government policies, a wave of aggressive antisemitism swept post-war Poland, resulting in clashes on university campuses and anti-Jewish pogroms in several cities. Moderate, democratic political leaders in Galicia belonging to UNDO, the

Ukrainian National Democratic Union (*Ukrainske Natsionalne-Demokratychne Obiednanie*) and the USDP, the Ukrainian Socialist Democratic Party (*Ukrainska Socialistychna Demokratychna Partiia*) condemned the antisemitic excesses but lost ground steadily to the OUN, which did not hesitate to exploit the anti-Jewish myths and stereotypes so pervasive in Eastern Europe.

Betty Einstein-Keshev, an eyewitness to wartime events in Galicia, writes of Bandera and the OUN:

> Bandera's program was to create an independent Ukrainian state covering the entire ethnographic Ukraine with Kiev as its capital. To reach this goal they had to fight many enemies: the Soviets, the Jews, Poles, Germans and even the Orthodox Church.
>
> The Banderists wanted to finish off all their enemies at once. Their method of waging war was murder and destruction with no quarter shown. The independent Ukraine promised death and destruction to Jews and brought death and destruction with it. The Banderists carried out precisely what the chorus of their anthem proclaimed: "Death! Death! Death!" They distinguished themselves with extraordinary sadism, which exceeded the atrocities of the Germans.[15]

Present day apologists for the OUN prefer to emphasize the organization's nationalist strivings and avoid mention of its fascist proclivities, its racism and its antisemitism. However, numerous scholars—Ukrainian and non-Ukrainian—have found it necessary to clarify the nature of the movement. Panias Fedenko, for example, a former professor at the Free Ukrainian University at Munich, states frankly: "The ideology, tactics and morals of German Nazism and Italian Fascism were adopted by the OUN."[16]

According to Fedenko, the OUN rejected democracy in principle and ridiculed the "outmoded liberal-socialist-democratic psychosis which enveloped Europe in the 19th century." Fascism was acclaimed as the "ideal" social order and State Syndicalism as the ideal of Ukrainian nationalism. The OUN dictatorship would tolerate no other parties.[17]

Canadian-Ukrainian scholar Ivan L. Rudnitsky describes the OUN's vision of a future independent Ukraine as a "dictatorial, one party state." The OUN's emphasis on violence, Rudnitsky observes, "led to a blunting of moral sensibilities, as demonstrated by the use of physical and moral terror against Ukrainian political opponents." The reliance on "myth" rather than knowledge "interfered with the ability to perceive reality objectively and therefore, with rational and responsible decision-making."[18]

In his massive history of Ukraine, Orest Subtelny states that Ukrainian integral nationalists envisioned a "political system...based on the rule of one nationalist party. A hierarchy of 'fighters' or 'better people' would form the core of the party and its leadership.

At the pinnacle of the movement and the future state was the supreme leader or *vozhd* whose authority was unquestionable and unlimited."[19]

From the start, OUN ideologues dreamed of a "Greater Ukraine" encompassing all ethnographic areas where the Ukrainian language was spoken. This included sizeable portions of the Russian Federation, Belarus, Poland, Slovakia, Romania and Moldavia. According to Polish historian Wiktor Polisczuk, numerous maps published by Ukrainian nationalists delineating the Ukrainian ethnographic areas would expand present-day Ukraine by at least a third or 200,000 kilometers.[20]

Dmitri Dontsov

OUN theoreticians were highly influenced by Ukrainian geopolitical thinker Dmitri Dontsov, who argued that democracy was not suited for Ukrainians. "The masses," he wrote, "need to be enlightened and led by a small, sophisticated elite through a process of creative coercion."[21] Mouthing typical fascist sentiments, Dontsov insisted: "Every great idea is irreconcilable, uncompromisable, brutal, fanatic and amoral."[22] Dontsov, who was to settle in Canada in 1950, wrote in the May 1939 issue of *literaturnonaukovy Visnik* that international Jewry had caused the collapse of Germany in the First World War by the introduction of Bolshevik ideas: "Having seized control of the press, theatre, the arts and cinematography, they castrated the soul of the German people, forcing their attention and their tastes towards hedonism, erotomania and internationalism."[23]

In other works, Dontsov claimed that scientific measurements proved the genetic superiority of the Ukrainian race over the Russians and all other Slavs. Ukrainians, therefore, were destined to form the "ruling caste" and rule over the "inferior races" who must be content to serve their masters. Accused of fascist and Hitlerite leanings by his critics, Dontsov replied: "Read the Rome and Berlin press. There the great problem of our time is placed exactly as I understand it... Fascism, this is the new, vital ideology of the present destined to revitalize the poisoned...spiritual atmosphere of Europe."[24]

Dontsov's ideas were as unequivocally fascist as the members of the OUN that espoused them. However, a number of Canadian and American scholars with close ties to the Ukrainian nationalist community have shied away from using the term "fascist" and its inevitable stigma by employing the more academic-sounding, less denunciatory term, "integral nationalist," to describe the OUN ideology. Despite considerable intellectual squirming, however, they have been unable to avoid recognition of the essentially fascist nature of its program.

John A. Armstrong, author of *Ukrainian Nationalism: 1939-1945*, whose book gave currency to the term "integral nationalism" offers the following description of the movement's beliefs:

1. A belief in the nation as the supreme value to which all others must be subordinated;

2. An appeal to mystically conceived ideas of solidarity of all individuals making up the nation, usually on the assumption that biological characteristics (have) welded them into one organic whole;

3. A subordination of rational analytic thought to the "intuitively correct" emotions;

4. Expression of the "national will" through a charismatic leader...

5. Glorification of action, war, and violence as an expression of the superior biological vitality of the nation.[25]

Take away the distancing effect of Armstrong's academic language and his description of the essential qualities of Ukrainian "integral nationalism" would serve just as well to describe the ideology of Hitler's *Mein Kampf*.

What kind of state would the OUN have created had Ukraine become independent? How would it have been governed? The answer can be clearly seen in the OUN's brief Transcarpathian venture into statehood. Isolated from their Ukrainian compatriots by the Carpathian Mountains, the Carpatho-Ukrainians were among the most politically, socio-economically and culturally underdeveloped of all Ukrainians. With the fall of the Austro-Hungarian empire in 1918, there came an end to Hungary's oppressive rule and the incorporation of the region into the Czechoslovakian Republic.

In 1938, Britain and France, in an attempt to appease Hitler, compelled Czechoslovakia to cede the Sudetenland to the German dictator. The German *Führer* now proceeded to dismember what remained of the Czechoslovak republic. For this purpose, German intelligence recruited Slovak nationalists to agitate for an independent Slovakia and called on members of the OUN to raise the political temperature among Carpatho-Ukrainians. Under pressure from its enemies and deserted by its allies, Czechoslovakia was forced to permit first, Slovakia and then Transcarpathia to declare their independence as "free, federated states" within the Czechoslovakian Republic. Six months later—after Hitler had occupied Bohemia and Moravia—the OUN engineered a coup to take over the government of Transcarpathia. On March 15, it declared the Carpatho-Ukraine an independent Ukrainian state. But, Hitler had lost interest in the Ukrainian nationalists and decreed that the Carpatho-Ukraine should be handed over to Hungary. The Ukrainian nationalists felt betrayed by Hitler's decision and rejected German advice to submit to Hungarian rule.[26]

Within weeks, Hungary moved in its troops and sent the OUN packing. But in those few weeks, the OUN fully showed its hand. Despite Hitler's betrayal, the German National Socialist State remained its model and guiding light. Since all political parties in Germany other than the NSDAP were banned, the OUNists in the Carpathian Ukraine followed suit and banned all parties other than their own. "It was the OUN forever," writes Mykyta Kosakivsky, "One party, one nation, one Führer, for this is what Germany has. Nazis had the Dachau camp. So OUNists had to have a camp too—and got it; the Dumen in Transcarpathia was the place for people with 'wrong thoughts,' 'subversives,' and 'suspicious characters.' Nazis were beating and torturing their political enemies. OUNists were doing the same... The Germans confiscated the property of foreigners and Jews; the OUNists were doing the same... The OUNists treated the Jews like the Nazis did. They taxed the Jewish shops in Transcarpathia...saying the Germans are doing it too."[27]

Ironically, the OUN's enthusiasm for fascist ideas and Hitler's 'New Order' did not affect in the least the German dictator's plans to eradicate millions of Slavs. Indeed, it can be said "in Hitler's and Himmler's plans for a Thousand Year Reich, the 'Final Solution of the Jewish Problem' was only a grand rehearsal for a much vaster 'solution'—the destruction of the Slav peoples." As early as January 1941, Himmler told a gathering of SS officials that the destruction of thirty million Slavs was a prerequisite for German planning in the East.[28] Following the sweeping Nazi military victories in 1941-42, Himmler's plans grew ever bolder and the number of "subhuman" Slavs to be driven beyond the Urals and exterminated reached the figure of 100 millions.[29] Only the ultimate victory of the Red Army prevented Himmler and his SS minions from fulfilling his plans.

OUN Connections with the Abwehr

Seductive though totalitarian ideas may have been in the 1930s, the OUN remained a minority, extremist movement, dependent for financing and success on great power sponsorship. Connections between radical-right Ukrainian groups willing to hire out to foreign intelligence services can be traced back to the time of the 1918 British and American intervention against the Bolshevik revolution. Leading figures in the British Secret Service were directly involved in operations in the White Sea ports of Murmansk and Arkhangelsk and the Pacific port of Vladivostok. E.H. Cookridge, who has written extensively on the convoluted intelligence culture, remarks: "In the mid-1930s, Admiral Sir Hugh "Quex" Sinclair, who had been head of naval intelligence during the 'Intervention' years and was now head of SIS [Secret Intelligence Service or MI6], patronized Stepan Bandera, the leader of the Organization of Ukrainian Nationalist Revolutionaries (OUNR), the most reactionary of the émigré groups."[30] Bandera, who boasted to Sinclair that he had the largest following among anti-Communist Ukrainians inside the Soviet Union, was unable to prove his effectiveness to the British and was dropped by the SIS.

The *Abwehr*, the German Military Intelligence, found better use for the OUN's services. Admiral Wilhelm Canaris, appointed head of the *Abwehr* in January 1935, had a great love for "everything that smelt of reaction" and did not hesitate to establish contacts with OUN founder Ievhen Konovalets and other right-wing Ukrainian exiles who had taken refuge in Germany after their defeat in the Civil War. When, in 1938, Konovalets was assassinated by the Soviet secret police (NKVD), the mantle of leadership passed to two, bitterly-opposed contenders: Andrii Melnyk, veteran officer of the Austro- Hungarian army and Deputy-Commander of the Ukrainian *Sichovi Striltsi* (Sich Riflemen) and the younger, more impetuously militant Bandera.[31] The latter, imprisoned by the Polish government for his involvement in the assassination of Polish cabinet minister Pieracki, continued to exercise leadership from his prison cell. Once the Germans had taken Warsaw, Canaris arranged Banderas' immediate release.

A consummate schemer, Canaris made room for both Melnyk and Bandera in the *Abwehr's* Second Department, which specialized in sabotage and subversion under the direction of General Erwin Lahousen and Colonel Erwin Stolze. Skillfully playing one man against the other, Canaris bestowed Konovalets' former *Abwehr* code-name, Consul I, on Melnyk while Bandera became known as Consul II. In advance of the 1939 campaign against Poland, Canaris ordered Ukrainian exiles smuggled into Poland to weaken Polish defenses by launching a terror campaign against the Jews and the Polish farmers. According to General Lahousen's testimony at the Nuremberg Trials, the mission was to provoke an uprising in which all Polish homes would be set afire and Jews killed.[32]

As it happened, the German advance against Poland was so rapid that the services of the Ukrainian saboteurs were hardly needed. However, there were more campaigns to come. Canaris recruited the Ukrainian nationalists who had served in the Polish army and were now held in German prisoner-of-war camps. To these he added Ukrainian exiles that had fled to German- occupied Polish territory, and placed them in the *Abwehr's* sabotage unit—the Brandenburg 800 Regiment—in preparation for the impending invasion of the Soviet Union. In the winter of 1940-1941, Canaris arranged his Ukrainian recruits in two separate terrorist units under the nominal commands of Consul I and Consul II. With typical cynicism, he bestowed poetic, romantic names on these formations while training them in murder and destruction. Melnyk's unit was named Roland after the medieval French knight who died in battle against with the Saracens and served as inspiration for numerous French *chansons*. Bandera's unit was given the utterly inappropriate designation, *Nachtigall* or Nightingale.

"After the outbreak of World War II," writes historian Philip Friedman, "the Germans constantly favored the OUN at the expense of more moderate Ukrainian groups...[but] to avoid open provocation of Soviet Russia, with which Germany at that time still maintained friendly relations, these Ukrainian divisions were called 'labor service' or 'labor divisions.' In reality, however, they had received full military training. When the Germans invaded Eastern Galicia in June 1941, they brought with them the Ukrainian formations

Roland and *Nachtigall* led by Bandera's [and Melnyk's] adherents under the supervision of the German *Abwehr*."[33]

In the spring of 1941, additional nationalists were recruited in Poland and Germany to form OUN "marching groups" (*Marschketten*) that would follow on the heels of the advancing German army. Their task was to help the Nazis establish the "New Order" by helping select mayors, police chiefs and town clerks in the occupied territories.[34]

Some ten days before the 1941 German invasion of the Soviet Union, Melnyk sent Hitler a detailed document in which he touted OUN/Melnyk as the most appropriate, most authoritarian nationalist organization in Ukraine, the one the Reich could rely on as the "sole counterweight" to Muscovite and Jewish aspirations.[35] Late in June 1941, Melnyk wrote again to the German *Führer*, requesting "the honour to be permitted to march shoulder to shoulder with the liberators, the German *Wehrmacht*." On July 10 of that tragic year, Melnyk pledged his full support of Hitler's plan to build a Europe "free of Jews, Bolsheviks and plutocrats."[36]

Notes

1. Subtelny, *Ukraine*. 29.

2. Armstrong, *Ukrainian Nationalism*, 3'd edition, 15.

3. Several versions of the Decalogue can be found in various histories of the Ukrainian Nationalist movement. Some have rewritten the more extreme statements to make them more acceptable to a democratic audience. However, the version above is provided by Alexander J. Motyl, *The Turn to the Right: The Ideological Origins and Development of Ukrainian Nationalism*, 1919-1929. (New York: East European Monographs, 1980), 142, is the most authentic.

4. *Ibid*. 143.

5. See Yury Boshyk, editor, *Ukraine during World War II: History and Aftermath* (Edmonton: Canadian Institute of Ukrainian Affairs, 1986), 173.

6. According to Pavel Sudoplatov, the former director of the KGB's Administration for Special Tasks, the OUN had contracted with Croatian Nationalists to carry out the assassination of King Alexander of Yugoslavia and Minister of Foreign Affairs Louis Berthou of France. See: Pavel and Anatoli Sudoplatov, *Special Tasks: The Memoirs of an Unwanted Witness - A Soviet Spymaster* (Boston: Little, Brown & Company, 1995 edition), 18.

7. Hans Höhne, *Canaris* (London: Secker and Warburg, 1979), 316.

8. David Dallin, *Soviet Espionage* (New Haven: Yale University Press, 1955), 350.

9. Tadeusz Piotrowski, *Poland's Holocaust* (Jefferson, N.C.: McFarland and Company, 1998), 192.

10. *Ibid*. 193.

11. It was Sudoplatov who planted the bomb in a box of chocolates that killed Konovalets.

12. Sudoplotov, 15.

13. Sudoplatov, 17.

14. Quoted in Panias Fedenko, "Remarks on Modern History," *Nashe Slovo*, Munich, 1977, 1.

15. Betti Einstein-Keshev, "The Story of Independent Ukraine," in *Fun Noenten Oiver*, (Out of the Recent Past), Vol. III, trans. B.G. Kayefetz (New York: Central Yiddish Cultural Association, 1957).

16. Fedenko, *op. cit.*

17. *Ibid.*

18. Ivan L. Rudnitsky, *Essays in Modern Ukrainian History*, Peter L. Rudnitsky, ed. (Edmonton: Canadian Institute of Ukrainian Studies, 1987), 107-108.

19. Subtelny, *Ukraine*, 442.

20. Wiktor Polisczuk, *Legal and Political Assessment of the OUN and UPA* (Toronto: Wiktor Polisczuk, 1997), 17.

21. Quoted in Myron S. Kuropas, "The Unity Thing," *Ukrainian Weekly*, March 28, 1993, 7.

22. Dmitri Dontsov, *Nationalism* (Lemberg: 1936), 224. Dontsov settled in Canada after World War II and obtained a teaching position at a Quebec university. He was a frequent head-table guest and speaker at Ukrainian-Canadian banquets and conferences.

23. Quoted from Michael Hanusiak, *Lest We Forget* (Toronto: Progress Books, 1976), 13.

24. Quoted in Paul Kovalchuk, *The Adopted Criminals*, translated from Ukrainian, (Kiev: Ukrainian Publishing House, 1973), 4-5.

25. John A. Armstrong, *Ukrainian Nationalism*, 3'd edition, 13.

26. *Ibid.* 16.

27. Mykyta Kosakivsky, *"Z Nedan'oho Minuloho"* (This was not so long ago), *Nashe Slovo Review*, No.5, 1977, 67-80. Reprinted in "Remarks on Modern History, " Part II, July 1978.

28. R. Ainsztein, "Final Solution? of the Slav Problem, Colonization with Assassination," *Wiener Library Bulletin*, Vol. IV, No. 2, March 1950, 36-38.

29. R. Ainsztein, *Ibid.*

30. E.H. Cookridge, *Gehlen, Spy of the Century*, (London: Transworld Publishers, 1972), 307.

31. In the inter-war years, the *Sichovi Striltsi* or Sich Sharpshooters was an illegal paramilitary organization consisting largely of Ukrainian veterans of the Austrian army and veterans of Petliura's armies.

32. Nuremberg Trials on the Main Nazi War Criminals, 7 volumes (Munich: 1958), Vol. 2, 99-100.

33. Philip Friedman, *Roads to Extinction* (New York: Jewish Publication Society of America, 1980), 179.

34. The extent to which the *Marschketten* were sponsored by the Germans is debatable. Armstrong sees them as possibly tolerated by the Wehrmacht, but intent, nevertheless, on proclaiming the *akt* of Lviv throughout Ukraine, organizing a Ukrainian state apparatus and recruiting a Ukrainian army from former soldiers of the Red and Polish armies. "They realized that the German authorities were not going to welcome them cordially; consequently they carefully skirted the large towns and concentrations of German troops... The Wehrmacht commanders, like all field soldiers, were annoyed at the presence of unauthorized civilians in their zone of operations. However, most had heard of the cooperation of the youthful movement with the Germans. Moreover, in many cases, they undoubtedly had real sympathy for Ukrainian nationalist aspirations, for they had seen the touching gratitude with which the Ukrainians welcomed their supposed deliverers from Soviet tyranny and their readiness to cooperate against the Bolshevik regime." Third edition, 61.

35. Alexander Dallin, *German Rule in Russia 1941-1945: A Study of Occupational Policies* (London: Macmillan & Co., 1957), 118.

36. Dallin, *Ibid.* footnote on page 121. Dallin's quotations are drawn from *Einsatzgruppen* (mobile killing squads) reports for July 7 and July 15, 1941. The heads of the four major *Einsatzgruppen* sent regular situation reports to SS headquarters in Berlin.

CHAPTER 4

SLAUGHTER IN LVIV

A FULL SEASON OF FATEFUL BETRAYALS PRECEDED THE ONSET of World War II. Hitler defied the Treaty of Versailles by remilitarizing the Rhineland. Next, he imposed an *Anschluss* on a more or less willing Austria and proceeded to bully Czechoslovakia into a state of helplessness. England and France betrayed the Loyalist government of Spain with a false pose of neutrality and abandoned their promise to defend Czechoslovakia against the Germans. In the name of "peace for our time" British Prime Minister Neville Chamberlain and French Premier Edouard Daladier signed the Munich Agreement on September 30, 1938, bestowing Czechoslovakia's Sudetenland on Nazi Germany. Robert T. Elson, in *Prelude to War*, recalls those bitter days:

> The Munich Pact spelled Czechoslovakia's doom. Loss of the Sudetenland not only stripped the country of its principal line of fortifications against Germany, but also whetted the appetite of Czechoslovakia's other enemies. Poland and Hungary simply walked in and took some 8,000 square miles of Czech territory. The provinces of Slovakia and Ruthenia demanded and got a large degree of autonomy.[1]

Hopelessly dismembered, Czechoslovakia could offer no resistance when Hitler declared Bohemia and Moravia German protectorates and moved his troops into what remained of Czechoslovakia. Hitler proclaimed: "Czechoslovakia has ceased to exist."

The world was stunned in August 1939, when the Soviet Union signed a non-aggression pact with Nazi Germany, ostensibly communism's most relentless ideological enemy. The pact promised free rein to both Hitler and Stalin in their respective spheres of influence while secret protocols set the stage for the destruction of Poland and the seizure of the Baltic States, Bessarabia and Bukovina by the USSR.

Prelude became grim reality on September 1, 1939, with the German attack on Poland. Polish resistance was heroic but futile. The German forces were vastly superior in numbers, aircraft, tanks and artillery. The German *Blitzkrieg*, previously untried, penetrated the Polish defenses, encircled it armies, smashed Polish communications and made it impossible for Polish generals to communicate with their troops.

On September 17, in accord with the Nazi-Soviet pact, the Red Army began to take possession of eastern Poland. Five days later Lviv and Bialystok were taken by the Russians. Faced with two simultaneous, overwhelming forces, the Polish military situation was hopeless.[2]

Warsaw, severely bombed and fully surrounded, fought desperately but was forced to surrender to the Germans on September 27. The *Black Book of Polish Jewry* reports:

> Warsaw capitulated after three weeks of resistance and heroic struggle. On September 29, 1939, the German army marched into the capital of Poland; the Jewish quarters of the city had been subjected to an especially heavy bombardment during the closing days of the siege... From beneath the ruins, the Jews began to drag out the corpses that had been buried during the long days of the bombardment.[3]

The completion of the German military campaign saw the beginning of a cruel program of persecution of Poland's three-and-a-quarter million Jews. As each locality was occupied, Jews were isolated from the remainder of the population, driven into overcrowded, unsanitary ghettos, weakened by hunger and physical abuse, deprived of medical assistance, and drafted for hard labour.

> The Germans treated the Jews with their customary brutality, they cut off the beards of the Jews, plundered Jewish stores and sent eighty Jews to the concentration camp in Krakow... Czestochowa, near the Polish-German frontier was occupied on September 3. Immediately upon their arrival, the Germans started a hunt for Jews, beating and killing them on the streets and looting their homes. The pogrom lasted several days during which 180 Jews were killed.[4]

Bielsko followed Czestochowa where some 2,000 Jews were beaten and tortured, synagogues and schools destroyed. Bygdoszcz, Kalisz, Aleksandrow, Piotrkow, Zgierz, Wloclawek, Mielec, were given similar treatment.[5]

The German march brought Hitler's forces to Krakow, Lodz, Lublin and Lviv; hunger and disease followed. The *Black Book of Polish Jewry*, compiled by a respected group of Jewish historians, describes the subsequent treatment of the city's Jewish inhabitants:

> The persecution of the Jews began on the very first day of the German occupation. German soldiers plundered Jewish homes, shot Jews dead in the streets and dragged off, tortured and insulted men, women and children... It was the German intention not only to ruin the Jewish inhabitants economically and make beggars of them, but to exterminate them physically.[6]

The plight of Warsaw's Jews in the years that followed has been detailed in numerous works by competent scholars and needs no recapitulation here. Polish diplomat Jan

Karski-Kozielewski made a secret visit to the Warsaw ghetto in 1942 and described the extremes of hunger and disease he witnessed in *Story of a Secret State*. Karski, deeply disturbed by what he had witnessed, notified British Foreign Secretary Anthony Eden and the Polish Government-in-Exile that 300,000 of Warsaw's 500,000 Jews jammed in the Warsaw Ghetto had been "resettled" in an obscure village about 60 miles from Warsaw where the Germans had established an extermination camp. His warning fell on deaf ears.[7]

Determined to exterminate all of Warsaw's Jews, the German administration ordered the Jewish Council (*Judenrat*) to deliver 6,000 Jews daily to a collection place (*Umschlagplatz*) for 'resettlement in the East.' The deportees were transported in cattle cars to Treblinka, Majdanek and Trawniki. Gerald Reitlinger, author of *The Final Solution*, observes: "Nearly half the ghetto population had gone by August 15, 1942."[8]

Increasingly aware that resettlement meant death, desperate groups of Jewish young people organized to resist the Nazis. Their decision to fight was an act of desperation without hope of victory or survival. Despite its hopelessness or perhaps because of it, Reitlinger characterizes the ghetto rebellion as "a Jewish epic in its own right."[9]

Himmler appointed *SS-Sturmbannführer* Jürgen Stroop to wipe out the resisters. The fighting began on April 19, 1943.The Jewish Combat Organization fought from cellars and rooftops against tanks, armored cars and flame throwers. Originally Stroop expected the action to take no more than three days, but it was thirty-three days before he could boastfully announce, "The Jewish Quarter of Warsaw is no more."[10]

The fighting, though sharp, was essentially small scale. The rebellion, though historically significant, was confined within the ghetto walls and posed no threat to the German army. Stroop's forces numbered no more than 2,090 men, including 105 German Police, 540 Waffen-SS personnel, 16 Security Police, 161 Polish Police and 160 Trawniki men.[11]

The presence of a contingent of Trawniki men, consisting of Ukrainian and Baltic auxiliary policemen, has led some to allege that the 14th Waffen-SS Division participated in the suppression of the Warsaw Ghetto Uprising. The Trawniki detachments were recruited by the Germans from the vast number of Soviet soldiers held in German prisoner-of-war camps under horrendous conditions following their capture in 1941-42. They were given rudimentary training at the Trawniki Transit and Labour camp on the railway line to Lublin and subsequently assigned to guard duty at concentration camp guard towers and ghetto gates. They frequently served as guards on trains headed for the death camps. Their brutality was notorious.

Although there were numerous Ukrainians among the Trawniki men, they were not a source of recruits to the 14th Volunteer Grenadier Waffen-SS Division. The Division had barely begun to be organized in the spring of 1943 when the fighting raged in Warsaw, so it was impossible for the full Division or any part of it to participate in the suppression of the 1943 Jewish uprising. However, the question remains: Did the Division or some part of it participate in the brutal suppression of the Polish Uprising in Warsaw that took place the following year? That question will be dealt with in a later chapter.

Hitler unleashed "Operation Barbarossa" on the Soviet Union early in the morning of June 22, 1941. His objective was to defeat the Bolshevik enemy, reap the vast wheat fields of Ukraine and command the oil and mineral wealth of the Caucuses. The occupation of the Soviet Union would also allow him to resolve the "Jewish Problem" in Eastern Europe, a matter of considerable importance to the *Führer* who defined the war as an ideological battle against Jewish Bolshevism.

From Finland to the Black Sea, some 3,500,000 German troops, organized in three army groups—North, Central and South—poured across the Soviet frontier.[12] Following on the heels of Army Group South, Bandera's *Nachtigall* formation, clad in *Wehrmacht feldgrau,* crossed into Soviet territory at Przemysl on June 29 and quickly made its way to Lviv in German transport trucks. Ostensibly led by its token Ukrainian commander, Roman Shukhevych, they were, in fact, under the direct command of *Abwehr* Senior Lieutenant D. Herzner and political adviser Theodor Oberländer.[13] Speeding ahead of the regular German forces, they arrived in Lviv at 3:15 a.m. on June 30, some seven hours in advance of the main German forces. Six civilian members of the OUN leadership, Jaroslav Stetsko, Lev Rebet, Iaroslav Starukh, Ivan Ravlyk, Stephan Lenkavsky and Dmytro Jaciv accompanied them.[14]

Melnyk's *Roland* battalion, under the command of *Abwehr* Colonel R. Jary, advanced from the village of Zaubersdorf, near Vienna, hard on the heels of the *Wehrmacht* in its drive on Kiev. In contrast to the field-grey uniforms of *Nachtigall,* Melnyk's forces wore the blue uniforms of the Galician *sich* armies of the revolutionary period.

Following both formations, cadres of young Ukrainian nationalists known as *Marschketten* (Marching Groups) sped eastward by train, truck and wagon to usurp the civic functions in hundreds of occupied towns and villages.[15] Working in concert with local underground members of the OUN they sought to create their own administration and organize a militia consisting of OUN members.[16]

No sooner did the *Nachtigall* formation enter Lviv than the killing began. Armed with a blacklist prepared by Oberländer, Bandera, Stetsko and Shukhevych, death squads rounded up hundreds of suspected communists, Soviet functionaries, Polish scholars and Jewish intellectuals and put them against the wall.[17] In keeping with the Nazi strategy of eliminating the intellectual and political leadership of countries it occupied, more than 700 university professors and 1,000 secondary school teachers and 4,000 elementary school teachers were exterminated by the German invaders.[18]

Joachim Schoenfeld, an eyewitness to many of these events states:

Jews were arrested in the streets or carried away from their houses and dragged to the Brigidky prison where they were brutally tortured, shot, hanged and viciously beaten to death. Six thousand Jews, young, old, lawyers, workers, doctors, merchants...among them the Chief Rabbi of Lviv, university professors, lost their lives in the pogrom. After the pogrom, a part of the building to which the corpses of the murdered Jews had been carried was burned down...with inmates still locked in their cells.[19]

Historian Philip Friedman, the most cautious and restrained of the Jewish historians who survived the Holocaust, offers a detailed account of the initial attack on the Jews of Lviv. He reports that from June 30 until July 3, German soldiers spread through the streets of the city in the company of Ukrainian nationalists and an unruly mob of local citizens. Soldiers and citizens fell upon the Jews in the streets, beat them murderously and dragged them away for "work," chiefly for cleansing the prisons filled with corpses and caked with blood. Thousands of Jews were seized and conveyed to jails on Zamarstynowska, Jachowicza and Lackiego Streets. Others were dragged of to the Brigidky Prison on Kazimierzowska Street and to the Gestapo headquarters at 59 Pelczynska.

Friedman recounts that a deadly fear gripped the Jews of Lviv:

They hid in cellars and ceased to show themselves on the streets of the city. Then the destroyers, chiefly the newly organized Ukrainian militia, began to roam through Jewish houses, to remove men—and frequently women also... Most of the Jews taken to prison courtyards never emerged again. Eyewitnesses who escaped the hoodlums...relate that the courtyard walls of the Brigidky Prison were spattered with fresh blood up to the second floor, and with human brains.[20]

Rabbi David Kahane in his *Lvov Ghetto Diary* confirms these accounts of the initial slaughter in Lviv. "The Germans seized Jews in their homes and forced them to work in the prisons. For that purpose they called upon the services of the Ukrainian police force, which they had set up recently. The Polish and Ukrainian populace rendered whole hearted assistance to the Germans."[21] Kahane was saved from annihilation by the Ukrainian Metropolitan of the Uniate Church, Archbishop Andrii Sheptytsky, who arranged to hide the young rabbi in a Sudite monastery under his jurisdiction. But before finding shelter in the monastery, Kahane witnessed the violence in the streets, the slaughter in the prisons and the promiscuous murder of Jews in *Aktion* after *Aktion*.

But there was worse to come. Three weeks after the slaughter in Brigidky Prison, the Bandera forces proclaimed July 25, Petliura Day in honour of the assassinated Ukrainian general. "To celebrate the holiday and avenge the death of their hero, a hunt for Jews began. Jews were arrested on the streets and carried from their homes," Schoenfeld writes. "Having arrested 5,000 Jews, the Ukrainians massacred and killed a majority of them, leaving others alive, badly wounded, who as the Gestapo asserted, were taken into custody and held as hostages."[22]

The Petliura Day celebration, in Friedman's account, was carried out with terrible zeal during the three-day period of July 25-27. "Thousands of Jewish men and women were seized by Ukrainian militiamen… [The] unfortunates were brought to the prison on Lackiego Street: intermittently Ukrainian mobs would burst in howling 'Revenge for Petliura' and would beat many Jews to death."[23]

German reports praised the "spontaneous efforts of the Ukrainian population to take vengeance on the Jews of Lviv and reported that similar massacres took place in the towns of Dobromil, Yavoriv, Ternopil, Zlochiv and Sambor in Eastern Galicia.[24]

Ukrainians in Lviv dispatched a telegram to Hitler expressing gratitude for their liberation and pledging to assist in the rebuilding of Europe freed from "the bloody Jewish Bolshevist rule and plutocratic oppression."[25] An OUN letter addressed to German police headquarters read in part: "Long live the greater independent Ukraine without Jews, Poles and Germans. Poles behind the San, Germans to Berlin, Jews to the gallows."[26]

Ukrainian historians, Orest Subtelny among them, attribute the fury of the attack on the Jews of Lviv to the sight that confronted the populace on the morning after the Russians had fled the city:

> The sudden advance of the Germans into Galicia caught the NKVD by surprise and it did not have the time to evacuate the prisoners. The solution applied was simple and brutal: during the week of 22-29 June 1941, the NKVD set about slaughtering the inmates of its prisons… It was not only the numbers of the executed (10,000 in Galicia and 5,000 in Volhynia) but also the manner in which they died that shocked the populace… It was evident that many of the prisoners had been tortured to death; others were killed *en masse*.[27]

That the NKVD committed the described acts cannot be denied. Alexander Dallin, dean of the historians of the Nazi occupation, Gerald Reitlinger, one of the earliest and most reliable of Holocaust historians and Rabbi David Kahane all document the same events and offer similar descriptions. However, Reitlinger adds significant details missing from the other descriptions, namely that large numbers of Jews and Poles as well as Ukrainians were among the NKVD victims. Reitlinger reports further that one of the first acts of the

SD (*Sicherheitsdienst*) on its arrival in Lviv was to exhibit large photos in the shops of what were purported to be mass murders committed by Jews.

Although unforgivable crimes were committed in Lviv by Soviet authorities against Ukrainian, Polish and Jewish citizens in the opening days of the war, it was the Jews who were made to pay the price for Soviet depredations by the invading Nazis. In this, the Germans were enthusiastically aided and abetted by their Ukrainian nationalist cohorts. While other populations resisted attempts to spur them into "spontaneous" attacks on the Jews, none proved more willing than the Ukrainian nationalist forces of Western Galicia.[28]

Approximately 540,000 Jews dwelt in Galicia in 1941. In Lviv itself, the estimate runs between 150,000 and 160,000.[29] But by the time the slaughter ended with the return of the Red Army on October 1, 1944, only 1,689 Jews are known to have survived. In the whole of Galicia, no more than 10,000 to 15,000 of the original 540,000 had the good fortune to come through alive.[30] However, a mere recital of population figures fails to convey the full horror imposed on Jewish communities in Galicia. One example should suffice although many others could be offered. On March 5, 1943, the Jewish Telegraphic agency published a detailed report describing the annihilation of the Jewish community of Kolomyja:

> When the German army entered Kolomyja there were 58,000 Jews there... By September 1942, only 8,000 remained in the Ghetto of Kolomyja... Thousands of Jews were burned alive when forced to leap naked into flaming fires. Others were driven into the forest where they were shot to death by Nazi firing squads. After witnessing 150 Jews shot before his eyes, Horowitz, the chairman of the Jewish community, committed suicide in the presence of the Gestapo. In order to make sure that not a single Jew would remain there, the Nazis sent the entire Jewish Ghetto up in flames.[31]

The Role of the Nachtigall Battalion

While granting that massive pogroms took place in Lviv and adjoining Galician cities in the first weeks of the war, some historians question whether the Nachtigall battalion played a significant part in these tragic events. For example, German historian Philipp-Christian Wachs (*Der Fall Theodor Oberländer, 1905-1998*) claims that Nachtigall's role was entirely marginal. The battalion, he reports was kept busy with ceremonial duties in the first days after its arrival in Lviv and had no opportunity to participate in the atrocities that swept over the city. According to Wachs, Nachtigall was confined to its quarters the night it arrived in Lviv (June 30, 1941) and spent the following day at a church service in honour of the KGB victims.

Many of the men, Wachs relates, had lost family members to the KGB and were understandably boiling with rage, but the unit's German leadership—Oberländer, Herzner, Stolze and Hans Koch—met with the men and made it clear that they were strictly forbidden to act on their feelings.[32] An occasional member of the formation, Wachs suggests, may have joined in actions initiated by the SD, but the battalion as a whole played no part in the pogroms.[33]

Despite Wach's account, one is compelled to ask: For what purpose was *Nachtigall*—a highly trained Special Operations regiment specializing in sabotage and subversion—rushed to the city in advance of regular army units? Surely not to serve as honour guards at funerals or to remain confined to barracks performing housekeeping duties.

To properly evaluate *Nachtigall's* role, one must be aware that after the unit left Lviv on July 7, it proceeded to Solochev, Ternopil, Prokurov, Zhitomar and Vynnitsa. Terrible slaughters of the civilian populations followed their arrival in each of these towns.[34]

Jewish eyewitnesses in Lviv recall beatings, stabbing and shootings by Ukrainian soldiers in German uniforms:

> We were escorted by uniformed Ukrainians and civilians wearing yellow or yellow and blue armbands...a double row, consisting exclusively of Ukrainians in German uniforms was formed at the entrance to the courtyard. They had bayonets fixed to their rifles. We were beaten and stabbed...[35]

> In the first days of the occupation, the Ukrainians, who had always been very anti-Semitic, were given a free hand as regards the Jews. We were led to Lacki Street. There were handed over to Ukrainians in German uniform, commanded by German officers who were present there... I was one of a group of some 500 Jews; the Ukrainians killed nearly all... I managed to escape death...[36]

Dallin in his study of German occupation practices supports these allegations. Bandera's followers, he says, including those in the *Nachtigall* regiment, displayed considerable initiative, conducting purges and pogroms.[37]

East-European Antisemitism

The participation of nationalist elements in the large-scale massacres that coincided with the arrival of the Banderist and German forces in Galicia has been largely ignored, skillfully minimized or cynically disclaimed by Ukrainian scholars of a nationalist bent. Subtelny, for example, writes: "Given the lowly position of Ukrainian collaborators in the Nazi apparatus and the SS monopoly on the actual extermination of the Jews, Ukrainian participation in the massacres was neither extensive nor decisive."[38]

Canadian-Ukrainian scholar Yury Boshyk prefers to attribute the atrocities to the actions of "some individuals [who] directly aided or abetted the Nazis in committing crimes against their own people as well as others."[39]

In many cases, Ukrainian nationalist scholars present the slaughter of Jews as a regrettable, but nevertheless understandable *quid pro quo* for the atrocities committed by the Soviets during the 1939-1941 occupation of the western Ukraine and the devastating famine visited upon the eastern Ukraine in 1932-1933. The presence of significant numbers of Jews among the initial leaders of the Bolshevik revolution, and the presence of Jewish commissars in Ukraine prior to and during the famine years, is said to have given rise to the perception among the peasants that Bolshevism is Jewish and that Bolshevik Jews were the chief Soviet agents in the persecution of Ukrainians.

For example, Taras Hunczak, Professor of History at Rutgers University, says: "The popular perception of Jews as agents of Bolshevism resulted in the violent mass outbursts against the Jewish people during the initial stages of the German war against the Soviet Union. The violence was more likely a response to a situation—the aftermath of Soviet rule—than to the OUN's political resolution."[40]

However, the perception of Jews as Bolsheviks is hardly a sufficient explanation for the ferocity of the slaughter that accompanied the OUN's arrival in Lviv. Had antisemitism been unknown in Ukraine before Marx wrote *Das Kapital* and Trotsky helped make the Russian Revolution, this theory might hold some water. But given the strong anti-Jewish sentiments endemic in Eastern Europe, one is compelled to regard the perception of Jews as Bolsheviks as a mere continuation of earlier demonological myths concerning Jews. In the 14th century the Jews of Poland were reviled as usurers. In the 15th, they were perceived as host-desecrators and well poisoners. In the 18th century, the Jews of Galicia were seen as agents of the Polish aristocracy, and as late as the 19th century the Jews of Tarnow were accused of ritual murder. At the turn of the 20th century, the Polish-Galician government instituted a "Buy from your own kind" boycott of Jewish merchants, a boycott in which many Galician Ukrainians readily participated.[41]

Despite the endemic nature of antisemitism in Eastern Europe, large-scale violence was both sporadic and periodic. It was seldom, if ever, spontaneous. In each case, when pogroms swept the land, it resulted from the machinations of specific political forces, specific parties and specific organizations. It is, therefore, nonsense to think that random individuals or an inflamed, unstructured mob committed the atrocities committed in Lviv in 1941.

Who then was responsible for these savage acts? Unquestionably, they resulted from a close partnership between the German *Einsatzgruppen*—which included members of the *Geheime Feldpolizei, Geheime Staatspolizei,* and *Wehrmacht Feldgestapo*—along with the returning Bandera and Melnyk forces and the local nationalists who volunteered their services as militiamen and auxiliary policemen. Erwin Schultz, commander of *Einsatzkommando 5* of *Einsatzgruppe C,* testified at the Nuremberg Trials that by the time his men arrived in Lviv "the military command had already organized a local militia in the city. Dr. Rasch, [commander of *Einsatzgruppe C*] who worked in close cooperation with the militia, ordered the *Sonderkommando* to support it."[42]

The Ukrainian militias—the men who donned blue and gold armbands and coursed the streets to round up Jews—were largely OUN members. Antisemitism was built into the nationalist program; the stereotype of Jews as the flag-bearers of Bolshevism was not just "peasant talk" but formally incorporated into the OUN charter at its April 1941 congress in Krakow. The resolution reads:

> In the USSR the Jews are the most faithful supporters of the ruling Bolshevik regime and the vanguard of Muscovite imperialism in Ukraine. The Muscovite-Bolshevik government exploits the anti-Jewish sentiments of the Ukrainian masses in order to divert their attention from the real perpetrator of their misfortune in order to incite them, in time of upheaval, to carry out pogroms against the Jews. The Organization of Ukrainian Nationalists combats the Jews as the prop of the Muscovite-Bolshevik regime and simultaneously educates the masses to the fact that the principal enemy is Moscow.[43]

Whatever interpretation one chooses to put on the 1941 OUN Charter provision quoted above, there are several inevitable conclusions:

- It is clear that in the eyes of the OUN, the Jews constituted the major "prop" of its principle enemy.
- The OUN recognized and endorsed the "anti-Jewish sentiments of the Ukrainian masses."
- The OUN leadership saw pogroms as a counter-productive distraction. A more effective way to deal with the Jews was to combat Muscovite-Bolshevism at its source. In other words, defeat the Bolsheviks and you simultaneously defeat the Jews.

In practical terms, the OUN could look forward to defeating the Muscovite-Bolsheviks some time in the future, meanwhile their "faithful supporters," the Jews of Galicia, were close at hand and defenseless.

Notes

1. Robert T. Elson, *Prelude to War* (New York: Time-Life Books, 1976), 198.

2. "Polish Campaign," *The Oxford Companion to World War II*, I.C. Bear, editor (Oxford: Oxford University Press, 1995), 903-906.

3. *Ibid.* 16.

4. Jacob Apenszlak, editor, *The Black Book of Polish Jewry; An Account of the Martyrdom of Polish Jewry under Nazi Occupation* (New York: The American Federation of Polish Jews, 1943), 5.

5. *Ibid.* 7.

6. *Ibid.* 17, 18.

7. Equally horrifying descriptions are offered by Yisrael Gutman (*The Jews of Warsaw, 1939-1943);* Emanuel Ringlbaum *(Notes from the Warsaw Ghetto);* Gerald Reitlinger *(The Final Solution);* Raul Hilberg *(Destruction of the European Jews).*

8. Gerald Reitlinger, *The Final Solution* (New York: Beechhurst Press, 1953), 263.

9. *Ibid.* 275.

10. Jürgen Stroop, *The Stroop Report; The Jewish Quarter of Warsaw is No More,* translated by Sybil Milton (New York: Pantheon Books, 1979).

11. *Ibid.* "Teletype Message from SS and Police Leader in the Warsaw District," May 8, 1943.

12. Army Group North, led by Field Marshal Ritter von Leeb was aimed at Leningrad; Army Groups Center, under Field Marshal Fedor von Bock, had Moscow as its goal; Army Groups South, under Field Marshal Gerd von Rundstedt was headed for Kiev and the Caucuses. Hungarian and Romanian forces operated in conjunction with the German 11th Army on a front along the Prut River and the Black Sea.

13. Oberländer, referred to as "The Hangman of Lvov" in *The Brown Book* issued by East German Democratic Republic, is reported to have participated in Hitler's 1923 *Putsch* against the Weimar Republic. When the Nazis came to power, he rose rapidly in the Party ranks. In 1933, he was appointed director of the Institute for East European Economic Affairs and head of the *Bund Deutscher Osten* (BDO) which organized German national groups in foreign countries on behalf of the Reich. With war imminent, he joined the *Wehrmacht's* counter-intelligence arm.

14. Aleksander Drozdzynski and Jan Zaborowski, *Oberländer: A Study in German East Policies,* (Poznan: Wydawn Zachodnie, 1960), 78-79.

15. Edward Prus, *Herosi Spod znaku tryzuba: Konowalec-Bandera-Szuchewyc* (Warsaw: Institut Wydawniczy Zwiaskow Zawodowych, 1985), 168-169.

16. Dieter Pohl, *Nationalsozialistische Judenverfolgung in Ostgalizien 1941-1944: Organisation und Durchführung eines staatlichen Massenverbrechen* (Munich: R. Oldenbourg Verlag, 1996), 47.

17. Reuben Ainsztein, *Jewish Resistance in Nazi Occupied Europe* (London: Paul Elek Publishers, 1964), 252.

18. *Ibid.* 89.

19. Joachim Schoenfeld, *Holocaust Memoirs* (Hoboken: KATV Publishing House, 1985), 47.

20. Friedman, *Roads to Extinction,* 247.

21. David Kahane, *Lvov Ghetto Diary* (Amherst: University of Massachusetts Press, 1990), 6.

22. Schoenfeld, *Holocaust Memoirs,* 47.

23. Friedman, *Roads to Extinction,* 249.

24. *Ibid.* 248.

25. Ronald Headland, *Messages of Murder: A Study of the Reports of the Einsatzgruppen of the Security Police and the Security Service, 1941-1943* (Toronto: Fairleigh Dickinson University Press, 1992), 111.

26. *Ibid.* 114.

27. Orest Subtelny, "The Soviet Occupation of Western Ukraine, 1939-1941: An Overview" in *Ukraine During World War II; History and Aftermath,* ed. Yuri Boshyk (Edmonton: Canadian Institute of Ukrainian Studies, 1986). 12.

28. Additional descriptions of events in Lviv can be found in the following: Lucy Dawidowicz, *The War Against the Jews 1939-1945* (New York: Bantam Books, 1981) 7th printing. 377-378; Ilya Ehrenberg and Vasily Grossman, *The Black Book,* edited and translated by John Glad and James Levine (New York: The Holocaust Library, 1981). 109,123; Alexander Dallin, *German Rule In Russia 1941-1945: A Study of Occupation Policies* (London: Macmillan & Co., 1957). 114; H. Jaeger, "Anti-Bolshevist Bloc of Nations," *Wiener Library Bulletin,* Vol. XVI, No.2, April 1962; Simon Wiesenthal, *The Murderers Among Us* (London: Heinemann, 1967). 29-30; Raul Hilberg, *The Destruction of European Jews* (New York: Harper and Row, 1961). 204-205; Martin Gilbert, *The Holocaust - A History of the Jews of Europe during the Second World War* (New York: Holt Rhinehart and Winston, 1986). 195-201 and Helmut Krausnick and Hans-Heinrich Wilhelm, *Die Truppe des Weltanschauengs Kriege* (Berlin: CDVA, 1981). 186-187.

29. Philip Friedman, "The Destruction of the Jews of Lwow, 1941-1944," in *The Nazi Holocaust: Articles on the Destruction of European Jews,* edited by Michael Marrus (London: Meckler, 1989), 659.

30. Pohl, 385.

31. *The Black Book of Polish Jewry,* 103.

32. Phillip-Christian Wachs, *Der Fall Theodor Oberländer (1905-1998)* (Frankfurt: Campus Verlag, 2000), 85-86.

33. *Ibid.* 88-89.

34. "The Hangman of Lvov," in *Brown Book; War and Nazi Criminals in West Germany* (East Berlin: Verlag Zeit im Bild, 1965), 287.

35. Drozdzynski and Zaborowski, 88.

36. *Ibid.* 88.

37. Alexander Dallin, *German Rule in Russia 1941-1945; A Study of Occupational Policies* (London: Macmillan & Co. Ltd., 1957), 119.

38. Subtelny, *Ukraine,* 472.

39. Yury Boshyk, ed. *Ukraine during World War II: History and its Aftermath - A Symposium* (Edmonton: Canadian Institute of Ukrainian Studies, 1986), xiii.

40. Taras Hunczak, "Ukrainian-Jewish Relations during the Soviet and Nazi Occupations," in *Ukraine during World War II: History and Aftermath.* 43.

41. Jacob Litman, *The Economic Role of Jews in Medieval Poland* (Lanham: University Press of America, 1984), 4-5.

42. Cited in Friedman, *Roads to Extinction,* 246.

43. There are several translations of Resolution 7, none of which alter the meaning in any significant way. The translation quoted above is taken from Taras Hunczak's article "Ukrainian-Jewish Relations" in *Ukraine During World War II.* 40.

CHAPTER 5

EINSATZGRUPPEN, POLICE AUXILIARIES AND THE WAFFEN-SS

HITLER WAS CONFIDENT THAT HIS MASSIVE SURPRISE ATTACK would succeed in defeating the Soviet army before winter set in. However, the German dictator and his generals recognized that with a fighting front stretching from Tallinn in the north to Sevastopol in the south, the *Wehrmacht* would have a difficult time maintaining order behind the lines. The Russian population was expected to be hostile and the Communists would organize resistance groups in the territories occupied by the German army. With every regular soldier required at the front, it would be necessary to create special auxiliary forces to intimidate the local population and discourage the growth of a partisan movement. This special force would root out the local Communist leadership and resolve the "Jewish Problem" by applying the "Final Solution."

Planful as always, the Germans came prepared with a plan developed by Reinhard Heydrich, Head of the SS Security Service (SD). Jews would be herded from the small towns into urban ghettoes and murdered in batches at the convenience of the German authorities. Once concentrated, the Jewish ghetto communities would be strictly governed, their wealth confiscated and their labour exploited until the "ultimate measures" could be undertaken. Heydrich was generally opposed to the isolation of Jews in large urban ghettos lest they become centres of resistance. However, it was necessary to distinguish between short-term measures and ultimate goals. Ghettos, Heydrich emphasized were a temporary step offering better control of the Jewish population and their efficient exploitation.

The plan required the Jews to be marched to a suitable killing ground out of sight of the local population, shot in batches and buried in mass graves. This task, this obligation, would be given the highest priority; no exigency of war, no economic consideration, no shortage of supplies would diminish the necessity of completing the assignment down to the last Jew.[1]

The Nazi hierarchy also dreamed of turning the conquered eastern territories into a German fiefdom. The Ukrainian peasantry would be displaced, one third would eventually be killed, another third would serve as serfs to German settlers and the remainder would perform menial tasks in German-owned industries.

Responsibility for executing the plan was assigned to Himmler and the SS. Four task forces known as *Einsatzgruppen* were organized; each designed to follow on the heels of the three major German armies as they stormed into the USSR. Their orders called on them to destroy the Soviet infrastructure by executing "all officials of the Comintern, officials of senior and middle rank, the central committee, and the provincial and district committees; the People's Commissars."[2] Also targeted for immediate execution were Jews, "in the service of the Party or the State."[3] Well equipped, highly mobile, these special formations were frequently referred to as "Slaughter houses on wheels." Although their total German personnel consisted of no more than 3,000 men, they succeeded in burning down hundreds of villages and murdering over a million and a half Jews in an eighteen-month period.[4]

The *Einsatzgruppen's* definition of Jews "in the service of the Party or the State" made little distinction between Communists and Jews. For example, Einsatzgruppe A stationed in Lithuania reported to its Berlin headquarters that Jewish children were being shot almost daily. It proudly reported that in operations conducted on August 29, 1941, 1,468 Jewish children were put to death along with 582 Jewish men and 1,731 Jewish women.[5]

The Recruitment of Local Police Auxiliaries

Such a thoroughgoing slaughter could never have been achieved without the recruitment of large numbers of local helpers organized into auxiliary police squads. Variously called "defence formations," "punitive battalions" or simply "auxiliary police," these police forces served as the chief agents for the annihilation of Jews in Poland and the territories in the Soviet Union occupied by the Germans.

Raul Hilberg, whose authoritative volume, *The Destruction of the European Jews* is based on an intensive examination of the *Einsatzgruppe* reports submitted by their commanders to SS headquarters in Berlin, writes:

... a Ukrainian militia (*Militz*) was operating in the area of *Einsatzgruppen* C and D. The Ukrainian auxiliaries appeared on the scene in August 1941, and *Einsatzgruppe* C found itself compelled to make use of them because it was repeatedly diverted from its main task to fight the "partisan nuisance." Moving with speed, the *Einsatzgruppe* organized a network of local Ukrainian militias, making them partly self-financing by drawing upon Jewish money to pay their salaries.. The Ukrainians were used principally for the dirty work—thus *Einsatzkommando*

4a went so far as to confine itself to the shooting of adults while commanding its Ukrainian helpers to shoot children.[6]

The auxiliary police battalions were not ordinary town and village policemen who directed traffic and arrested thieves. Their role was much more specialized and they were selected according to a different set of criteria. In order to ensure loyalty and a willingness to undertake the dirty job ahead, priority was given to candidates with pre-war, pro-fascist, nationalist credentials.

Ukrainians were not the only nationality group recruited by the Nazis. Similar police forces were organized in Estonia, Latvia, Lithuania and Belarus. In each case, priority was given to recruitment of men with pro-Nazi, pro-German records. In similar fashion, the Germans chose Ukrainian recruits for their political reliability and their willingness to join Hitler in creating his version of a New Europe. One such recruit was a member of the Savchak family in the village of Zbarazh in the Ternopil region. Within days after the start of the German invasion, one of the OUN's *Marchketten* reached the village. Passionate speeches were made and the villagers were called upon to support the German invaders. Patriotic young men were urged to enlist in local police units. Savchak expressed his eagerness to join the new police force and was immediately appointed a platoon leader. "He imagined himself as a representative of the 'New Order.' He admired his new uniform, feeling like a 'Superman.'"[7] On October 2, 1941, several truckloads of German SS-men and Ukrainian auxiliary policemen descended on the nearby village of Berezhany, Savchak among them. Civilians, Jews and non-Jews, were rounded up and transported to an adjoining village where they were executed. Savchak is reported to have curried favour with his Nazi bosses by tearing the clothes off the victims and laughing at their pleas for mercy.

Later that year, Savchak joined with other auxiliary police in the torture and murder of inmates of the Tarnopil prison. Again, he is reported to have shown such enthusiasm for the task that he drew the praise of the operation's SS Chief.[8]

In July 1943, Savchak enlisted in the Ukrainian SS Division *Galizien* as a machine gunner. After the defeat of the Division in a crucial battle against the Red Army near the town of Brody, Savchak deserted and took shelter with his parents who resided at the time in the village of Blajhiv in the Lviv District. There, with the help of forged papers he resumed civilian life but was exposed some years later, tried and punished.

In the first flush of the German occupation, the police recruits began their careers as arm-banded volunteers in civilian dress. If they exhibited the requisite ruthlessness, they could be advanced to the ranks of auxiliary policemen in local uniforms and subsequently promoted to police battalions in SS dress. When the need for fighting men at the front outweighed the need for personnel to police the rear areas, they were encouraged to join ethnic Waffen-SS brigades, either singly or as whole police units.

Philip Friedman, in his *Roads to Extinction* describes the auxiliary police units as the principal form of collaboration between the Germans and the local Ukrainian population. They functioned as assistants to the German police and the SS in their anti-Jewish campaigns. They maintained a watch over the ghettoes, guarded the transports conveying Jews to the extermination camps and served directly as the triggermen or executioners in the extermination of Jews.

The Ukrainian police auxiliaries did not serve exclusively in Ukrainian territories. Their German commanders dispatched them to Warsaw and various Polish and Lithuanian ghettoes. Friedman explains: "They were also used as guards to carry out the work of extermination in various concentration camps: Sasow, Ostrow, Grochow, Poniatow, Plaszow, the Janowska Street camp [in Lviv] and the death camps of Sobibor, Treblinka among others. Further Ukrainian policemen were used to guard prisons that held Jews, such as the notorious Pawiak Prison in Warsaw."[9]

According to Hilberg, the fearsome efficiency of the *Einsatzgruppen* which resulted in the death of one and a half million Jews on Soviet territory in the space of a year, was due entirely to the help given the Germans by the auxiliary police.[10] Recruited locally, they were familiar with the Jews in their villages and knew their houses. Having, in some cases gone to school with the Jews they could identify them readily and prevent them from passing as Ukrainians. If the Jews tried to hide, they could guess at their hiding places.

Ukrainian-American journalist Michael Hanusiak, who until his retirement wrote for a pro-Soviet Ukrainian newspaper in New York, received early access to USSR archives. He reports that in October 1941, SD officer Hans Krieger and his Ukrainian auxiliaries surrounded the Stanislaviv ghetto and ordered its inhabitants to assemble on Blavaderska Street. "All in all, there were 20,000 children, women and elderly people who were marched in column to the Jewish cemetery located near the local shoe factory. There the shooting began and continued for a large part of the day. Twelve thousand people—dead and alive together—remained lying in the ravine that became their mass grave. The remaining 8,000 were forced to return to the ghetto because the SS-men and the Ukrainian policemen, who carried out the action, grew tired of shooting."[11]

Similar reports tell of the inhuman cruelty exercised by the German-led police units in the wholesale destruction of Jews in thousands of towns and villages. One such unit, the SS-102 Punitive Battalion, was especially active in the Ternopil region. Its brutal killing methods were illustrative of the standard procedure laid down by the SS and followed meticulously in cities, towns and villages from Estonia to Crimea. A witness to the killings in Kremianets testified: "The trucks kept bringing people to the place of execution till 10 p.m. First they brought out children of various ages and also their mothers. When the tailgates of the trucks were removed, the police, cursing horribly, started pushing them off with their rifle butts and clubs. Everyone was undressed and lined up by fours. Then they were forced to approach the 'trench.' The horrible screams of the victims merged with the stutter of machine guns. The victims fell one on top of each other. One woman dropped her small daughter as she was falling in, but the policeman grabbed the child by the leg and threw her alive onto the pile of dead bodies."[12]

When there were hardly any Jews left to kill and the Red Army had advanced so far westward that little, if any, Ukrainian territory remained behind the battle lines, the SS-102 police unit was moved to France where it joined the *Gestapo* in hunting down the *maquis* (French resistance). Other units, such as *Roland*, *Nachtigall* and the 31st *Sicherheitsdienst* (Security Police), operating in the neighborhood of Lutsk, Kremianets and Volodymyr, carved out bloody careers before they made their way into the ranks of the First Division of the Ukrainian National Army—the designation adopted by the 14th Waffen-SS Division in the dying days of the war. Another police battalion with an equally miserable record, *Das Ukrainische Schutzmannschaft Battalion Nr. 204* (The Ukrainian Police Battalion No. 204) was transferred into the Galician Division on Himmler's order of January 11, 1944.[13]

The Police Battalions and the War against the "Bandits"

Efforts have been made by Ukrainian nationalist historians to portray the German-led Ukrainian police units as brave figures engaged in a heroic battle against armed guerrillas and the NKVD. According to Ukrainian encyclopaedist, Volodymyr Kubijovyc, the presence of the Ukrainian Division contributed to making Galicia "the only relatively peaceful island in the great expanse of eastern Europe conquered by the Germans."[14] According to German historian Helmut Krausnick, the mass shootings of unarmed Jews during this "peaceful" period in which 90 per cent of the Jewish population of Galicia was eliminated, was regularly misrepresented as "anti-partisan operations." In fact, the principal target of the operations was the "cleansing" of the crowded ghettoes established by the German authorities in the East.[15] Eric von dem Bach-Zelewski, the SS general in charge of anti-partisan warfare, testifying on his own behalf at the Nuremberg Trials, stated: "The fight against the partisans was gradually used as an excuse to carry out other measures such as the extermination of the Jews and Gypsies, the systematic reduction of the Slavic population by some thirty million souls in order to assure the supremacy of the German people, and the terrorization of civilians by looting and shooting."[16]

On those occasions when police units did engage armed guerrillas, relatively few of the policemen were killed or wounded while the partisans, generally, sustained heavy casualties. The high disparity in casualty rates indicates that the guerrilla forces were most often pitifully under-armed and extremely low in ammunition.[17]

Terror was the Nazi occupying power's chief weapon and its first principle was utter ruthlessness. Wint, in his volume, *Total War*, comments: "Although the details varied in practice from country to country, the overall pattern [of terror] was uniform because it reflected not individual initiative or local eccentricity but a policy devised on the highest level by the German state, the Nazi Party and the armed services."[18]

The determination to employ terror in all its awfulness to pacify the civilian population did not emerge as a response to atrocities committed by the Poles or the Russians. The terror was initiated by Hitler who decreed that the war against the USSR was an ideological crusade that required the extermination of the Bolsheviks and the Jews as bearers of the Marxist world-view. In a March 30, 1941 speech in the Reich Chancellery, Hitler demanded the same ruthlessness from the *Wehrmacht* as he required from the SS. Every traditional restraint on warfare, all chivalry towards opponents must be abandoned. No German soldier who committed offences against the enemy's civilian population would be court-martialed. The German soldier was free to shoot, torture and plunder at will.[19]

The following day, Field Marshall Wilhelm Keitel, head of the German Armed Forces High Command (OKW), issued the first of a series of infamous orders to the *Wehrmacht* that came to be known as the "Commissar Order." Officially titled "Guidelines for the Treatment of Political and Military Russian Officials" it required the German armed services to execute all Communists among the Russian prisoners-of-war since they constituted Bolshevism's driving force. The special conditions of the eastern campaign, he stated, demanded special measures, which the German forces must be free to carry out free from bureaucratic and administrative influences. Political representatives and commissars must be eliminated. Identification as a Communist political functionary was all the proof required for liquidation.[20]

The initial German attack sent the Soviet forces reeling. The Russians offered only sporadic resistance in the first weeks of the war. Yet, on July 16, 1941, the German High Command issued the "Jurisdiction Order," demanding complete ruthlessness from its soldiers. "The leading principle in all actions and for all measures that must be resorted to is the unconditional security of the German soldier," the order stated. "The necessary rapid pacification of the country can be attained only if every threat on the part of the hostile civil population is ruthlessly taken care of. All pity and softness are evidence of weakness and constitute a danger."[21]

This order was reaffirmed by General Keitel as Chief of the High Command of the Armed Forces in an order issued on July 23: "The troops available for securing the conquered Eastern territories will, in view of the size of the area, be sufficient for their duties only if the occupying powers meet resistance, not by legal punishment of the guilty, but by striking such terror into the population that it loses all will to resist."[22]

On October 10, 1941, Field Marshall Walter von Reichenau, Commander of the 6th Army that occupied Kiev, elaborated on the order for his troops:

> The most essential aim of war against the Jewish-Bolshevist system is complete destruction of their means of power and the elimination of Asiatic influence from the European culture... The soldier in the Eastern Territories is not merely a fighter...but also a bearer of a ruthless national ideology and the avenger of the bestialities which have been inflicted upon German and racially related nations. Therefore, the soldier must have full understanding for the necessity of a severe but just revenge on subhuman Jewry.[23]

This policy of terror and indifference to guilt or innocence was further reinforced in 1942 when Keitel ordered that every village sheltering partisans must be burned down and all victims suspected of offenses against German troops must be shot without trial. The Order, issued December 16, read: "This sort of fighting has nothing to do with soldiers' chivalry or the Geneva Convention. Unless the fight against the armed bands both in the East and the Balkans is conducted with the most brutal vehemence, the now available forces would soon not suffice to overcome this plague. The troops are, therefore, permitted and obliged to use all means without restriction, including against women and children... Not a single German participating in combat against armed bands can be subjected to disciplinary punishment or court-martialed for his behaviour in fighting bandits and their accomplices."[24]

As military historian Brian Bond points out in his biography of General Walther von Brauchitsch, leader of the campaign against the Soviet Union, the Commissar Order became an excuse for the wholesale murder of prisoners of war, while the Jurisdiction Order served to justify and condone the extermination of civilians on a vast scale.[25] Throughout 1941 and 1942, German Panzer groups corralled hordes of Russian prisoners. Thousands were summarily shot and over a million are estimated to have died in German camps from hunger, disease and exposure. British historian Alan Clark, in his account of the German campaign in Russia, states that atrocities committed by the Germans were so commonplace that "no man coming fresh from the scene could stay sane without acquiring a protective veneer of brutalization."[26]

The International Military Tribune, meeting at Nuremberg after the war, declared: "Mass murder, deportations, deliberate starvation of prisoner cages, the burning alive of school children, 'target practice' on civilian hospitals, were the order of the day."

Himmler and the Higher SS assumed the chief responsibility for anti-partisan warfare in 1943. As a result, collaboration between the *Wehrmacht*, the SS and the SD became closer as the partisans became increasingly effective in disrupting communications behind the lines. Unable and unwilling to withdraw hard-pressed army units from the fighting front, an *ad hoc* mix of local police, SS, SD, and Waffen-SS troops conducted anti-partisan warfare under the command of a Higher-SS and Police officer. *Wehrmacht* and *Luftwaffe* (air force) units participated chiefly in the larger sweeps.

The standard practice was to burn down villages suspected of harbouring Jews or assisting partisans. They slaughtered the male inhabitants, locked the women and children in churches and barns and burned them to death.[27]

"The pacification system proceeded on a uniform pattern," writes polish Historian Szymon Datner. "Usually a given village was surrounded in the early hours of the morning in order to prevent the escapes of the inhabitants. Next, individual buildings were entered. The persons found there were either killed on the spot, or everybody was driven to a central point where either all or certain groups were executed."[28]

Under a system and policy in which terror was deemed essential, concepts of justice were regarded as inconsequential if not laughable. Historian Eugene Davidson in his volume on the Nuremberg Trials *(The Trials of the Germans)* cites the case of Panzer Group 3, which was instructed to shoot all the villagers living along the Tilsit-Interburg railway line in the event the line was damaged. "If any doubt existed in the mind of the commander, suspicion would have to suffice."[29]

Himmler gloried in his troops' use of terror. In 1943, after units of the *Leibstandarte* and *Totenkopf* Waffen-SS regiments had massacred 20,000 inhabitants of Kharkov and murdered thousands of prisoners of war, Himmler exhorted his officers:

> We have only one task, to stand and pitilessly to lead this race-battle. I say now once more what I have already said today to men at another position: the reputation for horror and terror which preceded us in the battle for Kharkov, this outstanding weapon we want never to allow to diminish, but only to strengthen it. The world may call us what they will...[30]

As can be expected, the instruments of the terror campaign—the men who served in the police battalions and the Waffen-SS—failed to win the hearts of their countrymen. On the contrary, those who resisted, the partisans who took to the woods armed with nothing more than a pistol or hunting rifle, became heroes in the eyes of their neighbors.

Aware that he was losing the battle for hearts and minds of the people in the occupied territories, SS-Chief Himmler ordered a ban on the use of the term "partisan." In a letter to one of his officers, a Major Suchanek, he complained that all of Europe was falling prey to a propaganda swindle inflicted on Germany by the Jews and other lesser-breed Bolsheviks. Through their use of the term "partisan" to describe those who resisted the German invaders, they had succeeded in casting themselves in a heroic light. Therefore, he ordered that the term "partisan" no longer be used and that all who resisted should be identified by demeaning terms such as robbers, snipers, ambushers, poachers and bandits.[31]

The Nature of the Waffen-SS

Having dealt with the police, what of the Waffen-SS? Was it, as its apologists have averred an elite fighting force, a chivalrous body of warriors unlikely to participate in acts of barbarity? Was it truly different than other SS formations such as the *Gestapo* and the *Sicherheitsdienst*?

To begin with, it must be recognized that the SS was essentially a police formation. Although it grew gradually to number 600,000 men and took an active part in front line fighting, it set its own rules of warfare. Some *Wehrmacht* generals still imbued with the warrior's honour code protested against the ruthless behaviour of the SS. For example, General of Artillery Walter Petzel complained against the arbitrary arrests conducted by the Waffen-SS, its engagement in wholesale plundering, the internment of Poles and the public mistreatment of Jews who were beaten in their synagogues and driven through the streets by SS-men wielding heavy leather whips.[32]

The Nuremberg Tribunal found it impossible to distinguish between the actions of the Waffen-SS and the *Ordnungspolizei* (Order Police) and the *Sicherheitsdienst* (Security Service). Given the orders issued by the High Command to exercise extreme ruthlessness issued to all military units—including the *Wehrmacht*—the Tribunal found them all guilty of having participated in numberless crimes against humanity.

The Nuremberg Tribunal's task was further complicated by the close connections between front line units and the infamous SS police state. The editors of *Army, The Magazine of Landpower*, point out that virtually the entire prewar contingent of concentration camp guards was transferred into the Waffen-SS in October 1939. The new units created to replace them at the beginning of the war were equally notorious, conducting numerous deportations and executions in the period between 1939 and 1941 before they too were converted into SS infantry.[33]

Waffen-SS units played a major role in assisting the four mobile killing units called *Einsatzgruppen* that followed in the wake of the German armies. The *Totenkopf Waffen-SS* Division assisted *Einsatzgruppe "A"* in accomplishing its dirty work as it followed the Northern Army Group in its drive through the Baltic countries. In the centre, *Einsatzgruppe "B"* accompanied SS-Division *Das Reich* (The State) as the troops headed for Moscow. In Ukraine, the Nordic Division *Wiking* (Viking) and the "elite" Leibstandarte-SS *Adolf Hitler* assisted in the slaughter of thousands of innocent civilians.[34]

Waffen-SS troops were responsible for the massacre of U.S. troops at Malmédy and it was the *Hitler Jugend* (Hitler Youth) Waffen-SS Division under SS General Kurt Meyer that murdered surrendered Canadian soldiers in Normandy. It was SS General Wilhelm Möhnke who watched his men shoot down British prisoners at Wormhoudt. On the Eastern Front, the number and scale of SS atrocities was infinitely larger, in fact, almost a daily occurrence.

As we have stated, "anti-partisan operations" served as a cover for the murder of thousands of innocent civilians, particularly in the Balkans and behind the German lines in the USSR. Mass executions in Oradour, Minsk and Kharkov served no military purpose whatsoever except to inspire terror and confusion.

The military journal *Army, The Magazine of Landpower*, describes the Waffen-SS as "tough, savage, bloodthirsty, ruthless" and accuses the Waffen-SS of operating "in a moral vacuum, without any sense of limits." As a result, the whole of the SS—including the General SS, the Death's Head units, the Waffen-SS and the police forces (*Gestapo, SD,* and the Leadership Corps) were all found guilty and declared criminal organizations by the Nuremberg Tribunal. The court was careful and judicious, however, and refused to entertain any notion of collective guilt. The Nuremberg judges found mass punishment unthinkable and mere membership in one of these SS organizations insufficient to merit punishment.[35]

The court described the "criminal organization" as analogous to a "conspiracy" prosecution in criminal law. The normal protections available to defendants in such cases under Common Law would also apply to those charged with being members of a criminal organization. In charging conspiracy, the prosecution would have to prove three things:

- That the individuals named had themselves participated in a criminal act.
- That the individual knew he was joining a criminal organization.
- That the individual joined voluntarily.[36]

Generally, these rulings exempted draftees from facing criminal charges and excused those who were unaware that the Waffen-SS indulged in acts contrary to the rules of war and crimes against humanity.

By 1943, when the Division was organized, Galicia had experienced two years of Nazi rule. By then, every child of ten in Galicia knew what the Nazis were doing to the Jews and the role played by the Nazi-organized police formations in rounding up Ukrainian youths and transporting them to slave labour camps in Germany. Given that the members of the 14th Waffen-SS Division were, almost without exception, literate, mature men, they were unquestionably familiar with how the Waffen-SS behaved. Given all these givens, the Nuremberg Tribunal would not have hesitated to classify the Division a criminal organization.

Notes

1. Lucy Dawidowicz, *The War Against the Jews; 1933-1945* (New York: Bantam Books, 7th printing, 1981), 267-299.

2. Helmut Krausnick and Martin Broszat, *Anatomy of the SS State* (London: Granada, 1968), 80-81.

3. *Ibid.* 80.

4. *Ibid.* 82.

5. *Ibid.* 81.

6. Hilberg, *The Destruction of European Jews* (New York: Harper and Row, 1960 edition), 205.

7. An-Thon, "Over the Dark Precipice." In *Alliance for Murder*, ed. B.F Sabrin (New York: Sarpedon, 1991), 213.

8. *Ibid.* 213-215.

9. Friedman, *Roads to Extinction*, 185-186.

10. Hilberg, *The Destruction of the European Jews*, 205.

11. Michael Hanusiak, *Lest We Forget*, 33.

12. *Ibid.*

13. National Archives of the United States (Washington, D.C.) Microcopy T-175, Roll 74, Folder 263, "Records of the Reich Leader of the SS and Chief of the German Police."

14. Volodymyr Kubijovyc, "Ukraine during World War II," *Ukraine: A Concise Encyclopaedia*, Volume I, (Toronto: Shevchenko Scientific Society, 1963), 889.

15. Helmut Krausnick and Martin Broszat, *The Anatomy of the SS State* (London: Granada Publishing, 1968), 89.

16. See Robert E. Conot, *Justice at Nuremberg* (New York: Harper and Row, 1983), 281. Conot's reference is "Bach-Zelewski Statement in Bach Interrogation File," Bach-Zelewski was born in Pomerania, served in World War I and joined the Nazi Party in 1930. On July 21, 1943, he was given the task of subduing Polish partisans. In 1944, he commanded the German forces that crushed the Polish Warsaw Uprising. In 1945, he commanded an army group.

17. *Alliance for Murder*, 6.

18. Peter Callvocaressi and Guy Wint, *Total War*, (Middlesex: Penguin Books, 1972), 265.

19. Brian Bond, "Brauchitsch" in *Hitler's Generals*, edited by Corelli Barnett (London: George Weidenfeld and Nicolson, 1989), 89-91.

20. *Nazi Conspiracy and Aggression,* (Ten volume compendium of the Nuremberg Prosecution's documents) 1519 PS, "Treatment of Political Commissars," March 31, 1941.

21. Quoted in Alan Clark, *Barbarossa: The Russian-German Conflict 1941-1945* (New York: Morrow & Co., 1965), 152.

22. Quoted by Conot in *Justice in Nuremberg,* 219. Conot's reference is *Nazi Conspiracy and Aggression,* C52, Supplement to Order No. 33, July 23, 1941.

23. *Trial of the Major War Criminals before the International Tribunal, 14 November 1945 - 10 October 1946,* Volume IV, 459.

24. V.N. Nemyaty et al., *History Teaches a Lesson* (Kiev: Politvidav Ukraini, 1960), 105-106. This volume is a compilation of documents located at the Central State Archives of the October Revolution (CSAOR, USSR) and the Central State Archives of the October Revolution of the Ukrainian SSR. The Keitel order is cited as CSAOP USSR, fund 7445 and invt. 2, file 96, 86-87.

25. Brian Bond, *Hitler's Generals,* 91.

26. Clark, *Barbarossa,* 193.

27. Szymon Datner et al., *Genocide 1939-1945* (Warsaw: Wydawnictowo Zachodnie, 1962), 125-126.

28. *Ibid.,* 125.

29. Eugene Davidson, *The Trial of the Germans* (New York: Macmillan Co., 1966), 318.

30. "To Korpsführen in Kharkov," 24.4.1943; International Military Tribunal 1919-PS. Also cited in Peter Padfield, *Himmler, Reichsführer-SS* (London: Macmillan, 1990), 340.

31. National Archives of the United States (Washington, D.C.) Microcopy 1175, T-175, folder 332.

32. Davidson, *Trial of the Germans,* 314-315.

33. *Army, The Magazine of Landpower,* Volume 35, No. 6, June 1985, 7.

34. Padfield, *Himmler, Reichsführer-SS,* 339-340. See also Ronald Headland, *Messages of Murder* (Toronto: Fairleigh Dickinson Press, 1992), 37-38.

35. *Army, The Magazine of Landpower,* June 1985, 9. Similar evaluations can be found in Charles W. Syndor, *Soldiers of Destruction: The SS Death's Head Division 1933-1945* (Princeton: Princeton University Press, 1977), 318-335. Also, George H.Stein, *The Waffen SS: Hitler's Elite Guard at War* (Ithaca: Cornell University Press, 1966), 255-258; and Heinz Höhne, Trans. Richard Barry, *The Order of the Death's Head: The Story of Hitler's SS* (London: Pan Books, 1972; also, Helmut Krausnick et al., *Anatomy of an SS State,* trans. David Barry (New York: Walker, 1966) and Gerald Reitlinger, *The SS: Alibi of a Nation 1922-1945* (London: Arms and Armour, 1981).

36. Davidson, *Trial of the Germans,* 314-315.

CHAPTER 6

UNDER SOVIET AND GERMAN OCCUPATION

AS THE GERMANS BLASTED THEIR WAY EASTWARD INTO POLAND in September 1939, the Soviets drove westward to occupy a line previously agreed upon by German Foreign Minister Ribbentrop and Soviet Foreign Minister Molotov the previous August. The Red Army took possession of Galicia and, in the usual manner prescribed by the Soviets, Galicia's citizens "petitioned" to become an integral part of the Soviet Union—a wish Moscow readily granted.[1] Long a border region between Poland, Ukraine, Hungary, Romania and German-speaking Austria, Galician settlements were a patchwork of ethnic settlements; Polish towns neighbored on Ukrainian towns and towns that were primarily German-speaking mingled with towns in which Hungarian was the dominant language. In all these towns, Jews formed a large part of the non-rural population, varying between fifteen and fifty percent, totaling more than 600,000 people.

> From the cultural point of view, this community of 600,000 Jews was among the richest of all the eastern-European communities. Galicia was the cradle of *Hassidism*, a movement that sought to spread religious ecstasy, the comradeship of man to man, and the concept of the salvation of Israel through faith.[2]

The Soviet occupation of the Western Ukraine was relatively benign. Soviet authorities, determined to win over the Galician population, made Ukrainian the language of instruction in Galician schools, increased the number of elementary schools and opened the doors of the university in Lviv to Ukrainian teachers and students. Health care in the small towns and villages was dramatically improved and the large Polish estates were redistributed among the peasants. Industrial enterprises, largely Polish and Jewish-owned, were nationalized. However, in the spring of 1941, the Soviets instituted large-scale deportations of Ukrainians, Poles and Jews regarded as bourgeois "enemies of the people."[3]

The first wave of deportees, Subtelny reports, consisted of leading Polish, Ukrainian and Jewish politicians, industrialists, lawyers, priests and retired army officers. "Later, anyone identified with Ukrainian nationalism was liable to arrest... Without warning, without trial, even without formal accusation, thousands...were arrested, packed into

cattle cars, and shipped to Siberia and Kazakhstan to work as slave laborers under horrible conditions."[4]

Meanwhile, the Germans were busy reorganizing their segment of the newly conquered Polish territory according to their own grand design. Western sections of Poland were incorporated directly into the *Reich* while Hitler's plenipotentiary, Governor General Hans Frank, ruled the remainder of occupied Polish territory from his headquarters in a castle in Krakow. Frank's fiefdom was officially known as the *Generalgouvernment*. Jews, driven from the incorporated territories, were deposited in the *Generalgouvernment* where they were concentrated in the larger cities. A series of ordinances required Jews to wear yellow stars and forbade them from entering major sections of the city. They were allotted minimal rations and made subject to arbitrary levies of forced labour. Their synagogues were destroyed and thousands of Jews were killed at random in the streets, at work and in the local prisons.

Six months into the occupation, the Jews of Lodz were sealed into a narrow, overcrowded ghetto. A few months later, the Jews of Warsaw were walled into an old section of the city. By the year's end, almost all of Poland's Jews under German rule were separated from the rest of the population by high walls and barbed wire. Within those walls, Jews endured hunger, disease and impressment in forced-labour brigades. At least half a million Jews died in the Polish ghettoes from malnutrition, exposure, overwork, epidemic, and brutality.[5]

Meanwhile, nationalist Ukrainians, eager to escape Soviet rule in Galicia, hastened to join Frank's court in Krakow. In May 1940, under the sponsorship of the occupation authority, they formed the Ukrainian Central Committee (UTsK) headed by geographer Volodymyr Kubijovyc. Ostensibly a welfare agency organized to help the sick and the aged, the Central Committee published newspapers, approved theatre performances, manned radio stations, organized youth groups and appointed teachers and minor bureaucrats under the close supervision of the *Abwehr's* Krakow bureau. Essentially collaborative, Kubijovyc's committee was proud of its status as the only Ukrainian organization officially recognized by the German authorities. A one thousand-man Ukrainian auxiliary Police Service with headquarters in Zakopane was nominally sponsored by Kubijovyc but commanded by the Germans.[6]

In 1941, when the Germans unleashed Operation Barbarossa against the Soviet Union and drove the Soviet forces eastward, many Galician communities greeted the Nazi forces with bread and salt, the traditional Ukrainian symbols of welcome and hospitality.

Bandera, who had been released from his Polish prison cell in 1939 by the advancing Germans, saw his opportunity and seized it. No sooner did his *Nachtigall* detachment secure Lviv than a band of Ukrainian nationalist leaders descended on the city, intent on proclaiming an independent Ukrainian state. Time was of the essence; history favoured the bold. The blue and yellow nationalist banner needed to be raised in Lviv before his arch-rival Melnyk reached Kiev and claimed precedence by flying the OUN's banner over the golden dome of St. Sophia in the ancient Ukrainian capital.[7]

On June 30, 1941, a small group of German dignitaries was invited to a carefully staged rally in Lviv to witness the proclamation of an "Act" declaring the reestablishment of the Western Ukrainian state under the leadership of Stepan Bandera. Yaroslav Stetsko, Bandera's close friend and confederate, was designated Prime Minister.[8] Reitlinger describes it as a sudden and unexpected coup in which the responsible intelligence officer, Professor Hans Koch, an old friend of the nationalist Ukrainian cause, was invited to a rally where the Banderites (OUN/B) proclaimed an independent Ukrainian state. This attempt to "make history" was unanticipated by the *Abwehr* and did not earn its blessing.[9]

The proclamation issued by Stetsko on behalf of the Bandera faction of the OUN promised that the new Ukrainian state would faithfully "cooperate with National Socialist Great Germany, which under the leadership of Adolf Hitler is establishing a New World Order in Europe and the world."[10] The proclamation's closing flourish called for: "Glory to the heroic German army and its Führer, Adolf Hitler."[11]

Despite the proclamation's promise of ardent support for Hitler and the National Socialist state, the German authorities were exceedingly uncomfortable with this obvious attempt at a *fait accompli*. Some *Abwehr* leaders such as Professor Hans Koch could take the declaration in their stride since the OUN was the *Abwehr's* creature and its ultimate leaders *Abwehr* personnel. Whenever it pleased, military intelligence could ring down the curtain on the Ukrainian cabal. Meanwhile, there was no harm in allowing Stetsko and Company to strut about on the stage of the Lviv Opera House if it helped recruit Ukrainians to the war effort. But neither Koch nor Stetsko took into account the fierce rivalry between the SS and the *Abwehr*, between Himmler and Canaris.

Himmler's SS officers were well acquainted with Hitler's plans for the Ukraine, Byelorussia and the Baltic states. They were aware that it called for the ruthless exploitation of their people and resources—plans that left no room for self-rule of any kind. The SS saw Stetsko's proclamation as willful and dangerous, a gesture that must be promptly suppressed lest it be taken seriously by others. Lacking the *Abwehr's* sophistication and its willingness to toy with the Ukrainian nationalists, the SS ordered Stetsko and his colleagues to retract their "act of independence." Bandera and Stetsko, believing they had the protection of the powerful Admiral Canaris, defied the SS and continued to proclaim their independence. What they failed to realize was that the SS was gaining ascendancy and that one day Himmler would consume the *Abwehr* and garrote Canaris for his suspected support of the bomb plot against Hitler. Walter Schellenberg, the ruthless careerist who succeeded Heydrich as head of the German secret service after the latter's assassination, wrote in his memoirs:

> During the following years, Canaris' work grew continuously worse. In spite of his intelligence, his behavior aroused suspicion and many people became convinced he was involved in treasonable activities...[Himmler] saw to it that other leaders, both political and of the Wehrmacht, who for one reason or another were opposed to the Admiral, continuously kept the subject of Canaris in the limelight. Himmler regularly furnished this anti-Canaris clique with new material against him... From the middle of 1944, I took over the Canaris Military Intelligence Department... In March 1945, Hitler and Kaltenbrunner (head of the SD) jointly ordered the execution of Canaris.[12]

The OUNites, unaware of this deadly battle being waged in the background, scorned the orders of the SS. Himmler, brooking no nonsense, ordered the arrest of the nationalist leaders and the execution of several of their most adamant followers.

The detention of the OUN leaders was not particularly severe or injurious. Bandera was taken from Krakow to Berlin where he was placed under house arrest. On July 12, 1941, Stetsko and his crew were gathered up and sent to Sachsenhausen concentration camp, where, as befitted temporarily misguided allies, they lived in relative comfort in officers' quarters with other distinguished "guests." The Germans found it convenient to use Sachsenhausen to house a number of distinguished political detainees such as Romanian Iron Guard leader Horia Sima, German evangelical Pastor Niemoeller, the son of Italian Marshall Pietro Bodoglio, former Austrian Chancellor Kurt Schuschnigg, German industrialist Fritz Thyssen, French premier Edouard Daladier, Jacob Djugashvili, the son of Marshall Stalin who had fallen into German hands, and a host of European aristocrats who had carelessly criticized the Austrian corporal in the presence of his spies.

The quarters assigned to the Romanian Iron Guardists and the Ukrainian nationalists were relatively luxurious, equipped with radios, telephones, newspapers and libraries. Armstrong, in his volume *Ukrainian Nationalism* reports: "While nominally under house arrest, they were allowed to carry on their political activities."[13] The interned Ukrainian leaders kept in close touch with their colleagues and continued the murderous factional feud that divided the Bandera and Melnyk cadres. A Red Cross delegation sent to inspect the camp was shown through this section of Sachsenhausen to demonstrate how well inmates fared in concentration camps.[14]

Needless to say, not everyone fared so well in the Nazi concentration camps. Many of the lower ranking Ukrainian nationalists were sent to Auschwitz when arrested and suffered as severely as other non-Jewish prisoners. Bandera's younger brother was slain by Polish fellow-prisoners who chose him as an object of national vengeance. Melnyk's men also suffered badly. When the Melnykites organized a large conference to commemorate the anti-Soviet Ukrainian partisans killed by the Bolsheviks in the last months of the 1917-1920 civil war, the SS took the occasion to arrest and execute 20-odd conference organizers gathered in Zhitomyr. Considerably later—not until January 1944—they reached out for Melnyk himself and sent him to the same concentration camp where his rival, Bandera, still lingered.

The Roland and Nachtigall Detachments

With the arrest of Bandera and the neutralization of Melnyk, the OUN's *Nachtigall* and *Roland* detachments found themselves stripped of their political leadership. Their overall command was assumed by Theodore Oberländer who directed both units to give full support to *Einsatzkommando 4a* of *Einsatzgruppe C* which was actively fulfilling its assignment of eliminating the Jews in the southern sector of the Eastern Front. While *Nachtigall* did its dirty work in Lviv and surrounding districts, *Roland's* area of operation was in the region of Odessa, Izmail, and Mykolaiv.

Some of the *Roland* and *Nachtigall* officers were seriously disturbed by the arrests of Bandera, Stetsko and Melnyk, causing a number of them to ask to be relieved of their duties. However, most felt challenged to prove their loyalty to the Germans by intensifying their actions against the Jews who dwelt along the line of march from Lviv through Zlochiv, Ternopil and Brailov to Vinnytsia.

Nevertheless, the resignations did lead Oberländer to rethink the role of his "Ukrainian Legion." On August 27, 1941, he withdrew both formations to Germany and reconstituted them as *Schutzmannschaftbatalion 201* (Auxiliary Police Battalion 201) under the nominal command of Yevhen Pobihushchy and Vice Commander Major Roman "Tur" Shukhevych. On March 23, 1942, three thousand strong, they were placed under the command of Erich von dem Bach-Zelewski, the Higher SS and Police Leader of the Central Region. A professional soldier from a Junker family, Bach-Zelewski was another of those *Wehrmacht* officers who joined the *Freikorps* after World War I and went on to become an early member of the Nazi Party (NSDAP) and the SS. Handsome, well-educated, seemingly gallant, he was an efficient *Einsatzgruppe* commander, responsible for the deaths of thousands of Jews. On October 31, 1941, after 35,000 Jews had been massacred in Riga, he proudly reported: "There is not a Jew left in Latvia."[15]

Under Bach-Zelewski's ruthless command, the reconstituted *Roland* and *Nachtigall* formations destroyed the last remnants of the Byelorussian Jewish community. Major Shukhevych is credited with organizing the slaughter of the Jews of Pinsk and Luminets.[16] The formation helped suppress all opposition, burn down countless villages and murder thousands of innocent men, women and children. In 1943, their effectiveness increasingly circumscribed by the advance of the Red Army towards Minsk, they were withdrawn to Galicia and incorporated into the newly formed 14th Waffen-SS Division (Galician No. 1). Pobihushchy, having proven his loyalty to the Nazis, became a senior officer in the Galician Waffen-SS Division.[17]

The Division's Ukrainian Officers

Pobihushchy's career is typical of many of the Ukrainian officers and enlisted men that served in the Galician Division. An officer in the short-lived Ukrainian army that fought the Poles in 1918-1920, Pobihushchy made his peace with the Polish government and became a contract officer in the Polish army. When the Germans invaded Poland in 1939, he served in the Polish ranks until Poland surrendered and then offered himself to Canaris and the *Abwehr*. Taken on by the Germans, he was made field commander of the Roland detachment in 1940, became commander of the *Schutzmannschaftbattalion* 201 towards the end of 1941 and rose to the rank of regimental commander in the Galician Division in 1943. In the post-war period, Pobihushchy—under the alias of Eugen Ren—worked for British intelligence for a time and then organized a Ukrainian guard company that did sentry duty at American installations in Germany.[18]

The careers of Ukrainian officers who served in the 31st SD *(Sicherheitsdienst* or Security Service) Punitive Detachment was no more illustrious than those that served in the 201st. Organized in the late autumn of 1943, the 31st SD was made up mainly of Volhynia region members of the Melnyk faction of the OUN, including units from Lutsk, Kremianets and Dubno. Originally dubbed the Ukrainian Self-Defence Legion, its name was changed to 31st SD Punitive Detachment. Its first commander, *Hauptstürmführer* (Captain) Assmus, was ambushed and killed by Polish partisans on the road between Volhynia and Krakow. Its second commander—also a German—was Major Ewald Biegelmeyer, a long-time Nazi Party member and early recruit to the SS. The 31st SD's commander was posted in France and Belgium before being assigned in October 1941 to his eastern post as head of the Security Service in Lublin. A French military commission sought Biegelmeyer's extradition in 1945 for alleged war crimes in Lorraine. British interrogators accused him of responsibility for the deaths of 40,000 Jews in the Lublin ghetto. However, he managed to avoid extradition to both France and Poland. In the post-war years he served as a witness in numerous post-war, war-crimes trials in Germany, giving evidence against former colleagues, he, himself, was set free for lack of evidence.[19]

In time, the 31st SD absorbed a number of smaller police units such as the Chelm Self-Defence Detachment and Police Battalion 207 drawn from police units whose areas of operation had been overrun by the Red Army. Colonel Pyotr Dyachenko, a former of-

ficer in Petliura's 1918-1920 army and subsequently an officer in the Polish army, returned to service as the 31st SD's chief of staff.

In late December 1943, the unit tortured and shot a large number of Ukrainians and
Jews in the village of Pidhaitsi. On New Year's Eve of 1943, the 31st SD wiped out the last
Jews housed in the ghetto at Lutsk. (The Lutsk ghetto had lasted longer than most because Jewish craftsmen were needed to build army barracks and sew uniforms for Ukrainian police units.) Their bodies were buried in a mass grave hacked out of the frozen
earth on the playground of the Lutsk elementary school. A Soviet post-war commission
disinterred the victims and found signs of brutal torture on their bodies. The Commission
stated: "The first corpse pulled out from the pit was identified as Yuri Petrovich
Parfenjuk from the village of Kivertsi… Medical examination revealed that the Germans
had put out his eyes, cut off his ears, knocked out his teeth, broken his hands and frac-
tured his skull."[20]

In Ustalych—the birthplace of Igor Stravinsky—the Ukrainian policemen in German
uniform discovered a small band of Jews hiding in crude earth shelters and subjected
them to a horrible death. Women and children were beaten to death with clubs and gar-
roted with barbed wire. In revenge for the death of the unit's original commander at the
hands of Polish partisans, the 31st SD destroyed all the inhabitants of a small village not
far from Krakow. According to Herasym Makukh, a member of the legion and a partici-
pant in the attack, the order was given to spare no one in the village:

> We had to execute all the inhabitants regardless of their sex or age and set fire to
> their houses. When I arrived at the outskirts of the village, I witnessed a horrible
> picture. The local inhabitants—men, women and children—were running in
> panic and desperately trying to break through our lines. Our legionnaires killed
> them as they ran. The whole village was in flames and on all sides one could hear
> the terrible wailing of the inhabitants. I saw heaps of corpses alongside the road
> and in the yards of houses. I witnessed the killing of children, women, and old
> people. The legionnaires not only killed and burned but stole everything they
> could carry away from the villagers' houses.[21]

The slaughter did not cease with the organization of the Halychyna Division in 1943. Village after village was destroyed and its inhabitants tortured and shot in close cooperation
with special units of the 14th Waffen-SS Division. Soviet Journalist Valery Styrkul states:

> According to captured German documents, in March 1944, the 31st SD Punitive
> Division mounted anti-partisan operations along with elements of the SS
> Halychyna Division… Daily situation reports of the police commandant of the
> District of Lublin… mention repeatedly [the participation of] Assmus' special for-
> mation in fighting against partisans in the Hrubieszow District.[22]

Ukrainian Units and the Warsaw Uprising

On August 1, 1944, Warsaw rose a second time against the Nazi invaders. This time it was the underground Polish Home Army, the Armia Krajowa that signalled the uprising. The task of suppressing the uprising was given to Himmler who decreed that every Warsaw Pole, regardless of age and sex, should be shot, and every historic building, every palace, park and museum should be destroyed. Joanna Hanson, in her study of the Warsaw Uprising relates that from the very first days of the uprising, German soldiers performed indescribable crimes. "Rapes, loot and murder became the order of the day."[23]

World War II historian Alan Clark's description is equally graphic and equally horrifying. Prisoners, he recounts, were burned alive with gasoline; babies were impaled on bayonets and stuck out of windows like flags. Women were hung from balconies in rows. "The object, Himmler told Goebbels, was that the sheer violence and terror of repression would extinguish the revolt in a very few days."[24]

For the next two months, the Polish Underground Army, joined by a handful of "Rubblemen"—a pitifully small group of survivors of the previous year's Jewish Ghetto Uprising—fought a desperate but losing battle against the motley crew of plunderers, rapists and murderers assembled by *SS-Gruppenführer* Bach-Zelewski. Because front-line German troops could not be spared and the German garrison in Warsaw was small, Bach-Zelewski was forced to depend on a scattering of *Wehrmacht*, *Waffen-SS* and SS-led police units to reduce the city. Hanson's account underlines the mixed nature of Bach-Zelewski's forces. "The significance of these units lay not in their numbers but in their character and quality. Barely half of the men in these units—although they wore German uniforms—spoke German. They were Ukrainians, Russians, Kalmuks, Cossacks, Turkomans, Azerbaijans and Muslims."[25] Deschner, in his account of the uprising *(Warsaw Rising)*, specifically mentions the addition of Hungarians and Galicians to the German forces.[26]

From Czenstochowa, Bach-Zelewski brought his notorious *SS-Sonderkommando* (Special Detachment) Kaminski, a Russian anti-partisan militia unit. From Lyck, he brought the Dirlewanger Brigade, recruited from the dregs of German jails. So brutal was the behaviour of the Dirlewanger and Kaminski brigades that disgusted German field commanders prevailed on Hitler to withdraw them from Warsaw before the uprising was entirely crushed.[27]

Fighting at their side—at the side of brigades that had shed all traces of human decency—were elements of the 31st SD under the leadership of Colonel Pyotr Dyachenko. Survivors of the 31st SD, testifying before Soviet authorities, described Dyachenko as a grey-haired, former officer of both the Petliura forces and the Polish army who walked with a distinct limp.[28]

The potpourri of regular troops and locally raised police units, the variety of languages spoken and the difficulty of identifying specific units in the heat of battle, makes it difficult to document the 31st SD's record in Warsaw. There are numerous references in the records of the Polish Underground Army (AK) to Ukrainian troops that behaved with typical brutality, but it is not always clear to which of the various Ukrainian, Russian and Kalmuk units they refer. There are, for example, Polish reports of a unit in German SS uniforms that "spoke Polish or understood perfectly what they were saying." This unit, assumed to be Galician because of its knowledge of the Polish language, had barrels of gasoline and naphtha and threw gasoline grenades through the houses.[29]

There is also official Polish mention of a Ukrainian unit that took part in the assault on Aleie Shukha (Rose Lane), the scene of some of the most bestial fighting in Warsaw.[30] A Soviet source reports that the 31st SD participated in the murder of wounded Polish rebels in a Warsaw hospital.[31] Polish survivors tell of the mass slaughter of civilians by "German and Ukrainian" soldiers in the Wola section where some of the worst crimes were committed.[32]

Despite the confusion and the admitted tendency to blame "Ukrainians" for the sins of the Dirlewanger and Kaminski brigades, German historian Hanns von Krannhals concludes that there were genuine Ukrainians in the ranks of Bach-Zelewski's forces at Warsaw and among them were "two companies [of the 31st SD] under Colonel Dyachenko [who] fought in the Czerniakow area [of the city], but mostly in the Weichsel district.[33]

Given the cruelty and callousness exhibited by the 31st SD against their own people, given Bach-Zelewski's professional ruthlessness in suppressing rebellion; given German standing orders requiring the slaughter of all those suspected of armed resistance; and given the general behaviour of the German forces in Warsaw, there is little reason to believe that the members of the 31st SD exercised any more restraint in fighting the hated Polish Home Army than they did in fighting their own Ukrainian neighbors. That Pyotr Dyachenko and elements of the 31st SD participated in the suppression of the 1944 Warsaw Uprising is certain. It is equally certain that Dyachenko and many of his Warsaw veterans later served in the ranks of the 14th Waffen-SS Division.[34]

Major Heike's memoirs provide another source of reliable information on the 31st SD and its transfer to the Galician Division. The Ukrainian Division's executive officer wrote that February 1945, "In accordance with a plan to unify all Ukrainian military formations into a Ukrainian National Army, a battalion of Volynian Ukrainians arrived... This unit was associated with the Organization of Ukrainian Nationalists under the leadership of Colonel Andrii Melnyk."[35]

A major Ukrainian encyclopedia edited by geographer Kubijovyc confirms the transfer: "In the summer of 1944, the [Ukrainian Legion of Self Defence] joined the police guards of the 31st *Schutzmannschaft* Battalion... In March 1945, numbering over 600 men, it joined the First Ukrainian Division (14th Waffen-SS Division (Galician)."[36] Further confirmation can be found in the autobiography of General Pavlo Shandruk, the last wartime commander of the Division, who repeatedly refers to Dyachenko as one of his leading regimental officers and praises him for his courage and initiative.[37]

Notes

1. Shmuel Spector, *The Holocaust of Volhynian Jews, 1941-1944* (Jerusalem: Yad Vashem, 1990), 24-25.

2. Jacob Apenszlak, ed., *The Black Book of Polish Jewry: An Account of the Martyrdom of Polish Jewry Under the Nazi Occupation* (New York: The American Federation for Polish Jews, 1943), 97.

3. Subtelny, *Ukraine*, 456.

4. *Ibid.*

5. Lucy S. Dawidowicz, *The War Against the Jews 1933-12945* (New York: Holt, Rinehart and Winston, 1975), 396-397.

6. Volodymyr Kubijovyc, "The Ukrainians in German-Occupied Territory," in *Ukraine, A Concise Encyclopedia,* Vol. 1 (Toronto: University of Toronto Press, 1963), 874-876.

7. The *Tryzub* is the three-pronged emblem adopted by Volodymyr the Great who Christianized Ukraine. Placed on a blue and yellow background, it was adopted by the OUN as its emblem.

8. See Friedman, *Roads to Extinction*, 180.

9. Reitlinger, *The SS: Alibi of a Nation*, 119.

10. Kost' Pankivsky, *From State to a Committee* (New York-Toronto: 1957), 113-114.

11. Dallin, *German Rule in Russia*, 121.

12. Walter Schellenberg, *The Schellenberg Memoirs* (London: Andre Deutsch, 1956), 408-412.

13. Armstrong, *Ukrainian Nationalism*, 83.

14. Edward Prus, *Horosi Spod Znaku Tryzuba* (Warsaw: Instytut Wydawniczy Zwiazkow Zawadowych, 1985), 194-197.

15. Robert Wistrich, *Who's Who in Nazi Germany*, (London: Weidenfeld and Nicholson, 1982), 9.

16. Reuben Ainsztein, "The Myth About the Fatalistic and Helpless Galician Jew," in *Jewish Resistance in Nazi-Occupied Europe* (New York: Barnes and Noble, 1974), 252.

17. Prus, 167-168. See also Friedman, *Roads to Extinction*, 181 and *Ukraine, A Concise Encyclopedia*, 1087-1088.

18. Valery Styrkul, *We Accuse* (Kiev: Dnipro Publishers, 1984), 246-248.

19. According to Biegelmeyer's own statement before a magistrate in the Wiesbaden court, the 31st commander became a member of the *Schülerbund*, a Nazi youth movement, in 1929. He joined the SA and the NSDAP in 1931, was accepted into the SD in 1936, and became a member of the SS in 1937. This information is the result of personal correspondence with Wiesmann, Oberstaatsanwalt, Wiesbaden, April 1988.

20. Ukrainian State Archive, Lviv, "Statement of Witness," (ACT), May 24, 1944.

21. "Statement of Witness Herasym Mykytovych Makukh," October 20, 1967, Ukrainian State Archive, Lviv. According to Makukh's statement, many of his comrades in the 31st SD found shelter abroad after the war. The author has the names of several who took up residence in England and Canada. One of them serves as a priest in Canada.

22. Styrkul, *We Accuse*, 267. See also: Jerzy Markevitch, *Nie dali ziemi skad ich rod* (Lublin: Wydawnictwo Lubelskie, 1965), 202.

23. Joanna K.M. Hanson, *The Civilian Population and the Warsaw Uprising of 1944* (Cambridge: Cambridge University Press, 1982), 81.

24. Clark, *Barbarossa*, 391.

25. Hanson, 84-85.

26. Gunther Deschner, *Warsaw Rising* (New York: Ballentine Books, 1972), 66.

27. *Ibid.* 87-88.

28. Transcripts of their evidence are in my files.

29. Edward Serwanski and Irena Trawinska, *Zbrodnia Niemiecka w Warsawie 1944* (Poznan: Wydawnictwo Institutu Zachodniego, 1946), Protocol No. 246, 168.

30. Serwanski, Protocol No. 212, 173-174. Reference to the fighting in Rose Lane is also given in Hanns von Krannhals: "*Der Warschauer Aufstand* (Frankfurt: Bernard and Graefe, 1962), 265. The reference reads: *Die Sicherheitspolizei war, soweit ich mich einstinne, etwa 700 Mann stark; ihr gehörte eine kompanie Ukrainer (sog. Hiwis = Hilfswillige) an, die in der Kurt-Lûck-Strasse [Ulicka Koszykowa] Ecke Rosenalle (Rose Lane) lagen. Auch das Kommando der Schutzpolizei hatte meine Wissens ukrainische Hilfsmannschaften zu Bechaungszwecken (Starke unbekkant). Von Abteilungen des SS-Galizien weiss ich nicht.*" (Von Krannhals ignorance regarding the presence of the Galician SS Division is understandable since the Division as such did not serve at Warsaw. However, Dyachenko and a portion of the 31st SD did serve at Warsaw and were soon after transferred to the Division.

31. Interview: Polikarp Shapeta, historian, and journalist, Lutsk, September 1, 1987.

32. Hanson, supra, 87-89.

33. Von Krannhals, *Die Warschauer Aufstand*, 265.

34. Statement of witness Leontij Mykhajlovych Pasal'skij before the Senior Assistant Prosecutor, Volyn Region, May 22, 1967.

35. Heike, English edition, 104.

36. O. Horbatsch, "Ukrainians in Foreign Armies During World War II," in Chapter XII, "The Armed Forces," editor Volodomyr Kubijovyc in *Ukraine, A Concise Encyclopedia*, Vol. II. 1086-1089.

37. Pavlo Shandruk, *Arms of Valor*, trans. Roman Olesnicki (New York: Robert Speller and Sons, 1959) 25, 245. Also an affidavit sworn by P.S. Glinia before the Prosecutor of the Volynia Region, Ukrainian SSR, testifying that he served in the 31st SD and personally knew the Legion's leaders, particularly Colonel Dyachenko and Colonel Gerasimenko. Sworn at Lutsk, Ukrainian SSR, September 18, 1987.

CHAPTER 7

THE GALICIAN DIVISION

WHEN THE CALL WENT OUT IN THE SPRING OF 1943 FOR RECRUITS to join the Division, thousands of Ukrainian youth flocked to the Galician banner. Within the first month, 82,000 men had volunteered. Of these, 42,000 were selected for medical examination and 27,000—largely between the ages of 18 and 30—were accepted. From their ranks some 13,000 were called up in that first year.

What kind of men volunteered for service in the Galician Waffen-SS Division? To begin with, they were unanimously volunteers. (Given the speed with which they presented themselves, there was no need for persuasion and hardly time for coercion.)[1] The vast majority were ardent nationalists, deeply committed—not only to an independent Ukraine—but to a Ukraine that conformed to the totalitarian leadership principles and racist fantasies preached by the Ukrainian nationalist ideologues. They were, according to retired University of Toronto librarian Wasyl Veryha, the "most nationally conscious young men and women" as well as "students of institutions of higher learning and those of the older generation who had been brought up on the ideal of a sovereign and independent Ukrainian state."[2] They were predominantly urban and middle class, the offspring of priests, teachers, minor bureaucrats, shopkeepers, a sprinkling of professionals and veterans of the 1918-1920 Petlurian armies—hardly the simple sturdy, peasant-stock so romantically portrayed by post-war, nationalist lobbyists.

The impetus for the organization of the Division came from several sources; first and foremost the desperate need for manpower following the grim defeat suffered the previous winter by Hitler's armies at Stalingrad. (The Red Cross estimates that the Germans suffered 200,000 dead at Stalingrad and 30,000 wounded.) Even so, the decision to recruit Galicians was reluctantly agreed upon by Himmler who had no wish to see his Aryan SS diluted by the addition of Ukrainian *Untermenschen*. But given the horrible losses on the Eastern Front, he had no alternative but to make room for Ukrainians in his Nordic pantheon. To make their entry more palatable, Himmler seized upon Galicia's former membership in the Austro-Hungarian Empire. He rationalized that as former Hapsburg subjects, Galicians were endowed with just enough Germanic blood and Germanic culture to qualify them for a severely depleted Waffen-SS.

Himmler's decision to raise a Ukrainian division came after a bitter debate between those SS factions that saw Ukraine solely as a milch cow fit for milking, and those who sensed that the war was as good as lost without massive infusions of non-Germanic manpower—even if it came from a people slated for slavery and eventual elimination. Although the Germans maintained tight control of the recruiting procedures and ultimately selected all those chosen to serve, the nominal instrument appointed to raise the Ukrainian flag and rally the troops was the Ukrainian Central Committee headed by Kubijovyc.

Despite its official, German-sanctioned status, the Ukrainian Central Committee had a rival in the Ukrainian National Committee, organized in June 1941 by the Bandera wing of the Organization of Ukrainian Nationalists (OUN). In the bitter, unrelenting rivalry between Bandera and Melnyk, the Central Committee led by Kubijovyc favoured Andrei Melnyk and supported his claim to the title of Ukrainian Supreme Leader. The Bandera forces, however, had stolen a considerable march on Melnyk by organizing their own nationalist underground, the Ukrainian Insurgent Army or UPA. Although post-war nationalist Ukrainian historians describe UPA as fighting a two-front war against both the Nazis and the Bolsheviks, in effect they were freely armed by the Germans who saw a nationalist guerrilla force as the best means of countering the growing Soviet partisan movement. UPA attracted large numbers of nationalist youths who, while preferring to support the Nazis in their war against the Soviet Union, nevertheless wished to avoid forced labour drafts that would press them into German slave labour camps.[3]

Sharp divisions in the ranks of the Nazi occupiers further complicated the situation. While the *Abwehr* and the *Ostministerium* (Ministry for the East) were delighted to support the OUN and provide arms for UPA, their opposite numbers in the SS-SD despised Bandera and his talk of an independent Ukraine. In order to wean potential recruits away from the political leadership of the Bandera-led faction of the OUN, the SS dangled new bait before their noses, the signal honour of serving in a Waffen-SS division. *SS-Untersturmbannführer* Friedrich Buchardt who helped recruit Russian, Byellorussian and Ukrainian groups for service on the Eastern Front, states in his lengthy memoir: "The Germans hoped, in particular, to cut the ground away beneath the feet of the OUN or UPA with the formation of this [Waffen-SS] division."[4]

By 1943, the wishes of the Melnykites and SS-SD began to coincide. As early as July 1941, Melnyk had suggested to Hitler's headquarters that a Ukrainian combat unit be created to fight alongside the legions of Europe, side by side with the German *Wehrmacht*.[5]

In August of the same year, Kubijovyc made a similar suggestion to Hans Frank, Governor of the *Generalgouvernment*, a suggestion Frank scorned at the time. However, when Kubijovyc renewed the proposal in 1943, after the surrender of General Field Marshal Friedrich von Paulus and his armies before Stalingrad, it received a better reception.

Kubijovyc, writing on the origins of the Division, states that the combination of the catastrophic defeat at Stalingrad, the Red Army's recapture of the eastern borderlands and the successful Allied landing of troops in North Africa had a serious, sobering effect on German troops in the east. In particular, these events served to strengthen the position of those Germans who advocated cooperation with the non-Russian nations of Eastern Europe. "As the military situation grew more desperate by the day, Hitler publicly expressed the hope that other nations threatened by the Bolshevik onslaught would stand united on the Eastern, anti-Communist front."[6] Kubijovyc claims the announcement served as the first indication of an impending change in policy towards the recruitment of eastern troops and points to the formation of large Latvian and Estonian Waffen-SS units soon after.

Despite the pressing need for manpower, Himmler was not easily persuaded of the need for a Ukrainian Waffen-SS unit. Not only would his racial ideology be compromised by the presence of Ukrainians in his beloved SS, but there was the additional danger that a Ukrainian military unit might kindle further hopes for an independent Ukraine. The alternative, however, was even more horrendous in the eyes of the *Reichsführer*, namely the exhaustion of the Aryan gene pool through losses on the battlefield.

Meanwhile, a tug of war developed between those Nazi occupation officials who sought to direct the new recruits to Lublin where they could be trained as concentration camp guards and those who addressed urgent memoranda to Himmler demanding that the Ukrainian recruits serve as a local militia to protect the German administration from the rapidly growing danger of partisan attacks. Whatever its official designation, German officials understood that the need of the moment was for a militarized police formation capable of patrolling the large, increasingly incendiary area behind the front lines.[7]

However, an "image problem" confronted the German occupation officials. The governor of Galicia, *SS-Brigadeführer* Otto Wächter, was keenly aware that the locally raised Ukrainian auxiliary police units were feared and despised by a majority of the Ukrainian people. It was well known that they had served as the chief instrument in the extermination of the Jews. They were also responsible for rounding up thousands of Ukrainian young people for slave labour in Germany. At a meeting of the SS, police and Party representatives on April 12, 1943, Wächter insisted that for "political-psychological reasons" the term "police" should be avoided in the Division's official designation and that it should be known as the "*SS-Freiwilligen-Division Galizien*."[8]

The Ukrainian political leadership was acutely aware that the Division was to be, first and foremost, a police formation. In a telegram to Governor Frank, Kubijovyc as chairman of the Ukrainian Central Committee thanked "the leader of the Great German people" for organizing the "SS-Police Division Galizien."[9] In a June 13, 1943, letter addressed to Himmler, Gottlob Berger, Chief of the SS Main Office, called on the Order Police to supply training officers for the new division so that it could acquire police skills that would make it effective in fighting "bandits" before being moved to the front lines.[10]

Wächter, sensitive to Germany's manpower needs, did his best to persuade Himmler that it would be to the Reich's advantage to organize a Ukrainian Waffen-SS division. He also recognized that the creation of a Ukrainian Waffen-SS might cause considerable anxiety on the part of Nazi occupation officials if it blurred the distinction between the Master Race and its underlings. There was a further danger that it might stir up intense nationalist strivings. To allay those fears he circulated a secret memorandum on April 28, 1943, to his *Kreishauptleute* (District Chiefs) and *Stadtkommissaren* (City Officials) in Lemberg (Lviv), instructing them to avoid any references to "brotherhood" between Ukrainians and Germans. Under no circumstances were they to refer to Ukrainians as "allies" or give the impression that Germany was in any way dependent on Ukrainians for assistance. It would be sufficient, the memorandum stated, to stress that Ukrainian soldiers would receive the same treatment as German soldiers. All talk of independence was to be avoided. The recipients of the message were warned not to reveal its contents to Ukrainians on the recruiting commission and were ordered to destroy the memorandum as soon as it had been read.[11]

In a second memorandum of the same date, Wächter spelled out the precise relationship between the German occupation authorities, the Ukrainian Central Committee and the Military Council that was to serve as the nominal "board of directors" for the Division. The organization of the Division, he said, represented a fresh opportunity to enlist the Ukrainian people in the struggle against Bolshevism. He called on his officials to work with the Military Council at every opportunity and to avoid the impression that the Council was solely an organ of the German authorities. Recruitment, he predicted, would be difficult since most able-bodied men had been utilized for forced labour, but recruitment commissions, consisting of local priests and schoolteachers, would be able to help in the selection of recruits.[12]

Himmler, in turn, had sound reasons for insisting on Waffen-SS status for the new *SS-Schutzen* (police) division. As a Waffen-SS unit it would remain directly under his control, officered by men he personally appointed and ready to serve in ways he dictated. Above all, their primary allegiance would be to the Führer and the Waffen-SS. There must be no politics, he insisted, no talk of national independence by members of the Division. Indeed, the use of the terms "Ukrainian Division" and the term "Ukrainian people" were forbidden on pain of punishment. Himmler's solution to the Division's identity problem was to decree that it should march under the "Galician" banner.[13]

When all was in readiness, an "Act" proclaiming the organization of the Division was declared with considerable fanfare on April 28, 1943. Simultaneously, a military council under the chairmanship of *Abwehr* Colonel Alfred Bisanz was appointed by Wächter to encourage Galician youth to enlist in the Division and assist the families of the newly recruited soldiers.[14] Kubijovyc, in a spirited speech reported in the Lviv newspaper *Lvivski Visti* (Lviv *News*) thanked the German occupiers for their confidence in the Ukrainian people and promised that the Halychyna Division would "struggle shoulder to shoulder with the valorous German soldiers and the SS."[15] A few weeks later, Kubijovyc supplied *Lvivski Visti* with the following proclamation:

> Now arrives the long-awaited moment for the Ukrainian people to once more seize the opportunity to join the struggle, with arms in hand, against its most dangerous enemy, Moscow-Jewish-Bolshevism... The Führer of the great German state has agreed to the creation of a separate Ukrainian volunteer military formation under the name of SS-Grenadier Division *Halychyna* (Galicia). We must utilize this historic opportunity. We must immediately take up arms because it is demanded by our national pride and national history.[16]

As a symbolic gesture, Kubijovyc signed the first enlistment form to become an honorary member of the *14. SS-Freiwilligen-Division "Galizien."* [17]

In the months ahead, the Division's official designation was to undergo numerous changes, most related to efforts by the German military to rationalize the inconsistent SS numbering and nomenclature that had befallen Himmler's rapidly expanding forces. Other changes grew out of the persistent desire of the Division's members to be recognized fully as Ukrainians rather than provincial Galicians.

Wächter first dubbed the Division the *SS-Freiwilligen Division 'Galizien'* at a meeting on April 12, 1943. His colleague, the chief of the Order Police, referred to the Division familiarly as the *Galizische Division* in an April 14 letter to *SS-Gruppenführer und der Generalleutnant der Polizei* (SS-Group leader and Lieutenant-General of the Police) Otto Winkelman. But in his official proclamation announcing the Division's formation on April 28, Wächter referred to it as the *SS-Schutzen-Division"Galizien"* (Galician Police Division).[18]

The following designation changes are reflected in official German military records:

Date	Designation
June 30, 1943	*14. SS-Freiwilligen-Division "Galizien"*
October 22, 1943	*14. Galizische SS-Freiwilligen Division*
June 27, 1944	*14. Waffen-Grenadier-Division der SS (galizische Nr. 1)*
November 12, 1944	*14. Waffen-Grenadier Division der SS (ukrainische Nr. 1)*
April 25, 1945	*1. Ukrainische Division der Ukrainischen National-Armee*

The Relationship of the Division to the Waffen-SS

From the chart above, two things are clear: first, the Division was entirely a volunteer unit—a point that becomes crucial when we come to examine the Division's subsequent treatment by the British—and second, it remained officially an SS formation throughout its lifetime. Only in the final days of the war, two weeks before its surrender to the British on May 8, 1945 did the *14. Waffen-Grenadier Division der SS (ukrainische Nr. 1)* become *1. Ukrainische Division der Ukrainische National-Armee*. Subsequent efforts by Ukrainian nationalist groups to distance the Division from the SS and its excesses by describing it as a *Wehrmacht* or regular army unit are a sham. A 1948 memorandum addressed to the British government by G.R.B. Panchuk, the former Royal Canadian Air Force officer who led the campaign to admit the members of the Halychyna Division to Canada, states: "In accordance with the general policy for all non-German 'foreign' units, the [Halychyna Division] was termed Waffen-SS. This should not, however, be mistaken for the actual German SS in which only 'pure bred' Germans could serve."[19]

Nothing could be more misleading. The Galician Division remained on the roster of Himmler's forces throughout its career. The German officers who led the Division held SS ranks and were addressed by their SS nomenclature: *SS Obersturmführer* instead of the army's *Leutenant; SS Hauptsturmführer* for *Kapitan;* and *SS Sturmbannführer* for *Major*. The Division's helmets, banners and regimental standards all bore the swastika and the runic SS. At no time did the Division's emblems, the Galician Lion and the Trident take precedence over the SS symbols. The Division's Ukrainian officers were trained at the same *Junkerschulen* (officers' training school) as their German colleagues. Officers, non-commissioned personnel and enlisted men were given the same National Socialist ideological indoctrination. Ukrainian personnel were taught the necessity of "hardness" and drilled to the same degree of callousness as their German comrades-in-arms.[20]

Nationalist apologists have made much of the appointment of Uniate Church chaplains to service the Division, pointing to it as proof-positive that the Galician Division was not a genuine Waffen-SS division but the forerunner of a truly national Ukrainian army.

Himmler, the argument goes, preached a form of Aryan paganism which denied Christianity. As a result, most Waffen-SS divisions disdained the use of chaplains. Therefore, the presence of chaplains markedly distinguished the Ukrainian Division from all other SS divisions. They also argue that the presence of the Uniate priests throughout the Division served not only to provide spiritual and moral counsel for the young recruits but inoculated them against Nazi indoctrination as well. Historian John A. Armstrong states: "From the latter standpoint, at least, ecclesiastical efforts were entirely successful. Not only was the Ukrainian Division the only SS-sponsored formation of Eastern Europeans including Christian chaplains; direct Nazi propaganda was virtually excluded."[21]

However, Armstrong was probably unaware of photographs and films of the time that show Uniate chaplains celebrating mass at altars flanked by huge, swirling swastika banners, a practice that served to legitimize and even sanctify Nazism and its symbols rather than inoculate the young recruits against Nazi propaganda. The presence of Uniate priests with the Galician Division proves nothing except that German manpower needs were so drastic following the debacle at Stalingrad that Himmler was prepared to make any number of compromises with his pagan faith and racial beliefs in order to recruit the necessary manpower—compromises which in no sense altered the fundamental nature of the SS.[22]

The claim that the Waffen-SS was exclusively German is also nonsense. American historian George H. Stein, author of *Hitler's Elite Guard at War: The Waffen SS 1939-1945*, reminds us that Himmler's legions included Caucasian, Georgian, Turkomen and Cossack divisions of as early as April 1941. Later, Ukrainian and Russian units were added so that by the end of the war, approximately one million *Osttruppen* (Eastern troops) were serving in the German forces.

Stein explains that "having openly compromised its racial exclusiveness by the formation of the Moslem "Handschar" Division, the Waffen-SS no longer had a good reason for denying itself a share of the Slavic manpower pool." On April 28, 1943, a call went out for volunteers for a "Galician" SS Division. Although some effort was made to limit recruiting to that part of German-occupied Poland that had been Austrian Galicia, the fact remained that the division was composed of Ukrainians from both sides of the pre-war border. Stein insists that "the euphemistic designation of 14th SS-Freiwilligen-Division 'Galizien' fooled no one" but after years of Slav-baiting it was difficult for SS leaders to admit they had created an SS division of 'subhumans.' "[23]

The same view is elaborated by military historian John Keegan who points out that Himmler never deviated from the orthodox racial lines set by Hitler. However, starved for manpower to fight Tito's men [in Yugoslavia], he authorized the recruitment of Christian-hating Muslims from Bosnia-Herzegovina. Dubbed the 13th Handschar SS Division, they wore the fez and were led in prayer by regimental imams overseen by the Grand Mufti of Jerusalem.[24] Cossack units were allowed to retain their Cossack regalia, yet none of this tempered their ruthlessness in the anti-partisan campaign or quickened their sense of mercy while wiping out whole villages.

The Division's Police Antecedents

Many of the young men who joined the Division were raw recruits, fresh from the gymnasium (secondary school) with no previous police or military experience. The majority, however, transferred from previously recruited SS police units such as the 201st and 204th Ukrainian Schutzmannschaft battalions to form the core of the Division's personnel.[25] In addition to the SS-Freiwilligen Grenadier Regiments (numbers 29, 30 and 31), four regiments of Ukrainian police that had seen action against Jews and Poles were incorporated into the Division in the summer and fall of 1944. Included in that roster were:

1. Galician Volunteer SS-Police Regiment No. 4, which had been organized by ORPO (Order Police) in July 1943, and disbanded in June 1944, when its personnel was transferred to the Division.

2. Galician Volunteer SS-Police Regiment No. 5, which had been formed by ORPO in July 1943, and transferred into the Division in June 1944, after seeing action against Polish partisans.

3. Galician Volunteer SS-Police Regiment No. 6, which was formed by ORPO on August 6, 1943, from cadres dismissed from the *Polizeischutzregiment Nr. 32*. This unit was disbanded in southern France on January 31, 1944 and 1,200 of its members sent to join the Division at its divisional headquarters at Heidelager, Poland. During its training in France, the regiment was deployed against French partisans.

4. Police Regiment No. 7, formed on December 8, 1943, from the Headquarters Company and two additional companies of the 1st Battalion of Police Regiment No. 8. This regiment was similarly taken off the rolls in September 1944, its older members dismissed and 745 of its younger members transferred to the Division at Heidelager.[26]

Notes

1. The Germans could—and did—draft persons of German descent (Volksdeutsche) that had settled in various occupied countries, however, they had neither the power nor the desire to include those categorized as "lesser breeds" in their ranks. As a result, the various ethnic units of the Waffen-SS were almost without exception volunteers.

2. Wasyl Veryha, "The Galician Division in Polish and Soviet Literature," *The Ukrainian Quarterly*, Vol. XXXVI, No. 3, Autumn 1980, 256.

3. Friedrich Buchardt, *The Treatment of the Russian Problem during the Time of the National-Socialist Regime in Germany*, mss. The Buchardt manuscript is a voluminous personal account of the recruitment and secret collaboration of various Russian, Byelorussian and Ukrainian groups with Nazi intelligence during World War II. Its author, *SS-Sturmbannführer* Buchardt, helped coordinate the

Einsatzgruppen on the Easter Front. His account, long classified as "Top Secret" by the United States government, has only recently been declassified. I am grateful to John Loftus, author of *The Belarus Secret* and other challenging books for having introduced me to the report.

4. Buchardt, *Ibid*, 160.

5. Styrkul, *We Accuse*, 32. Also see Dallin, *German Rule In Russia*, 121, n. 3.

6. Volodymyr Kubijovyc, "The Origins of the Ukrainian Division 'Galicia'" in an appendix to Wolf-Dietrich Heike, *The Ukrainian Division Galicia 1943-1945: A Memoir* (Toronto: Schevchenko Scientific Society, 1989), 137-138.

7. Telegram from Dr. Hasse, Governor of the Lublin District to Dr. O. Losacker, Minister of the Interior of the General Government, February 6, 1943. Kiev State Archives.

8. U.S. National Archives, T-175-74. See also Roger James Bender and Hugh Page Taylor, *Uniforms, Organizations and History of the Waffen-SS*, Vol. 4, 1st edition, 2nd printing, (San Jose: R. James Bender Publishing Co., 1982), 17. Also valuable is Basil Dymytryshyn, "The Nazis and the SS Volunteer Division 'Galicia'," *The American Slavic and East European Review*, No. 15, 1956, 1-10.

9. U.S. National Archives, T-175, folder 263.

10. *Ibid.*

11. U.S. National Archives, T-580-89.

12. U.S. National Archives, T-580-89. Governor of the District of Galicia to the *Kreishauptleute, Stadthauptman, Lemberg Stadt und Landkommissare*, Lemberg April 28, 1943.

13. U.S. National Archives, T-175-74.

14. *Ibid.*

15. *Lvivski Visti*, No. 93, April 28, 1943.

16. *Lvivski Visti*, Vol, 2, No, 5, May 1943.

17. State Archives of Ukrainian SSR, Kiev. Copy of original in author's files.

18. Roger James Bender and Hugh Page Taylor, *Uniforms, Organizations and History*, Vol. 4, 7-58. See also: George Tessin, *Verbände und Truppen der Deutschen Wehrmacht und Waffen-SS im Zweiten Weltkrieg 1939-1945*.

19. Panchuk, *Heroes of the Day*, 154.

20. U.S. National Archives, T-175-94. Records of the Reich Leader of the SS and Chief of the German Police (Himmler).

21. John A. Armstrong, introduction to Wolf-Dietrich Heike, *The Ukrainian Division 'Galicia' 1943-1945: A Memoir* (Toronto: The Shevchenko Scientific Society, 1988), XIX-XX.

22. This issue is treated in George H. Stein, *Hitler's Elite Guard at War: The Waffen-SS 1939-1945* (Ithaca: Cornell University Press, 1966), xxxi : "The better SS divisions were recognized as the elite of the German army...[but] by 1943, the exigencies of war had forced the Waffen-SS to give up some of its exclusiveness. Large numbers of foreigners were recruited or conscripted, so that by the end of 1944 more than half the men wearing Waffen-SS uniforms were not native Germans. Those foreigners who could not meet SS racial standards (in general west Europeans and Volksdeutsche, or ethnic Germans) were used as replacements in elite SS divisions... The rest (mainly east Europeans) were segregated in special national formations labeled Waffen-Grenadier Division der SS."

23. Stein, 185.

24. John Keegan, *Waffen-SS: The Asphalt Soldiers* (New York: Ballentine Books, 1970), 104.

25. Centralle Stelle der Landesjustizverwaltungen (Ludwigsburg, Germany), *Die Waffen-SS: Einem Auszug über die SS-Division Galizien*.

26. Tessin, *Verbände und Truppen*, 313. Also letter from Simon Wiesenthal, May 8, 1989; and Bender and Taylor, 47.

CHAPTER 8

OFFICERS AND ADMINISTRATORS

ALL THE SENIOR OFFICERS OF THE DIVISION, FROM ITS COMMANDER, General Fritz Freitag down to the company level, were German nationals transferred from other SS police units, almost all of them long-time Nazi Party members. A few examples will suffice:

- *Obersturmbannführer* Friedrich Beyersdorff, commander of the 14th Waffen-SS Artillery Regiment, served as a Major in the *Schutzpolizei* and Waffen-SS Police Division before joining the Galician Division on January 30, 1943.[1]

- *Sturmbannführer* Otto Beissel, Battalion Commander; served in France before being transferred to the Viking Waffen-SS Division and the 14th Galician Division. After the war, the French sought his extradition on suspicion of murder. Tried *in absentia* by a French military court in Metz on January 27, 1956, he was condemned to death. The United Nations War Crimes Commission (UNWCC) lists him as a suspect in acts of murder and other crimes committed by the 51st SS Armored Brigade in Troyes, Buchers, and Briviades, France. He joined the 14th Waffen-SS on December 20, 1944.[2]

- *Hauptsturmführer* Otto Blankenhorn, Battalion Commander, served in police units utilized as security troops wherever needed. He was accused of participation in the death of Jews and Russian prisoners-of-war in Lemberg (Lviv) and in Zamosc in the Lublin district prior to being posted to the Waffen-SS.[3]

- *Sturmbannführer* Karl Bristot, Battalion Commander; joined the *Allgemeine SS* in 1933; became *Ordnungspolizei* lieutenant in 1937; assigned to 14th Waffen-SS in December 1943; arrested by American forces after the war but escaped from internment camp.[4]

- *SS Brigadeführer und General major der Waffen-SS* Fritz Freitag, the commander of the Ukrainian Division was a dour, bulky man, frequently contemptuous of his Ukrainian colleagues. Born in East Prussia in 1894, he served in the trenches in World War I and commanded the 4th SS Police Division in the 1940 invasion of France. An ardent National Socialist, he was given command of the 14th Galician Volunteer SS

Division in November 1943. Highly demanding and rigid in his thinking, Freitag was unpopular with both his German and Ukrainian fellow officers. Like many of the German officers who served under him, Freitag was an unsuccessful discard from another unit, not good enough to command a German division but adequate to direct a division consisting of non-Aryan foreigners. In German eyes, this was the equivalent of commanding black African troops *(Askari)*. At every turn, Freitag showed his preference for his German officers and underlined the failings of his Ukrainian soldiers. In one reported incident, Freitag approved the execution of an eighteen year-old Ukrainian recruit whose only offence was to cover his head with a blanket while standing to attention beside his barracks bunk. Despite the pleas for mercy from his Ukrainian officers, Freitag interpreted this minor prank as "disrespectful conduct" and allowed his court martial and execution to proceed.[5]

Wächter and Company

Since the men of the Division took an oath of blind obedience to the Führer and his appointed officers, the careers of the Division's tactical commanders—Wächter as Governor of Galicia and Oberländer as chief liaison with the *Abwehr*—take on additional significance. Wächter was the Division's guiding light and most ardent German supporter. Not only did he urge the Division's formation but he remained the unit's chief political advisor until its ultimate surrender. According to United Nations War Crimes Commission (UNWCC) records, Wächter served as Governor of Krakow from October 1939 until February1942 when he took up his duties as Governor of the Galician District with headquarters in Lviv. While serving in Krakow, he ordered 30,000 Jews out of the city in June 1940 and 20,000 more in November of that year. Only those Jews considered "useful" to the German war effort were allowed to remain, barricaded in a dismal ghetto known as Podgorze. Each day, the Jewish community had to supply 3,000 workers for forced labour; each week the boundaries of the ghetto were drawn tighter, forcing the inhabitants to live in closer, more crowded, less sanitary quarters.

In June 1940, the German authorities announced that by August 15, all Jews must leave Krakow. The numerous petitions and appeals made by individual Jews asking to be allowed to remain, served only to hasten the arrest of Mark Biberstein, the German appointed head of the Jewish Community Council. Biberstein, who had done his best to cooperate with the occupation authorities, was sent to the extermination camp at Oswiecim (Auschwitz) with all of the Council's members.

The last extension for the Jews of Krakow came to a brutal end in February 1941. *The Black Book of Polish Jewry* records that "Jews were seized on the street and taken to the railway station without a chance to gather any of their belongings or communicate with their families. The deportees were locked in freight cars without ventilation, water, food or sanitary facilities."[6]

Wächter and his colleagues stand accused by the United Nations War Crimes Commission (UNWCC) of "murder and massacre," "torture of civilians," and "internment of civilians under inhuman conditions" in relation to events at Auschwitz and Rajsko (Birkenau) from June 1940 to 1943. The United Nations committee describes these events in the following terms:

> More than a million Polish citizens, Poles and Jews, were deported to these camps during the period of 1939-1943. The internees were exposed to systematic extermination by means of mass executions, poisoning, injections and gas, and to physical torment by continuous flogging, kicking and all sorts of pestering... The main feature of the German occupation regime in Poland is sadistic terrorism exercised on a huge scale... The Jews are exposed to unimaginable persecution and pitiless extermination.[7]

The UNWCC report holds Wächter and his crew directly responsible for these depredations "because they were chiefs of administration, or leaders or commanders of the SS Police and Gestapo in occupied Poland, and in this leading capacity [they] not only ordered [but] carried out mass arrests as part of the systematic persecution of Polish citizens in the camps of Oswiecim and Rajsko (Birkenau)."[8]

The UN dossier emphasizes that Wächter and his staff possessed full knowledge of the tortures and massacres inflicted on the camp internees and were, therefore, full-scale accomplices in the commission of their crimes.[9]

Wächter is additionally charged by the UNWCC with participating in the persecution of the Roman Catholic clergy in Poland. "Doubtlessly aware of the clergy's great influence among the population of the General Government, and especially among the peasants, the occupant tried to...obtain compulsorily some sort of collaboration between the clergy and the occupation authorities."[10] Wächter and his colleagues threatened priests with dire punishment if they failed to report information on potential resistance gathered in the confessional to the Nazi authorities. "To render the clergy more accessible to this form of collaboration...the German authorities ordered mass arrests of clergy in several places, including Warsaw."[11]

Wächter's crimes did not end in Krakow. The UNWCC places him sixth on the roster of twenty-one Nazi officials in the Galician District responsible for crimes committed at the death camps of Belzec, Sobibor, Kosow, Podlaski and Chelmo. As General Government chiefs and leading officials of the districts incorporated into the Reich, Wächter and his colleagues were guilty of having participated in the mass killing of Jews by ordering their deportation from their respective provinces and districts to the extermination camps.[12]

Transferred from Krakow to Lviv in 1942, Wächter became administratively responsible for the systematic murder and massacre of civilians at Treblinka. The UNWCC charged that "responsibility for these crimes must be borne by all who devised and developed the plan for exterminating the Jews."[13]

Wächter was never tried for his crimes. He is reported to have died in 1949 in the Monastery Maria dell' Anima in Rome where he benefited from the protection of the infamous, pro-Nazi Bishop Alois Hudel, rector of the German church in Rome.[14]

Also intimately bound with the Halychyna Division was *Oberleutenant* Theodor Oberländer, head of *Abwehr-2*, the sabotage and subversion department of Army Group South and chief political officer to the *Nachtigall* and *Roland* Battalions. Given that the two units were integrated into the Halychyna Division in May 1943, Oberländer's record is of considerable significance to this inquiry.

An early Nazi, Oberländer took part in Hitler's 1923 *putsch* against the Weimar Republic. After Hitler took power in 1933, Oberländer specialized in "eastern affairs" as head of a state-sponsored organization, *Bund deutscher Osten* (Federation of the German East). The *Bund* sought to influence political events in Eastern Europe on behalf of the Nazis through espionage, subversion and provocation. German minorities in Poland, the Baltic countries and Ukraine were encouraged to draw up lists of "anti-German-minded persons" for future extermination. They were instructed to classify their country's population into "racially valuable" and racially inferior inhabitants.

Oberländer became a post war target of the East German government in its effort to embarrass the West German government of Chancellor Conrad Adenauer by demonstrating that his administration was riddled with Nazi war criminals. The German Democratic Republic published the *Brown Book* listing the numerous Nazis still serving in the judiciary, army, parliament and diplomatic corps of the Federal Republic. The *Brown Book* identified Oberländer as the "leader of special mass murder units in Lviv and other Soviet towns."[15]

After the war, Oberländer became a member of the *Bundestag*, arousing controversy for his habit of carrying a loaded gun on the assembly floor. From 1953 to 1960, he served in Chancellor Adenauer's cabinet as West Germany's Minister of Refugee Affairs. Denounced as a war criminal by the East Germans, he was tried *in absentia* and sentenced to life imprisonment by the East German Supreme Court. In the judgment of the court, Oberländer, as the real commander of *Nachtigall*, had participated directly in the massacre of three thousand Polish intellectuals and hundreds of Jews in the first days of the occupation in Lviv. In the end, the West German government found it too embarrassing to retain him in the face of the East German accusations and forced him to resign.[16]

Despite his dismissal from office, the West German government staged a "counter-trial" to clear Oberländer's name and deny the East German charge that numerous Nazis were playing prominent roles in Chancellor Adenauer's government. The Chief Public Prosecutor of the District Court in Bonn conducted the proceedings. The court found that as a liaison officer rather than a direct commander, there was insufficient evidence to hold Oberländer responsible for the atrocities committed by the *Nachtigall* forces in Lviv. During the trial, no fewer than 150 former Ukrainian Nazi collaborators testified to the good character of their former chief.[17]

Incidentally, the one possible exception to this pattern of early National Socialist Party membership and SS police service among the Divisions major officers was Major Wolf-Dietrich Heike, the Division's chief executive officer. A regular army officer (*Wehrmacht*), Heike's military experience and organizational skills were invaluable to a division officered largely by military amateurs whose ideological fervor outdid their martial know-how.[18]

The Training Period

The first batch of Lviv recruits entrained for training camps in Brno, Czechoslovakia and Debica in Poland on July 16, 1943. After passing in review before a large coterie of Nazi officials, including Wächter and Bisanz, they mounted railway carriages on which they had chalked Nazi slogans and crude anti-Semitic cartoons.[19] German newsreels of the event show the recruits and their political leaders with their arms extended in stiff-armed Nazi salute as they marched by a reviewing stand bedecked with SS and Swastika banners.[20]

As they marched, the recruits sang the Division's anthem:

Death, death to the Poles,
Death to Moscow-Jewish Communism,
We march proudly with OUN
And as we march
We kill the Communists and the Poles.[21]

For the remainder of 1943, the Division was scattered from Debica to Biarritz. Two hundred and forty men were selected for officer-training at *Junkerschulen* in Germany. Others were sent to artillery and field engineering schools in Hamburg, Oldenburg, Osnabrück and Neuhammer. A scout battalion trained at Karlsruhe and Koblenz. Some 5,000 Halychyna Division recruits—transferred from existing Ukrainian police regiments—were given further police combat training in France. While still in training, they joined other German-led troops in tracking down French resistance members and arresting downed Allied fliers.[22]

The Oath

In November 1943, Wächter, Bisanz and Military Council member L. Makarushka journeyed to France to swear-in the Ukrainian troops. In a field ceremony that followed a divine service, the men of the Halychyna Division took an oath of absolute obedience to Hitler as leader of the German armed forces and organizer of a new Europe:

> I swear by God this holy oath that in the struggle against Bolshevism I will give the C-in-C of the German Armed Forces, Adolf Hitler, absolute obedience, and as a fearless soldier, if it be his will, I will always be prepared to lay down my life for this oath.[23]

Atrocities

Valery Styrkul, author of the booklet *We Accuse* published by Dnipro Publishers (Kiev), states that sub-units of the Division participated in a variety of death-dealing activities while still in training. He cites the execution of Soviet prisoners-of-war at Szebnie, the liquidation of Poles, Gypsies and Jews in the town of Moderowka and the reinforcement of German units guarding the concentration camp at Szebnie. "On November 6, 1943, [SS-men from the Galician Division] helped shoot some 500 Jewish inmates in a forest near the village of Dubrocow. "Cadets of the Halychyna Division were involved in a similar action in the forest near Wawrzice."[24]

By March 1944, the scattered units of the Division had completed their training and reassembled at Neuhammer where they began divisional maneuvers. Although the Red Army was drawing closer, the growing strength and boldness of the Soviet partisans made it necessary to divert large segments of the Division to the task of keeping order behind the lines. Himmler, in a letter to Koppe, the Supreme SS and Police Chief in the East, gave his permission to use the Galician Division in any way necessary to hold down resistance.[25]

In February 1944, two of the Division's three available regiments consisting of some 2,000 men, were separated from the rest of the Division and assigned to fight the Soviet partisans. Organized as a special battle group (*SS-Kampfgruppe*) under the command of Division officers *SS-Obersturmbannführer* Friedrich Beyersdorff and Battalion Commander *Hauptsturmführer* Bristot, they were dispatched to the Chelm area to counter the partisans that had penetrated the *Generalgouvernement*.[26]

Chief Executive Officer Wolf-Dietrich Heike reports: "Not surprisingly, the afore-mentioned task force did not perform its duties well. Soon after reports of the unseemly behaviour of the unit began to arrive at the Division." Heike attributes this "unseemly behaviour" to the soldiers' lack of training and the "age-old antagonism between Poles and Ukrainians." These factors may have played a role in the cruel slaughter visited on numerous Polish villages, but the promiscuous use of terror as a weapon to suppress opposition—a practise with which Heike was undoubtedly familiar—offers a better explanation.[27]

On November 23, 1943, the Beyersdorff detachment—along with other police units—is reported to have raided the village of Kokhanivka. Eleven villagers were shot, five hanged and thirty-nine tortured to death. Twenty old people and fifty children were locked in a village home and burned to death. One hundred persons were taken for brief rides in *Gaswagens*. The *Gaswagens* were trucks fitted with hoses that brought the asphyxiating carbon monoxide fumes from the engine's exhaust into the passenger chamber. Styrkul claims: "Legal bodies investigating the war crimes of the Nazi occupiers estimated that the special company of the SS Halychyna Division had tortured more than 2,000 civilians to death in Poland, shipped 20,000 persons off to Germany and burned down 20 villages."[28]

By early June 1944, the detachment took up position in the Lviv region. That same month it staged a reprisal raid on the village of Ozhidiv in which twenty-five villagers were shot, seven hanged and fifteen beaten and tortured to death. On July 13, a raid on the Olesko district resulted in the deaths of 162 residents by gun, rope and club while gas vans accounted for another 120. The village of Pidhirtsi received similar treatment in a series of mid-June actions. Ozhevits was destroyed on July 10 and more than 595 residents of Zolochiv were murdered between July 12 and July 20 by Beyersdorff's special squads. All in all, it is estimated that the special detachment shot, hanged, gassed and burned more than 1,500 men, women and children between February 1943 and March 1944 when it rejoined the Division. It also rounded up thousands of able-bodied young men and women for forced labour in Germany.[29]

A United Nations War Crimes Commission file alleges that a Dr. Nickolay Terlicki of Borislav, an organizer and recruiter of Galicia Division personnel, led members of the "Ukrainian SS Division Halyczyna" (Polish spelling) in a brutal attack on the Jews of the Borislav ghetto. "The accused organized a pogrom of the Jewish population of Borislav in the course of which 180 citizens were beaten to death with iron bars and about 75 died within a few days from injuries." As well as organizing the pogrom, Terlicki took a personal part in carrying it out. He encouraged the SS-men, crying to them: "We must now play in this way." Six eyewitnesses swore to the accuracy of the description and claimed that Terlicki took part personally in the slaughter.[30]

While Bolsheviks and "kikes" were the primary targets of nationalist auxiliary police and military units, by 1943 the number of Jews in Galicia had been seriously reduced through pogroms, mass shootings and "resettlement" in concentration camps. This left the nationalists free to concentrate their attacks on the Polish villages that dotted the western Ukraine. Since the Poles were almost entirely Roman Catholic, this meant frequent attacks on Catholic institutions by the predominantly Ukrainian Catholic (Uniate) members of the nationalist police and military groups.

SS Chief Heinrich Himmler and Higher SS and Police Leader Odilo Globocnik were eager to put into effect their plan to colonize Ukraine with German landowners who would be served like medieval barons by land-bound Ukrainian peasants. "The main operation began on November 28, 1942, affecting mainly Skierbieszow, Stary, Zamosc and Wysokie Districts, altogether some thirty villages. Apart from their own forces, the Germans used large detachments of Ukrainian nationalists in this ethnic cleansing exercise. Most of the inhabitants were driven to a concentration camp at Zamosc... From the Zamosc camp, the Polish peasants were sent to work as forced labourers to Germany or to Auschwitz or to Majdanek. By July 1943, of the 691 villages in the Zamosc area, 279 were wholly or partly cleared of Polish inhabitants."[31]

The Majdan Starj district came under attack on July 3, 1942. Fifty-eight people were killed and 76 farms set afire. A twelve year-old that survived the action, recalled that on the afternoon of July 3, the village suddenly went up in flames and Ukrainian SS-men began rounding up all the residents. His father was in a group of men the SS ordered into a field where they were bound and machine-gunned while the people wept and begged for mercy. The women and children were ordered to lie down in the grass while two SS-men shot them from behind. "I heard the shots and fainted from fear," the boy reported. "When I came to I felt a terrible pain in my leg where I had been shot. I lay still without breathing until the SS-men left and I could hear their conversation grow dim in the distance."[32]

"The attacks on Polish villages grew more frequent and more intense the closer the Red Army approached," said Roman Catholic priest, Fr. Waclaw Szetelnicki. "On Sunday, March 4, 1944, a combined UPA and SS Volunteer Division rounded up some 2,000 people who were hiding in the Dominican Monastery in the Podkamien parish of Brody. Fr. Stanislaw Fialkowski and three Dominican priests were murdered. Altogether they murdered 600 people in the villages of Palikrowy, Malinska and Czernicy."[33]

In March 1944, the Soviet partisans made a daring attack on the city of Ternopil. An important railway hub before the war, its citizenry was composed equally of Ukrainians,

Poles and Jews living in their own distinctive neighborhoods. By 1944, there were few if any Jews left in Ternopil, but Poles still occupied important parts of the city.

The arrival of the partisans touched off a celebration in the Polish district. Red and white national flags were unfurled from the cathedral and the windows of Polish homes. Unhappily, the partisans were too few and too weak to occupy the whole city and were forced to retreat in the face of a German counter-attack. Once the Soviet forces had been driven off, the Germans and their Ukrainian allies took a terrible revenge on the Poles. SS Patrols ordered the Polish residents out of their homes and herded them into the cathedral square. *The Chronicle of the SS Halychyna Division* reports on their fate: "When the Germans and our SS-men cleared part of the city of Bolsheviks, we rounded up every single Pole and locked them into the cathedral, after which we exterminated them." The *Chronicle* reports further that it was the 3rd Battalion of the 4th Regiment of the Galician Division that participated in the battle with the Bolsheviks for Zbarah-Ternopil.

The *Chronicle* is a running account of the activities of the Division for the years 1943-1944, written and maintained by officials of the nationalist Ukrainian Central Committee in Krakow. A difference in handwriting and the periodic use of a typewriter indicates that at least three different officials were assigned the task of logging the Division's history. Not quite a formal war diary, the document is an unembellished account of the Division's actions. Many of the incidents recorded in the *Chronicle* can be substantiated by matching accounts published in the Halychyna Division's newspaper, *Do peremohy* (To Victory).[34]

Attacks on Polish villages were marked by special savagery. "Entire Polish villages were wiped out, their inhabitants invariably tortured and raped before being slaughtered with knives and axes; babies and children murdered with the same savagery as had been the fate of Jewish children."[35]

Not far from Lviv lay a cluster of villages settled by ethnic Poles: Huta Pieniacka, Huta Werchbuska, Hucisko Pieniacka, Majdan and Huta Broddzka. Constantly assailed by UPA bands, the villages joined together to form a self-defence unit and devised plans to evacuate their populations into the nearby forests in case of a major attack by Ukrainian forces. Small bands of unarmed Jews and poorly armed partisans visited these villages in search of food and medical supplies. On cold winter nights, they sometimes took shelter in the villagers' barns and sheds. German intelligence reports identified the villages as partisan havens which, according to standing orders, had to be mercilessly wiped out. The Ukrainian nationalists were eager collaborators in the eradication of Polish communities because with each village destroyed, the region became more purely Ukrainian. On October 10, 1944, a combined force of OUN "Banderites" and elements of the Halychyna Division wiped out Hucisko Pieniacka.

The next to fall was Huta Pieniacka. David Kruitkov, who served as a partisan scout, was familiar with the insignia of the various military units operating in the area. He recalled in an interview how he arrived at the village an hour or two after the Division's soldiers had withdrawn, taking the peasants' cattle with them. Kruitkov recalled the corpses strewn through the village and described with special poignancy the infant still seeking to suckle at its dead mother's breast.[36]

The Chronicle of the Halychyna Division relates how a small patrol of 14th Waffen-SS Division soldiers approached the village of Huta Pieniacka in mid-February 1944. Partisans hiding in the village fired upon the patrol and struck three of the soldiers, killing two and seriously wounding a third who died several days later. The Division staged an elaborate military funeral for the dead soldiers and then took its revenge on Huta Pieniacka.

On February 27, a mixed force consisting of a Ukrainian police regiment, a sprinkling of *Wehrmacht* reserves and a strong contingent from the SS Halychyna Division set out to pacify Huta Pieniacka. At dawn on the 28th of February, the German-led forces surrounded the village. Once in place, they opened fire with machine guns and hand grenades. Zvi Weigler, a Jewish schoolteacher who was hiding in the nearby forest, witnessed what followed:

> Only a few of the farmers succeeded in escaping to the forest; the rest of the inhabitants remained in the village... After firing and throwing hand grenades from the outskirts, the murderers went into the village, assembled all the farmers together with their families and locked them up in their barns. They even locked the cattle in the stables. Then, they set fire to the entire village... The German bandits stood guard to make sure no living thing, human or animal, would escape from the burning buildings. The village burned all day, and only at night did the murderers finally leave.[37]

More than 1200 villagers died in the raid on the village; only 200 survived. Three weeks later, the same fate befell Huta Werchbuska. Forewarned this time, three quarters of the villagers took shelter in the wood. However, those remaining received the standard treatment—all its occupants, human and animal, were slaughtered and their homes and barns burned to the ground.

Again, *The Chronicle of the Division* confirms the account provided by other sources. The entry for March 3, 1944 describes the death of the three soldiers as they approached Huta Pieniacka and reports that they were given a full military funeral at which Wächter and Bisanz served as pall bearers. The *Chronicle* records that "the villages of Huta Pieniacka and neighboring Benyaki were burned down, pacified and rid of its populace."

In the margin, the chronicler scribbled the following note alongside his description of the slaughter: "Not by our fellows but by the other guys." Whatever the intent of the marginal note, it fails to absolve the members of the Division. Even if the Halychyna Division merely stood guard while the *Wehrmacht* and the Ukrainian Police Regiment massacred the villagers and set their homes on fire—there is nothing in any of the accounts to suggest this was so—it would still fail to remove the stain of guilt from the Division. The criminal who pins the victim's arms so that his confederate can cut his throat is just as guilty of murder as the man who wielded the knife. He cannot claim: "It was the other guy."

Himmler Visits the Division

SS Reichsführer Heinrich Himmler had no illusions and no qualms about the role of the Halychyna Division when he addressed its officers at their Neuhammer headquarters on May 16, 1944. "Your homeland has become so much more beautiful since you have lost—on our initiative, I must say—the residents who were so often a dirty blemish on Galicia's good name, namely the Jews," he assured them.[38]

In an obvious effort to further endear himself to the men of the Division, Himmler added: "I know that if I ordered you to liquidate the Poles in this or that district, I would be giving you permission to do what you are eager to do anyway."[39] But, the *Reichsführer* of the Police and the SS warned that the privilege of enforcing order on the Poles belonged solely to "the saviour of Europe, Adolf Hitler and cannot be presumed by anyone else." The fate of the Ukraine was also in Hitler's capable hands, so there was no room for talk of an independent Ukraine. Indeed, he forbade the use of the term "Ukrainian" and urged them to bear the regional designation "Galician" with pride.

Himmler closed his speech with a demand for absolute obedience, order and loyalty to the man "who will become the Saviour of Europe and the creator of your future."[40]

On May 17, 1944—the day following Himmler's visit to Division headquarters—the command of the Polish resistance movement, the *Armia Krajowa* (Home Army) notified the Polish government-in-exile in London that "units of the SS Halychyna Division appeared recently in the county of Hrubieszow where they stepped up terrorist attacks on the civilian population. Six Polish villages were burnt down." A further report, dispatched on May 24, stated: "The terrorist actions of the SS Halychyna Division and the UPA continues in the region of Chelm. These actions are opposed by our self-defence and partisan units." And on July 7, the Home Army informed London: "The terrorist activities of the SS Halychyna Division increased in the region of Lublin."[41]

Notes

1. Public Record Office (PRO) London, TS 26/903; also Berlin Document Center; also Heike, *Sie Wollten die Freiheit*, 57-59; Bender and Taylor, Vol. IV, 47.

2. United Nations War Crimes Commission (UNWCC) 4645/FR/G/1880, and Correspondence of the U.S. High Commissioner for Germany, July 1, 1953, to Commander-in-Chief, U.S. Army Europe; Berlin Document Center; also *Centralle Stelle des Landesjustizverwaltungen*, Ludwigsburg, Germany. *Staatsanwaltschaft* Karlsruhe; correspondence May 19, 1987; also Berlin Document Center; also U.S. Army, 1st Infantry Division Civilian Internment Camp, September 9, 1946.

3. *Staatsanwaltschaft* Karlsruhe; correspondence May 19, 1987; also Berlin Document Center; also U.S. Army, 1st Infantry Division Civilian Internment Camp, September 9, 1946. Berlin Document Center; also Public Record Office (PRO) 26/903; also United States Army Intelligence and Security Command, March 13, 1987; also *Centralle Stelle*, Ludwigsburg.

4. Berlin Document Center; also PRO TS 26/903; also United States Army Intelligence and Security Command, March 13, 1987; also *Centralle Stelle*, Ludwigsburg.

5. Michael O. Logusz, *The Waffen-SS 14th Grenadier Division 1943-1945* (Atglen, PA,: Schiffer Publishing Ltd., 1997), 160.

6. Jacob Apensziak, editor, *The Black Book of Polish Jewry: An Account of the Martyrdom of Polish Jewry under Nazi Occupation* (New York: The American Federation of Polish Jews, 1982), 78-86.

7. UNWCC, 214/P/G/26

8. *Ibid.*

9. *Ibid.*

10. *Ibid.*

11. *Ibid.*

12. UNWCC, 214/P/G/21.

13. UNWCC, 79/P/G, April 1944, pages 10791-10792.

14. Hilberg, *Destruction of the European Jews,* 1st edition, 714. Hudal played an ambiguous role during the war and its aftermath. In 1943, when the Germans were organizing the arrest and deportation of the Jews in Trieste to Auschwitz, Bishop Hudal appealed to the German military commander to order the deportation of the Jews in Rome to be stopped. "I would be very grateful if you would give an order to stop these arrests in Rome and its vicinity right away; I fear that otherwise the Pope will have to make an open stand, which will serve the anti-German propaganda as a weapon against us."

15. Anonymous, *The Brown Book: War and Nazi War Criminals in West Germany*, English edition (Berlin: Verlag Zeit am Bild, 1965) 273-274, 305.

16. *Brown Book,* 305.

17. Scott Anderson and Jon Lee Anderson, *Inside the League* (New York: Dodd, Mead & Co., 1986), 44-45.

18. Material on the officers of the 14th Waffen-SS Grenadier Division was compiled from documents in the London Public Record Office (TS 26/903), the Berlin Document Centre, United States Army Intelligence and Security Command, the archives of the United Nations War Crimes Commission, the *Centralle Stelle der Landesjustizverwaltungen,* Heike's *The Ukrainian Division 'Galicia'* 1943-1945 and Landwehr's *Fighting for Freedom.*

19. Veryha, *Along the Roads of World War II*. See the photograph of troops embarking on page 18.

20. Recorded by German newsreel cameras, the film of the march past the reviewing stand erected before the Opera House was captured by the Red Army when it retook the Galician capital. The original is stored in the Central State Archives in Kiev. A direct copy is stored in the author's files. Still photographs, taken from the motion picture film, illustrate this book.

21. Antoni B. Szczesniak and Wieskaw Z. Szota, *Drogo Do Nikad* (Warsaw: Instytut Wydawniczky Zwiakzkow Zawadowych, 1985), 295.

22. Styrkul, *We Accuse*, 129-130. The English version of Heike's *The Ukrainian Division 'Galicia' 1943-1945*, states: "In France the soldiers finished their training in the Spring and most of them were sent to rejoin the Division at Neuhammer. During training they were also used against French partisans. After the dissolution of police regiments in France, some soldiers deserted to the ranks of the French partisans." Landwehr (*Fighting for Freedom*, page 27) and others make reference to a revolt of Ukrainian troops training in France "when it appeared that they might be used against the Western Democracies instead of the Soviets." Landwehr states: "Eventually the Ukrainians in these regiments found their way into the Ukrainian Division." Other versions of this "brief revolt" claim that the whole regiment deserted to join the French underground. The citations on this matter are vague and contradictory.

23. Styrkul, 130. Also Bender and Taylor, 28. David Littlejohn, *The Patriotic Traitors*, gives a slightly different version of the oath: "I swear to you, Adolf Hitler as leader, loyalty and courage. I pledge to you and those you place in authority over me, obedience even unto death. So help me God." Styrkul, on page 49, quotes the diary of the Division's journalist, Haj-Holowka: "We repeated the words of the oath of allegiance to Hitler and then sang songs. Well, now we are real SS-men."

24. Styrkul, 134-135.

25. Himmler file, U.S. National Archives, T-175-74.

26. References to the Beyersdorff Detachment and its activities can be found in Wolf-Dietrich Heike, *Sie Wollten die Freiheit: Die Geschichte der Ukrainischen Division 1943-1945* (Dorheim: Podzun, Vig., 1973), 59; Vasyl Veryha, *Along the Roads of World War II* (Toronto: New Pathway Publishers, 1980); Bender and Taylor, *Uniforms, Organizations and History of the Waffen-SS*, Vol. 4, 30-31; Styrkul, *We Accuse*, 167; Michael O. Logusz, *Galicia Division: The Waffen-SS 14th Grenadier Division 1943-1945* (Atglen, PA: Schiffer Publishing Ltd., 1997), 144-151 and 457 fn.

27. Heike (English version), *The Ukrainian Division 'Galicia' 1943-1945: A Memoir* (Toronto: Shevchenko Scientific Society, 1988), 22.

28. Styrkul, 171. In a personal interview with Styrkul in Kiev on September 4, 1987, the Ukrainian writer stated that "the legal sources" mentioned above were primarily the Reports of the Extraordinary Commissions appointed by the Soviet government as the war drew to a close. These commissions investigated atrocities, interviewed witnesses and performed forensic examinations on the victims.

29. Styrkul, 206-211.

30. UNWCC, 4889/P/G/166. Terlicki and his role as recruiter for the Division is also described in Styrkul's *We Accuse* on page 163. According to *The Black Book of Polish Jewry*, N.M. Gelber, Editor, in the article "Memorial to the Jews of Drohobycz, Boryslaw and Surroundings," 224, the ghetto in Borislav survived as an *Arbeitslager* (work camp) until liquidated in 1944.

31. R. Ainsztein, "The Final Solution of the Slav Problem," *The Wiener Library Bulletin*, Vol. IV, No. 2, March 1950. 36.

32. Markewicz, *Nie Dali*, 215.

33. Fr. Waclaw Szetelnicki, *Zapomniany Lwowski Bohater KS* (Polish Library, London), 132. This document, stored in London's esteemed Polish Library commemorates the Polish priests martyred at the hands of nationalist Ukrainians during World War II. A footnote in the document identifies the SS Division in this reference as the Ukrainian Volunteer SS Division Galicia.

34. The author has a full copy of the *Chronicle* obtained at the State Central Archives in Kiev.

35. Reuben Ainsztein, "The Myth of the Fatalistic and Helpless Galician Jew" in *Jewish Resistance in Nazi Occupied Europe*, 254.

36. I met with Kruitkov on two successive visits to Galicia. I questioned Kruitkov rigorously to determine if his story was true or Soviet propaganda. I cross-examined him carefully on details of the insignia worn by the attacking soldiers and came away convinced that his knowledge and recall were genuine. He identified members of the Galician Division by the Tryzub on their caps and the lion-rampant on sleeve and collar.

37. Zvi Weigler, "Two Polish Villages Razed for Extending Help to Jews and Partisans," *Yad Vashem Bulletin*, Jerusalem, 1957, 18-20. Weigler taught school in the nearby town of Zlochow until the Nazis arrived. Then, he took to the woods near his village. Weigler was approximately thirty years-old at the time. His testimony was recorded by Dr. Nathan Eck in November 1952. Reuben Ainsztein in *Jewish Resistance in Nazi-Occupied Europe* gives a similar account of the massacre at Huta Pieniacka, as does Szczesniak in *Drogo do Nikad* (Road to Nowhere). 127. Ainsztein also notes that the SS Galician Division was stationed in the Lviv area in January 1944, and was actively engaged in skirmishes with partisan General Medvedev's detachment while the partisans were making their way towards the Galician capital.

38. The full test of Himmler's speech is available in German in its original form in the National Military Archives, T- 175-94, "Records of the Reich Leader of the SS and Chief of the German Police."

39. *Ibid.*

40. *Ibid.*

41. *Armia Krajowa w Dokumentach 1939-1945*, Volume 3 (London:: Studium Polski Podziemnej), 447, 458, 507.

CHAPTER 9

FROM BRODY TO TAMSWEG: DEFEAT AND SURRENDER

THE RED ARMY'S 1944 SUMMER OFFENSIVE BROUGHT THE SOVIET forces within reach of the Lviv, Brody, Rava-Russka triangle defended by the Northern Ukraine Army Group consisting of the Hungarian 1st Army and the 1st and 4th Panzer armies. In late June and early July, the Galician Division was transported by train from its training base at Neuhammer to the Brody area where it was incorporated into the 13th Corps of the 4th Panzer Army.

The Division's officers were understandably apprehensive about going into battle against front line Red Army troops. Dealing with unarmed civilians and lightly armed partisans were one thing; contending with an attack by a surging Red Army was another. Wächter and the divisional staff begged Field Marshall Model, C-in-C of Army Group 'North Ukraine' to assign the Division to a relatively quiet sector of the front for completion of training and acquisition of battle experience.[1] Model paid them scant attention. As a result the Division found itself facing the very center of the Soviet advance.[2]

The Battle of Brody

On July 13, Soviet troops launched a massive attack against the 900,000-man Nazi force dug in on a 30-kilometer front that backed on Brody. By July 27, the Soviets—having executed a classic pincer movement—had liberated Lviv and Stanislav and trapped eight Nazi divisions in a rapidly narrowing pocket centred on Brody.

Caught in a cauldron of fire, the trapped German forces fought desperately to escape and in the process suffered heavy losses of 50 to 70 percent of their personnel. The 14th Waffen-SS Division bore the brunt of the attack as it tried to hold the line while the German divisions sought to break out. Military historian Michael Logusz graphically describes the Division's situation:

> Bombarded with overwhelming firepower, repeatedly strafed, bombed and rocketed by low and high flying aircraft, massively struck by enemy armor, reinforced with mechanized, criminal penal battalions and NKVD troops, the Division began to fold.[3]

The Division's losses are hard to estimate. It has been generally held that two thirds of the Division was destroyed at Brody. Others claim the Division was completely destroyed and no longer existed after Brody. However, Logusz—intent on proving that the Division fought heroically—insists that at least 5,000 of the 10,000 officers and men committed to the Brody battle succeeded in breaking out. "If one takes these figures into consideration, then it becomes clear that under extraordinarily tough conditions the Division executed a successful breakout, rather than being destroyed at Brody, as is the popular belief."[4]

However, Bender and Taylor, publishers of an oft quoted series of books on the German-led *Osttruppen*, hold that the Ukrainian Division's first engagement against front line troops proved a complete disaster. Bender and Taylor blame the lack of proper training for the Division's poor performance: "While part of the blame can be laid on the Division's inexperience in the field, one can hardly say that a formation with a year's training behind it went into battle 'inadequately trained.' A better assessment could be that its prolonged training was perhaps unsuited to the tough defensive warfare encountered at Brody, for the fact should not be ignored that originally it had been intended as a police division and its initial training had been for police duties."[5]

In any event, at least half of the Division's soldiers were killed, wounded or captured in a week of relentless fighting. On July 21-23, the surviving remnants of the Division managed to slip through the battle lines and beat a retreat towards the Carpathian Mountains. While the largest number of the Division soldiers that escaped the Brody pocket headed for safety in the Carpathian Mountains, a much smaller group deserted to the OUN's UPA forces that now found themselves cut off behind the Red Army lines.[6] One group passed through Sambor and the Uzhotsky Pass into Hungarian-occupied Carpatho-Ukraine where they rested briefly before being returned to Germany. Another contingent made its way from the Carpathian Mountains through Czechoslovakia to the American zone of occupied-Germany where they surrendered to the American forces. There they received a warm welcome from the short-memoried Americans who hired many of the former Division members as guards and drivers for the post-war Displaced Persons camps.

General Freitag was instructed to return with the battered remnants of his division to the old headquarters at Neuhammer. Here the Halychyna Division was brought back to full strength in record time. How was this accomplished? Where did they find the manpower now that all of Galicia had returned to Soviet control? Himmler used the simple expedient of transferring men from a variety of Ukrainian police units that had become redundant now that there was no Ukrainian territory left for them to patrol. To these he added personnel from reinforcement and training units, as well as a sprinkling of Ukrainian youngsters who had volunteered to serve in anti-aircraft batteries now overrun by the Red Army.

In its overwhelming appetite for manpower, the Division cared little whether the new recruits were Galicians or came from other parts of Ukraine; policemen who had served in the various German-formed *Schutzmannschaften* in the Kiev region and Ukrainian auxiliaries who had served the *Einsatzgruppen* were welcomed into the ranks. Former concentration camp personnel from Belzec, Treblinka and Sobibor were thrown into the Division once these death camps were overrun. Ukrainian members of the 'Trawniki' detachment—some of whose members had taken part in the suppression of the 1943 Warsaw Ghetto Uprising—were later absorbed into the Galician Division as were the members of *Nachtigall* and *Roland*.[7]

To make up for the shortage of trained non-commissioned officers, plans were made to transfer 1,000 German non-commissioned officers to the formation.[8]

The Division in Slovakia

Pressured by Hitler, betrayed by France and Britain, and undermined by pro-fascist forces from within, the Czechoslovakian Republic crumbled. Slovak nationalists, urged on by Hitler, Göring and Ribbentrop, declared their independence on March 14, 1939, and called on Germany to serve as its protector.

Often referred to as the "Parish Republic" because of its leadership by Roman Catholic Fr. Jozef Tiso, head of the Hlinka People's Party, the new regime hastened to install severely repressive legislation that muzzled the press, abolished all other political parties, and contracted with Eichmann to rid Slovakia of its 70,000 Jews at the price of five hundred German marks a head. Hlinka Party officials boasted that Slovakia's hastily installed *Codex Judaica* was more severe and more repressive than Germany's forbidding Nuremberg laws.

Fr. Tiso's regime, employing the SS-like Hlinka Guard and supported by German troops stationed in Slovakia, beat down all opposition. However, democratic ideals ran deep in Slovakia; many Slovaks were deeply ashamed of Slovakia's subservience to Hitler and resented their status as a Nazi puppet state. Slovak historian Jozef Lettrich holds that "No despotism can silence a nation's natural yearning for liberty... The great majority of the Slovak people disapproved of Slovak separatism, of the authoritarian regime of the (Hlinka) People's Party, of the Slovak government's pro-Nazi policy and its inhuman anti-Semitism."[9]

On August 23, 1944—the day on which Paris was liberated by the Allies and Romania surrendered—Slovaks joined in a heroic revolt signaled by both the Czechoslovakian government-in-exile in London and the partisan movement commanded by Moscow.

Slovak partisans, Soviet partisans, the general citizenry and elements of the Slovak army led by Chief of Staff Lt. Col. Ján Golian joined in the uprising. To the Germans, the Slovak Uprising was far more dangerous than the Polish uprising in Warsaw since it threatened to eliminate the Carpathian ranges as a vital defense line against the advancing Russians, and promised to cut the line of retreat of the German 8th Army retreating from Galicia.[10]

The German reaction was fierce. Armored divisions stationed in neighboring Bohemia and Moravia moved quickly against the poorly equipped and poorly organized rebels gathered in the Hron Valley region centered on Banská Bystrica. On October 1, 1944, the reconstituted 14th Waffen-SS Division, augmented by redundant Ukrainian police battalions, auxiliary military units and assorted Ukrainian refugees, was ordered out of its barracks at Neuhammer and dispatched to Slovakia along with the 18th "Horst Wessel" Division. There they joined the crack Adolf Hitler SS-Tank Division that had been dispatched from Bohemia. Additional Waffen-SS, Mountain Artillery and *Wehrmacht* divisions from other locations were added to the order of battle.

Despite a spirited defense, the Slovak forces were rapidly overpowered by vastly superior German forces supported by Hlinka Guard and German *Ordner* units; Banská Bystrica was captured and many of the Slovak leaders were taken prisoner. The remnant of the rebel forces, consisting of regular soldiers of the Slovak army, Czechs from the First Czechoslovak Army flown in from the USSR, isolated Jewish groups that had taken refuge in the mountainous border area, and a small contingent of escaped British and French prisoners-of-war, fled to the Slovak side of the Carpathian Mountains where they continued fighting until Slovakia was liberated by the Red Army at the end of April 1945.

Hitler exacted a horrible revenge on the Slovak rebels. Himmler's *Sicherheitsdienst* and the Slovak Hlinka Guards joined to hunt down every man, woman and child who had participated in or aided the unsuccessful revolt. "A terrible terror gripped Slovakia... the German Army put scores of communities to the torch...[and] shipped [their inhabitants] to concentration camps, to prison camps or to forced labor...[11] It was reported to Berlin that 2,257 persons had received 'special treatment' (*Sonderbehandlung*) which meant that they had been murdered on the spot." In the process, they flushed out the unarmed Jewish families that had taken shelter in the woods and mountains. Some 9,000 Jews and 530 other persons were captured and sent to concentration camps according to German reports. Heike, incidentally, makes no mention of these atrocities in his account of the Slovak campaign but boasts instead of the Division's success in maintaining a "courteous relationship" with the Hlinka Party and the Hlinka Guard."[12]

The Galician Division did not ennoble itself in Slovakia. On German orders, a special battle group consisting of one battalion of the 29th Regiment supported by artillery, anti-tank and sapper units was separated from the Division and sent ahead to suppress the Slovak insurrection. Lieutenant Colonel Wildner, a *Volksdeutscher* from Slovakia, was assigned to command it. Still under-armed and under-trained, the bulk of the Division was assigned to defend the town of Zilina and the surrounding district where it would face forces whose "battle strength was rather insignificant."[13] Its chief task, underlined by the receipt of a Führer order, was to secure the main railway line running between Ruzemberok and Zilina and to conduct search and destroy missions against partisans.

In the uneven battle between the Slovak rebels and the German forces, the Division suffered almost no casualties during its stay in Slovakia and won few battle honors.[14]

The Division did prove particularly effective in teasing Jews out of their hiding places and in "hunt and destroy" missions against rebel bands. Since the Division members were Slavs who spoke a Slavic language, they were adept at luring partisans out of their hiding places by calling to them in Russian. No sooner did the trusting rebels come within range, then they were shot or captured and turned over to the SD and Hlinka Guard for disposal. Heike, the Division's chief executive officer, makes clear that the commanders of the Division's individual units frequently conferred with the regional commander in Bratislava.[15] Soviet sources claim that "the Division's command kept in close touch with General Hermann Höfle, the SS chief in charge of the punitive elements in Bratislava, accounting to him for the progress of their work" and cooperated closely with the vengeful Hlinka Guard.[16]

While in Slovakia, the Division added to its reputation for rape and pillage. In the opinion of Colonel Irvin Pauliak and Major V.F. Stefansky of the Military Historical Institute of Slovakia, the Galician Division was among the cruelest of the troops serving the Nazis in Slovakia. "If we are to compare them to regular *Wehrmacht* units, the way they behaved, the cruelty and the pillage by the Galician Division was much worse. The Galician Division was the most cruel, the worst of all."[17]

Heike blames much of this reputation on the members of the Dirlewanger Brigade which was attached to the Galician Division during the Brigade's sojourn in Slovakia. Heike notes that the Brigade's personnel were unruly and undisciplined and that its commander—usually drunk in his quarters—made little effort to control his men.[18]

Heike describes Dirlewanger as a heavy drinker who refused to follow Division orders and spent the most crucial moments of battle in his bed without regard to the fate of his unit. As a result, the Dirlewanger Brigade was in the hands of the worst criminal element recruited by its commander. Heike admits that they committed numerous outrages against civilians and earned a bad reputation wherever they went. Later, Heike claims, the Dirlewanger Brigade tried to place the blame on the Ukrainian Division for the atrocities they committed.[19] He insists, however, that the Division has always emphatically denied these accusations: "Certain transgressions against the civilian population might have taken place here and there. Although it is regrettable, it could not be completely avoided since the partisans enjoyed considerable civilian support."[20]

It must be noted, of course, that Heike was put to the task of writing the Division's history by the British military authorities while Heike was still a prisoner-of-war in a British prison camp. Under the circumstances, he was hardly likely to record events or offer interpretations that might make him liable to war crimes charges. Similarly, the Ukrainian edition of Heike's book, *Ukransk'ka dyvisia 'Halychynma': istoria formuvannia I boiovykh dii u 1943-1945,* edited by Dr. Volodymyr Kubijovyc, is also unlikely to divulge anything damaging to the Division's reputation.

As for the Dirlewanger Brigade, its most notorious crimes were committed after the unit had finished its dirty work in Slovakia and joined the forces engaged in suppressing the 1944 Warsaw Uprising. Dirlewanger encouraged the utmost brutality in his troops and even shot some of his own men in a contest for plunder he coveted for himself.

His brigade, swollen with a variety of Muslim, Cossack, Turkomen, Hungarian, Galician, and German renegades recruited directly from prisons, behaved like demented men as they stormed into house after house to murder and rape whoever came to hand. So shocking were their crimes that Colonel-General Guderian, Chief of the German General Staff, persuaded Hitler to withdraw the unit from Warsaw.[21]

It should be mentioned that Dirlewanger Brigade's chief rival in wanton terror was the Kaminski Brigade, composed largely of Russians and a few Ukrainians. Ironically, while both units so sickened their Nazi masters with their excesses at Warsaw that they were ordered to withdraw from the city. Kaminski was subsequently shot for his crimes while Dirlewanger, a favorite of Himmler, went on to receive one of Nazi Germany's most coveted military awards, the *Ritterkreuz.*

As a high-ranking officer of the Halychyna Division, Heike understandably sought to absolve his formation from responsibility for atrocities against Slovak civilians and to place the blame on the Dirlewanger Brigade as well as the partisans and the civilian population itself. While Dirlewanger unquestionably committed his share of misdeeds, the Galician Division still bears the major responsibility for the crimes committed by Dirlewanger in Slovakia. It is clear from Heike's account that Dirlewanger and his brigade were an integral part of the Division for the brief time they served together in Slovakia. It is clear that before the brigade was ordered to Warsaw, it operated under the command of the Division's officers—including Heike himself. As Heike states in his book: "All units that were not part of the Division but were still operating in that area were placed under its command for use in anti-partisan and area-securing actions."[22]

Despite the Dirlewanger Brigade's wildness, drunkenness, and cruelty, no effort was made by the Division's officers to discipline Dirlewanger and curb his troops.. Heike, who clearly had no love for Dirlewanger and his rabble, admits that Dirlewanger was never reprimanded and never removed from his post.[23]

It would be overstating the case to say that the Galician Division was indistinguishable from the Dirlewanger Brigade, but there is no question that the Division as a military formation must bear much of the responsibility for the excessively cruel behaviour indulged in by the most notorious unit in the SS command.

From Neumark to Zilinia; From "Galician" to "Ukrainian"

By November 1944, the Soviet armies were poised on Czechoslovakia's eastern borders and were hammering away at the Baltic States. The German high command, recognizing that Neuhammer could no longer serve as a safe headquarters for the Division, ordered General Freitag to move his headquarters to Zilinia in Slovakia. Three months later, the Division was required to retreat further and take up positions in Slovenia and the lower Steiermark. After a further month's inaction, the Ukrainian Division was dispatched to Yugoslavia where it sought vainly to counter Tito's partisans in a frontless battle on both sides of the Austrian border.

Repeatedly, Heike raises the question of the Division's relationship with the local population. He claims that relations between his Ukrainian soldiers and the Slovenes were good and there were almost no excesses committed against the civilian population. Nevertheless, he adds: "Any [atrocities] that might have occurred took place in the course of fighting partisans, when it was often difficult to separate innocent civilians from the enemy."[24] Again he suggests that German units sought to transfer the blame for their misdeeds to the Ukrainians. However, with every section of the Division engaged in action against Tito's partisans alongside German police and military units, it inevitably participated in numerous atrocities perpetrated by German-led military and police formations in Yugoslavia.

Along with its transfer to Slovenia, the Division received belated recognition as a "Ukrainian" formation. Rather late in the game—in the war's final months—Himmler permitted the Division to change its designation from 14th Waffen-SS Division (galizische Nr. 1) to 14th Waffen-SS Division (ukrainische Nr. 1). The change was more cynical than real. With all of Ukraine, including Galicia, now in Soviet hands, the issue of Ukrainian independence no longer threatened German plans to displace the Ukrainian population of Ukraine and resettle the land with *Volksdeutsche*.[25]

In practical terms as well, the change in designation was meaningless to the men of the Division who continued to wear the same SS uniforms, follow the same German officers and obey the same commands issued in the German language. Nevertheless, urged on by their nationalist Ukrainian political advisors, the German high command hoped that the name change would improve the Division's morale and persuade its personnel that there was still something worth fighting for.

In any event, the change came much too late to evoke much enthusiasm. By now the military situation allowed little room for hope and even less for self-deception. The war was clearly lost and surrender was at most a few weeks away. With the situation worsening daily, the Division's political leaders were desperate to salvage whatever they could from the disastrous bargain they had struck with Hitler's Third Reich.

Under a New Guise: 1st Ukrainian Division of the Ukrainian National Army
By the spring of 1945, thousands of SS-men prepared to lose themselves, to abandon their SS uniforms, erase their SS insignia, hide their SS documents and disappear into the general population. Some donned Wehrmacht togs and sought shelter as ordinary soldiers in POW camps; others joined the vast stream of refugees in the hope of escaping Allied notice. Above all, they sought to move west, to reach the British and American lines in order to avoid being taken prisoner by the Soviet forces.

The Red Army, they reasoned, was familiar with the devastation they had inflicted on the territories the German armies had occupied, the towns they had burned to the ground, the hostages executed and the millions of lives they had cruelly terminated. Soviet retribution was sure to be swift and stern while the crimes they had committed in eastern forests and steppes were still largely unreported in the West. They also assumed, quite correctly, that the Allies would be more inclined to "plea bargain," particularly if they played skillfully on the Allies anti-Communist heartstrings.

Wächter, Kubijovyc, Bandera and Melnyk knew the end was near. The chief question that confronted them was how to disengage the Ukrainian Waffen-SS Division from the fighting, refurbish its image and rewrite its history so as to make it palatable to Allied eyes. At the same time, they dreamt of reversing the fortunes of war by unleashing the anti-Bolshevik fervor and nationalist strivings of the thousands of Ukrainians, Balts, Byelorussians, Cossacks and Caucasians concurrently retreating towards Germany. All too late, Wächter and his colleagues sought to meld the rivalrous, dispirited nationalist groups into a semblance of a "national liberation" movement.

Veryha recalls that it was not until late in November 1944, with the defeat of the Third Reich almost in sight, that the German leadership showed any inclination to deal with the Ukrainians and other people of Eastern Europe. Their first overture was to encourage the Ukrainians to set up a Ukrainian National Committee that would serve primarily as a branch of the KONR, the Committee of Liberation of the People of Russia headed by

General Andrei Vlasov. However, the Ukrainian nationalist leadership wanted no part of Vlasov's pan-Slavic movement since they had no intention of fighting the Soviets only to become part of a new, post-war Russian empire. Instead, they insisted on their own national army, headed by a general of their own choosing. Now that the dream of a German empire on the Ukrainian steppes had vanished with the advance of the Red Army, the German leadership was happy to accede to the nationalists' wishes.

Pavlo Shandruk: A Ukrainian General

In late November, 1944, Andrii Livytsky, President of the Berlin-sponsored Ukrainian People's Republic-in-Exile, invited Colonel Pavlo Shandruk to the German capital to inform him that a National Ukrainian Committee was being formed under German auspices, and that he, Shandruk, had been suggested as its head.[26]

Born in the western Ukrainian province of Volhynia in 1889, Shandruk decided early on a military career and became an officer in the Czar's Imperial Russian Army. He served in the front lines in World War I, received six military awards and achieved the rank of captain. Following the 1917 Russian Revolution, he joined the anti-Bolshevik forces of General Skoropadsky. As an officer in the Zaporozhian Division under the General's command, he helped drive the Bolsheviks from Kharkov.

By January 1919, however, the Red Army had expelled all nationalist forces from Kharkov and Kiev, so that by winter of 1919-1920, the nationalists were driven back to the Austrian-Russian border. Shandruk's allegiances seem to have shifted with the fortunes of war. By May of 1919, he had deserted Skoropadsky and joined Petliura's forces where he was appointed commander of the 9th Ukrainian Riflemen. However, Petliura's forces also fared badly and Shandruk transferred to the rapidly disintegrating 7th Brigade of the 3rd Iron Brigade under General Udovychenko.[27]

During this period, the attacks on the Jews in Ukraine intensified and units under Shandruk's command participated in some of the worst of them.

The all-Ukrainian Central Committee of Relief attached to the Directory's Ministry of Jewish Affairs, submitted a report on September 2, 1919, accusing Udovychenko of responsibility for two separate pogroms, at Ourinine on May 21st and at Podolia on June 24th. In the former, Udovychenko's Cossacks killed sixteen Jews; in the latter, they killed five. Holocaust historian Saul S. Friedman, in his book on Petliura, titled *Pogromchik: The Assassination of Simon Petliura*, states that military units under the command of Colonel Pavlo Shandruk, devastated the region of Moghilev in September, 1919. "Tongues were cut away, eyes plucked out. Hundreds lay dead in Shargorod as a result of the activities of [Udovychenko's] regular troops."[28] According to Friedman, Colonel Pavlo Shandruk, commanded the regular Haidamak Cossacks and the 9th Sharpshooters Regiment which

carried out a massacre of Jews in Verkhovka-Bibikov, Snitkov and Shargorod in
June-July, 1919.

Shandruk is also accused of initiating the pogrom staged at Sanielkov in the summer
of 1919.[29] In his autobiography, written years later while resident in the United States,
Shandruk represents himself as the heroic protector of the Jews and claims to have severely disciplined the officers and men of the Ukrainian units that engaged in pogroms.[30]
However, Professor Friedman denies Shandruk's claims. In Friedman's version of the
history of the period, Petliura's overture to the Jews in the shape of a Ministry of Jewish
Affairs was a mere facade. In fact, he says, the Ukrainian leader looked on the pogroms
with a tolerant eye, taking the attitude, "Let the boys have some fun." Rather than punish
the leaders of the military units such as Udovychenko, Palienko and Shandruk, who
countenanced the massacre of Jews, Petliura rewarded them with promotions.

As for Shandruk, Friedman states that after he had fled from Ukraine, Shandruk con-
cocted a myth whereby *he* was the Savior of the Jews of Proskurov. In Shandruk's version
of the story, he hastened to Proskurov at the head of the Zaporozhian Rifle Battalion to
quell the disorder, but no sooner did he arrive at the head of troops than the "bandits"
mysteriously disappeared. Friedman claims that Shandruk made no real effort to punish
the perpetrators and failed to arrest Cossack Ataman Semosenko, who led the rampaging
troops.[31]

In April 1920, Petliura succeeded in arranging an alliance with Poland and launching
the combined Ukrainian-Polish attack that moved rapidly eastward and recaptured
Kiev. For his services to the Directorate in this campaign, Petliura promoted Shandruk to
the rank of Colonel. However, the Polish-Ukrainian courtship soon soured as the Poles
negotiated a separate peace with the emerging Soviet Union and the Soviet Ukrainian
Republic.

Left to themselves, the Ukrainian nationalist forces continued the fight until November 1920 when they were forced to retreat to western Ukrainian lands annexed by Poland. They were disarmed and interned by their former ally; among the internees was
Colonel Shandruk.[32]

Following his release from internment, Shandruk undertook a number of assignments for the Ukrainian Government-in-Exile, but soon shifted his allegiance once again.
Early in 1936, he enrolled in the Polish High Command and General Staff College. On
graduation, he entered the Polish army as a contract officer with the rank of Major. In the
brief 1939 Polish defence against the German invasion, Shandruk served as Chief
-of-Staff of a disorganized Polish brigade that saw little action. As stated in the introduction to his autobiography, the capitulation of the Polish army delivered Shandruk into
German hands.[33] The future general was interned only briefly. On his release he re-

turned to civilian life and took up residence in the Polish town of Skierniewice. For the next four years he quietly earned his living as the manager of a local movie theatre.

A confidential U.S. Central Intelligence Corps report dated November 2, 1948, describes Shandruk as a counter-intelligence agent in the post World War I Polish army and a double agent working for both the Poles and the Germans in 1937. The report adds: "After the collapse of Poland in 1939, he began working for the intelligence section of the Gestapo and was thus instrumental in the denunciation of many Polish ex-officers and partisans hiding from the Germans."[34]

When summoned by Livytsky, Shandruk questioned the viability of the proposed Ukrainian National Committee. He expressed grave doubts regarding its ability to advance the Ukrainian cause at a time when the days of the Third Reich were so obviously numbered. Livytsky agreed there was no hope of turning the tide. Shandruk's major task, he explained, was to save whatever was still salvageable.

To succeed, Shandruk must avoid any effort by the German administration to fold the Ukrainians into the pan-Slavic movement led by the former Russian General, Andrey Vlasov. Captured by the Germans in July 1942, Vlasov—angry because the Soviet General Headquarters had failed to provide his surrounded Second Shock Army with the necessary support—agreed to form an anti-Stalinist Russian Liberation Movement recruited from the vast number of Russian prisoners held in German prisoner-of-war camps.[35] The Germans must grant Shandruk full equality with Vlasov and recognize the full independence of the Ukrainian nation. As for the Halychyna Division, Shandruk's task was to prevent the Division from falling into Soviet hands and do whatever he could to lead to safety the many thousands of Ukrainians serving in German police and military units.

Shandruk was not readily persuaded. It was not until he had received assurance of full support from both Bandera and Melnyk and held lengthy conversations with high-ranking SS officials, that Shandruk agreed to head the Ukrainian National Committee and serve as commander of the Ukrainian forces. Having given his consent, Berlin announced his appointment on March 15, 1945 as Lieutenant General of the General Staff and Commander of the Ukrainian National Army. Shandruk, in his autobiography, states that the newly-named unit's membership was to consist of "Ukrainians who are in the German army, and in other military formations."[36]

In executing his mandate to keep Ukrainians out of Soviet hands, Shandruk included a number of German-led Ukrainian units with no prior attachment to the Division. Amongst them was the 31st SD, the Volhynia-based Ukrainian Self-Defence Legion led by Colonel Pyotr Dyachenko.[37] Also included was the 281st Reserve Regiment stationed in Denmark, two infantry regiments stationed on guard duty in Belgium and Holland, three battalions of military police, and four hundred men from the Brigade for Special Tasks under Commander T. Bulba-Borovets.[38]

Despite Shandruk's elaborate title, his role was more titular than real. The Division, despite the name change, remained attached to the SS and continued to receive its orders from the *Reichsführer-SS* and the German High Command. Fritz Freitag continued as its Commander-in-Chief, the men continued to wear Waffen-SS uniforms and were ordered about by the same German officers and N.C.O.s. Shandruk's order to replace the prescribed Halychyna Lion shoulder patch with a badge bearing a yellow trident on a blue background was largely ignored.

Only the military oath was changed. As SS representatives looked on benignly, the men swore a new oath addressed to God, the Ukrainian homeland and the Ukrainian National Army. The first unit to embrace the new yellow and blue banner and swear to the new oath was a 1,900-man detachment assigned to the defence of Berlin. Its commander was Colonel Pyotr Dyachenko who led the 31st SD at Warsaw and subsequently became one of Shandruk's most trusted regimental officers.[39]

The "in-gathering" of defunct and redundant units meant that the Division incorporated in its ranks some of the most vicious of the German-led Ukrainian formations: the *Nachtigall* and *Roland* Battalions, the 207th and 201st Police battalions, the 31st SD Punitive Detachment, the Beyersdorff Detachment and elements of the Dirlewanger Brigade.

If the Division's name inspired fear and loathing before its ranks were decimated at the Battle of Brody, the reconstituted post-Brody division deserved an even worse reputation. Augmented by police battalions, punitive detachments and auxiliary military units, drawn from the whole of Ukraine, it embraced a higher percentage of men who had served as informers, torturers, executioners, plunderers and murderers than before.

Preparations for Surrender

Towards the end of April 1945, Shandruk, Wächter and Bisanz visited the Division. General Freitag, unwilling to recognize that Shandruk nominally outranked him, sulked in his quarters and left it to Heike to deal with the newly appointed Ukrainian general. Always militarily correct and respectful, Heike reported in detail on the status of his Ukrainian troops. After visiting each of the units at the front and appealing to their conscience and honour as Ukrainian soldiers, Shandruk left to set up his headquarters with the reserve training regiment rather than the Division. Heike comments in his memoirs that this was a very good idea since direct and frequent contact with the dour, resentful General Freitag would have made Shandruk extremely uncomfortable. "In general, relations between Shandruk and the Division commander were not very good," Heike comments, "which is not surprising considering their difference in character."[40]

Although the Slovenian front remained relatively quiet with neither side ready to launch major attacks, the Division's command recognized that Germany's defeat was imminent and its chief preoccupation was how to avoid being taken prisoner by the Red Army. With the Soviet forces pushing in from the east and Tito's Yugoslav partisans advancing northward, the choices available to the Division grew increasingly limited. Wächter, who maintained close liaison with the Division he founded and nurtured, recommended pulling out of the line and crossing the Alps to Northern Italy. There were rumors of a "last stand" in the Austrian mountains, supposedly in accord with the plans of the Reich administration. There was also talk of slipping behind the enemy lines to engage in guerrilla warfare.[41]

But Yugoslav and Italian partisans controlled the route to Italy and, in any event, the Division was seeking a safe surrender rather than prolonged warfare. There was, therefore, no alternative except surrender to the British and American forces advancing into Austria from the west. Moreover, it had to be done speedily, before the Soviets arrived.

Crisis in Klagenfurt

As World War II wound down, the Western Powers faced a new, unexpected political crisis that brought Europe to the brink of a fresh war—this time with former ally, Yugoslavia. Tito, emboldened by his success against the Germans and confident of Soviet support, was determined to redraw Yugoslavia's boundaries by forcibly seizing the Istrian Peninsula (Fiume, Trieste, Paola) and portions of southern Austria. His partisan army, now strong and well-equipped, surged across the pre-war Yugoslav frontier into Carinthia and the Venezia Giulia area of northern Italy. Since these districts contained a high percentage of people of Slovenian descent, Tito insisted that they deserved to be part of "Greater Yugoslavia."

The situation was delicate. The British government definitely wanted the Yugoslavs out of both Italy and Austria, but preferred to avoid a pitched battle with its erstwhile ally. Much depended on who "made history" by being the first to occupy the disputed territory. The British Eighth Army, having finally disposed of the stubborn German resistance in Italy, sped crack troops towards the disputed territories. In a close race, the New Zealand Division reached Trieste on May 2, a half-step ahead of the Yugoslav forces. On May 8, Lieutenant-General Charles Keightly's 5th Corps arrived in the southern Austrian provincial capital of Klagenfurt, barely two hours before Slovene irregulars swarmed into the disputed city.[42] The British took adroit advantage of this brief interval between their arrival and the appearance of the Slovenes to occupy most of the important buildings and strategic areas of the town.

For the next few days, the opposing forces sought to intimidate each other without resorting to violence. The Yugoslavs claimed a *fait accompli* while Keightly faced them down with daily parades of well-fed, well-equipped, highly-disciplined British troops. Out-maneuvered, out-gunned, and "out-bullshitted," the Yugoslavs withdrew from Klagenfurt on May 18, and moved back across the Mur, the river that formed Austria's southern boundary.[43]

Final Surrender

In the first days of May, convinced that the end was near, the Division dispatched SS *Hauptsturmführer* Lubomyr Makarushka, head of the Division's personnel section and member of the Military Council, to make contact with the British who were advancing rapidly into Austria from the west and southwest. On May 5th or 6th Makarushka located an English unit and began to negotiate the Division's surrender. The Ukrainian representative asked the British commander to designate the Völkermarkt district as the mustering point for the Division's scattered units. The British officer readily acceded to this request since, as Makarushka explained, the reserve regiment and several of the Division's sub-units were stationed nearby. However, the British were still some distance from Völkermarkt and Tito's men, who were distinctly hostile to the Division, occupied part of the town. The British officer, although cordial, showed little concern for the Division and told Makarushka that the Ukrainians would have to hold the town as best they could until the British troops arrived.[44]

Makarushka's misgivings were valid. Tito's partisans did not allow the Division free passage to Völkermarkt but harassed it severely on the march. The reserve-training regiment, in particular, took heavy casualties as it tried to force its way into the town and disintegrated completely under partisan pressure.

Meanwhile, the Division's main force, flanked by the German 4th SS Panzer Corps and the 1st Cavalry Corps, remained in the battle line. On May 6, General Shandruk, Dr. Wächter, Colonel Bisanz and Military Council member, Dr. Arlt, returned to the Division. Bisanz made an impassioned speech to the officers in which he called on all commanders to conscientiously fulfill their duties. At the same time, Wächter visited army headquarters in an effort to persuade the commanding general to allow the Division to be the first unit to withdraw from the line. He argued that the Russians, who regarded every man in the Division a traitor, would subject them to severe punishment if captured. The request was refused, and in the end, the Division had to fend for itself, completely disregarded by the German command.

According to Heike, the order to disengage from the line was delivered on May 8th. As soon as the order was delivered, the Division abandoned all its heavy equipment and marched day and night, without rest, in a race to reach territory occupied by the Allies. The march was difficult and conditions were confusing. Vital crossroads were jammed with German units in full retreat. Divisional command broke down as Ukrainian SS units scattered in the rush to escape the Red Army. On May 10th, the Allies announced that all foreign troops and national Waffen-SS units would be interned at Tamsweg, in southern Austria. For the officers and men of the Division, the war was blessedly over, but a period of uncertain captivity loomed ahead.

In the days that followed, General Freitag, unable to accept defeat and suffering a personal sense of failure, fell into despair and committed suicide. Wächter disappeared in an unknown direction only to re-emerge some months later as Fr. Otto Reinhardt in Rome's Maria dell' Anima monastery.[45] Colonel Bisanz declared his work with the Division completed and fled with the remainder of the Division's German officers.[46] Only Heike, the sole *Wehrmacht* officer to serve with the Division, continued to show concern for his men and sought to maintain contact with them in their captivity.

General Shandruk also separated himself from the main body of his men. Heike reports that the General went to meet with the Americans at Radstädt.[47] The details of Shandruk's surrender to the Americans are vague. What is known is that the general and the 1,300 men who accompanied him to Radstädt were permitted to proceed via Salzburg to Bavaria. There they were confined in POW camps in the American zone, held for six months to a year and released.[48]

The main force camped for a short time in an open field in Tamsweg before being moved to Spittal and then to Rimini, a charming resort town on Italy's Adriatic coasts. The march from Spittal to Camp 357 on Rimini's outskirts began on May 28, proceeding through Udine and Balaria. Curiously, the Division was not compelled to give up its arms. Bohdan Panchuk, the Royal Canadian Airforce officer who befriended the Division in its captivity, writes: "Arms were not removed from the unit; in fact, in many cases more arms were issued and the unit was instructed to cross over to Italy."[49]

While at Tamsweg, the command of the Ukrainian troops was assumed by Major Pobihushchy, the former commander of the Roland Battalion who came to command *Schutzmannschaftbattalion* 201 and served as a leading regimental officer in the Galician SS Division.[50] It is doubtful, however, if Pobihushchy accompanied the Division in its march to Rimini. The prisoner-of-war camps in Austria were crowded and loosely guarded. It took little effort to escape and disappear into one of the numerous refugee camps organized by the Allies. In all likelihood, Pobihushchy was one of the five thousand members of the Division who chose to remain in Austria where they entered directly into civilian life or joined friends and relatives in Displaced Persons camps in Germany.[51] What is known is that Pobihushchy, under the alias "Colonel Ren", recruited and drilled Galician veterans to serve as hired guards in Displaced Persons camps in the American Zone of Occupation. As sworn enemies of the Soviet Union and late converts to democracy, the Americans regarded them as suitable personnel to guard refugee camps and other USA installations in Germany. In 1948 and 1949, Pobihushchy was hired to help train spies for the British and American intelligence services.[52]

Shandruk's career also took a predictable course. A "top secret" American Counter Intelligence Corps (CIC) report, dated November 2, 1948, contains considerable information on Shandruk's various careers as a Czarist, Ukrainian and Polish officer.

When Poland collapsed in the face of the German *Blitzkrieg*, Shandruk began working for the intelligence section of the *Gestapo*.

Shortly before the German capitulation in May 1945, Shandruk sent Colonel Smosvski-Rayevski to establish contact with American intelligence services—probably the 7th Army—to discuss a merger of forces and the continuation of hostilities against the Soviet Union. The Americans contacted by Shandruk's emissary did not warm to the proposal and placed Smosvski-Rayevski under arrest.[53]

Three years later, however, with the shooting war over and the Cold War intensifying, the United States intelligence apparatus was playing a very different game. Now they were intent on finding allies among the east European émigrés crowding the Displace Persons camps. Shandruk, by this time had taken up residence in Munich and was deeply involved in underground Ukrainian émigré activities. Previously regarded with the suspicion due a former German agent, he was now seen in a different light by American intelligence agents hungry for information. Political background mattered little so long as the agent was staunchly anti-Communist.

A United States Counter Intelligence Corps (CIC) agent's report dated May 29, 1950 praises Shandruk as one of the few influential Ukrainian leaders who has given abundant proof by "action, deed and expressed attitude" of a consistent anti-Communist course. The Soviet attacks on Shandruk's character broadcast over Moscow radio were interpreted by the agent as added proof of the General's steadfast anti-Communism. "In any event," the agent concludes, "there is nothing in the information filed at this headquarters which would indicate that Shandruk's continued presence in the United States would affect materially the security of that country."[54]

After having served in four armies and an agent for both the Germans and the Poles, Shandruk now became a "source" for the Americans, continuing his career in the shadowy world of spy, counter-spy and covert network.

It is now common knowledge that the United States made frequent use of former Nazi collaborators to obtain information and conduct assassinations behind the Iron Curtain.[55] The CIC organized a network of former SS-men to ferret out Soviet infiltrators and recruit agents to drop behind Russian lines. Some, like Klaus Barbie, the *Gestapo* agent who broke the back of the French *resistance* in Lyons through torture and murder, worked their way onto the CIC payroll. In the meantime, another branch of the U.S. government was seeking to arrest them for war crimes.[56]

Shandruk's history of collaboration with the Nazis should have barred him from entering the United States, nevertheless, he arrived in October 1949 and took up permanent residence soon after. It is clear from his CIC file that the agency was well aware of his activities and whereabouts, yet no action was taken to deport him.[57] His undisturbed presence is best explained by the plethora of covert, anti-Communist organizations financed by the Central Intelligence Agency (CIA) after the war such as Intermarium, Assembly of Captive European Nations (ACEN) and the Anti-Bolshevik Bloc of Nations (ABN). This last was dominated by Ukrainian nationalist veterans of the OUN and UPA, Shandruk among them.[58]

Notes

1. Michael O. Logusz, *Galicia Division: The Waffen-SS 14th Grenadier Division 1943-1945* (Atgen, PA: Schiffer Military History, 1997), 191.

2. *Ibid.* 195-259.

3. *Ibid.* 218.

4. *Ibid.* 259.

5. Bender and Taylor, 35.

6. Logusz, 260.

7. See: "Report on the Entry of War Criminals and Collaborators into the UK, 1945-1950," All Party Parliamentary War Crimes Group, House of Commons, London, 1986, 26. For references to "Trawniki-men" see: Jürgen Stroop, *The Stroop Report: The Jewish Ghetto of Warsaw is No More*, trans. Sybil Milton and A. Worth, (New York: Pantheon Books, 1979).

8. Bender and Taylor, 38.

9. Jozef Lettrich, *History of Modern Slovakia*, second edition (Toronto: Slovak Research and Study Centre, 1985), 193.

10. *Ibid.* 203.

11. *Ibid.* 216.

12. Heike, English edition, 85.

13. *Ibid.* 75.

14. *Ibid.* 78.

15. *Ibid.* 78.

FROM BRODY TO TAMSWEG /99

16. Styrkul, *We Accuse.* 220-221.

17. Interview, Colonel Irvin Pauliak, Major V.F. Stefansky and Dr. Pavel Simunic, Military Historical Institute, Bratislava, 1984.

18. Wolf-Dietrich Heike, *Sie wollten die Freiheit: Die Geschichte der Ukrainischen Division 1939-1945.* (Dorheim: Podzun vlg., 1973), 150-152.

19. Heike, English edition. 80.

20. Heike, German edition, 150.

21. Helmut Krausnick and Broszat Martin, *The Anatomy of an SS State* (London: Paladin, 1970), 192-195.

22. Heike, English edition, 76.

23. *Ibid.* 81.

24. Heike, English edition, 100-101.

25. George H. Stein, *Hitler's Elite Guard at War: The Waffen-SS 1939-1945* (Ithaca: Cornell University Press, 1966), 187.

26. *Ibid.* 169.

27. *Ibid.* 166.

28. Friedman, *Pogromchik,* 219-221.

29. Friedman, *Ibid.* 217.

30. Pavlo Shandruk, *Arms of Valor,* trans. Roman Olesnicki (New York: R. Speller and Sons, 1959), 74-77, 124.

31. Friedman, sSupra, 151.

32. Veryha, *General Shandruk: An Appraisal.* 167.

33. Roman Smal-Stocki, "Introduction," Shandruk, *Arms of Valor,* xxv.

34. CIC (Counter Intelligence Corps, USA) Agent Report, File No.4490, Subject OUN/B Re: Sluza Bezpeky. (Probably Sluzhba Bezpeky. CIC agents were not accurate spellers.)

35. Oxford Companion to World War II, "Vlasov," 1247.

36. Shandruk, *Arms of Valor,* 244.

37. Heike, English edition, 104.

38. Shandruk, 254.

39. Shandruk, 235. The brigade commanded by Dyachenko was dubbed the 2nd Ukrainian Division by Shandruk and consisted of scattered Ukrainian units that had served previously in a variety of defunct German formations. These men were gathered together at Camp Nimek sometime in February and March, 1945.

40. Heike, English edition, 127.

41. *Ibid.* 128.

42. Anthony Cowgill, Thomas Brimelow and Christopher Brooker, *The Repatriations from Austria in 1945: The Report of an Inquiry* (London: Sinclair-Stevenson Ltd. 1990), 14.

43. James Lucas, *Last Days of the Reich: The Collapse of Nazi Germany, May 1945,* (Toronto: Stoddart Publishing Co. Ltd., 1986), 130.

44. Heike, English edition, 129.

45. Wächter died in Italy in 1949.

46. Colonel Alfred Bisanz, born in the Lviv region of German parents, served as officer in the Austrian-Hungarian army. He also served in every version of the Ukrainian and Galician armies that campaigned between 1918 and 1920. The Ukrainian-Galician Army (UHA) and the Ukrainian National Republic Army (UNR). Between the wars, he returned to his family estate in the Lviv region. With the German occupation of Poland, he joined Frank in the operation of the *Generalgouvernment*, providing assistance and advice to Governor Wächter. At the war's end, he was captured by the Soviets in Vienna and dispatched to a Siberian *gulag*. There the trail ends.

47. Heike, English edition, 135.

48. Bohdan Panchuk, *Heroes of their Day: The Reminiscences of Bohdan Panchuk* (Toronto: The Multicultural History Society, Ontario Heritage Foundation, 1983), 162.

49. Panchuk, 156.

50. Heike, English edition, 136.

51. Panchuk, 162.

52. Styrkul, 247. Also see: Thomas M. Baker, *Social Revolutionaries and Secret Agents: The Corinthian Slovene Partisans and Britain's Special Operations Executive* (New York: East European Monographs, Columbia University Press, 1990), 56-57.

53. Freedom of Information Request, CIC Agent Report, Dossier No. ZF010016, Vol. 1, "Shandruk, General commanding 1st Ukrainian Army." Submitted November 2, 1948. (The spelling of place names has been left as they appeared in CIC agents' reports.)

54. Declassified CIC document, dated May 29, 1950, obtained through Freedom of Information.

55. Christopher Simpson, *Blowback* (New York: Weidenfeld and Nicholson, 1988), 148.

56. Tom Bower, *Klaus Barbie, Butcher of Lyons* (London: Michael Joseph, 1984), 131.

57. Simpson, *Blowback.* 170.

58. *Ibid.* 269.

CHAPTER 10

FROM TAMSWEG TO RIMINI: THE DIVISION IN CAPTIVITY

ON MAY 7, 1945, THE MAIN GERMAN FORCES IN CENTRAL EUROPE surrendered uncondition-ally. The surrender agreement, which took effect the following day, required the de-feated armies to stand down and hand over their arms to the nearest Allied army. But that isn't how it happened. The Germans and their Ukrainian, Cossack and Croatian Ustasha allies, fearing retribution at the hands of the Soviet Union, sought desperately to surrender to the advancing British and the Americans armies. The result was a mad scramble to evade the Russians and reach the British and American lines.[1]

The Yalta Agreement and the Cossacks

No sooner had the British Fifth Corps made its way from Italy to Austria than it found it-self responsible for hundreds of thousands of surrendered enemy personnel, camp fol-lowers and civilian refugees. Although the greatest numbers of these were Germans, they included more than 100,000 Hungarians, Italians, Poles, Romanians, Ukrainians, Cossacks, Yugoslavs and others.[2]

Among them were thousands upon thousands of *Hiwis (Hilfswillige)*, Soviet citizens who volunteered to serve the Germans as drivers, cooks, ammunition carriers, and trans-lators. Mainly Red Army deserters who chose the role of dogsbodies to the *Wehrmacht* rather than starvation in a German prison camp, they were utilized as local militias to combat Soviet partisans as German manpower dwindled. As the war progressed, the *Wehrmacht* organized them into regular military units dubbed *Osttruppen* (Eastern troops) under the command of German officers.

Remnants of six *Ostlegionen* (Eastern Legions) recruited by the Germans in their march through the Caucuses had also fled to Austria to escape Soviet vengeance. Arbi-trarily categorized by Hitler as non-Slavs, they included Armenian, Georgian, Azerbaijani, North Caucasian, Turkestani and Volga Tatar ethnic legions.

In yet another category were the Cossacks with their cavalry sabers, fleece hats and traditional heel-length coats decorated with false cartridge tubes. Like the cowboys of the

American West, the Cossacks represented the romance of the frontier for Russia's vast, downtrodden population. Composed originally of runaway serfs, defrocked priests, adventurers and petty entrepreneurs, they developed a reputation as freedom-loving defenders of the peasants and staunch devotees of the Orthodox faith. Mounted frontiersmen, brawlers and drinkers, they gathered in the lower reaches of the Don and Dnieper Rivers, well beyond the reach of the Polish nobility intent on exploiting the Ukrainian lands. In time, the fugitive Cossacks coalesced into a distinct society with its own leaders (*Hetman*), values and customs.

Russian history records that the Cossacks created military settlements resembling American frontier forts along the southern perimeter of Russia from Ukraine to Siberia. They defended their settlements against the Muslim Ataturks and brought the steppes under their control. Fiercely independent and defiant of authority, the settlements were largely self-governing. Despite numerous revolts against Polish magnates and Russian Czars, their society eventually gave way to Russian imperial expansion. By 1917, when the Russian Revolution broke out, only remnants of the Ukrainian Cossacks still survived, namely the Zaporozhian, Registered and Ukrainian Cossacks. However, the Russian Cossacks, the Don, Kuban, Terek and Siberian Cossacks lent their loyalty to the Czar and formed the toughest, most ruthless formations in the White Armies in the 1917-1920 Civil War.[3]

Hitler, too, was imbued with the romance of the Cossacks. According to his idiosyncratic racial theory, the Cossacks were not despised Slavic *Untermenschen* but Aryans descended from the ancient Goths and Vikings. Although he frowned upon the organization of a distinctly Ukrainian military formation, he readily agreed to the recruitment of a Cossack cavalry corps under the leadership of Lieutenant-General Helmuth von Pannwitz. Additional units, several thousand strong, were organized under various Cossack generals, including Generals Domanov and Konev.

Bitterly anti-Bolshevik during the Civil War and hostile to Soviet efforts at collectivization, the Cossacks of the Don, Kuban and Terek, welcomed the German armies as they advanced towards the Caucasus. But the German military gains of 1942 turned into the massive retreat of 1943 as the Red Army advanced on all fronts. The Cossack legions, having committed themselves irretrievably to the Nazi cause, had no alternative but to gather up their wives, children and camp followers and join the German retreat.

The British forces were not only unprepared to deal with the deluge of surrendered enemy personnel, they were also completely unprepared for the acute moral dilemma imposed on them by the agreement reached by Churchill, Stalin and Roosevelt at Yalta in February 1945.

At a subsidiary conference concluded on February 11, 1945, it was agreed that all nationals accused of being deserters and traitors would be returned to their country of origin.[4] It was also stipulated that all surrendered personnel holding Soviet citizenship before the Hitler-Stalin Pact of 1939, must be repatriated to their homeland. At the same time, there were an estimated 50,000 British Commonwealth prisoners detained in seven German camps that had been overrun by the Red Army. In addition another 50,000 German, Polish, and French prisoners had been liberated by the Red Army from various German camps.

Yalta was intended to be a two-way street. Not only were Soviet nationals to be returned to the Soviet Union, but the Russians were equally obliged to return British and American subjects liberated by forces under Soviet command. Foreign Secretary Anthony Eden explained the necessity of adhering to the agreement as follows:

> It is most important that our own prisoners in Germany and Poland be well cared for and returned as soon as possible. For this we must rely to a great extent upon Soviet goodwill and if we make difficulty over returning to them their own nationals it will react adversely upon their willingness to help in restoring to us as soon as possible our own prisoners.[5]

On the other hand, a number of Cabinet ministers felt a great mistake had been made in agreeing to hand over any of the military detachments that had surrendered to the Allies. Lord Selbourne, Minister for Economic Warfare earnestly reminded Eden of Stalin's statement that "Russia acknowledges no POWs—Russia has only soldiers in her army, dead soldiers, or traitors." He predicted that any men returned would receive extremely rough treatment by the Soviets.[6] In the end, because of the large number of British and American prisoners of war held in German prison camps liberated by the Russians, Eden's view prevailed. With a minimum of thought, screening or investigation, the British command in Austria prepared to honour the terms of the Yalta Agreement by repatriating the Soviet nationals they held prisoner.

Six military formations required the British command's immediate attention:

Unit	Approximate Strength
Domanov Cossacks	22,500
Cossack Training Unit	1,400
Caucasians	4,800
15th SS-Cossack Cavalry Corps	25,000
White Russian *Schützkorps*	4,500
1st Ukrainian Division	11,000[7]

Four out of the six units clearly originated in territories unambiguously part of the Soviet Union prior to September 1939, namely the Domanov Cossacks, the 5,000 Caucasians, the 15th SS Cossack Cavalry Corps, and the small Cossack training unit.

The White Russian *Schützkorps* was declared exempt because of its unique history. It was, in a sense, the last remnant of the Czarist army having originated as a Cossack regiment that served in the Crimea under General Wrangel in the 1920 Russian Civil War. Shattered by the Red Army, they withdrew to Yugoslavia where King Alexander gave them asylum. Loyal to their imperial memories, they stayed together as a military unit dedicated to overthrowing the Bolsheviks and restoring the Czar. When Hitler invaded Yugoslavia in 1941, they volunteered their services to the Germans who used them chiefly to guard railway yards and bridges against the forays of Tito's partisans. In May of 1945, they joined the mass exodus of pro-German troops to Austria where they surrendered to the 1st Guards Brigade under the 6th Armoured Division.[8]

Why this 4,500-man unit was spared despite having served the Germans and worn the German uniform is nowhere specifically stated. In all likelihood, the British regarded them nostalgically as comrades-in-arms from Civil War days. It is well to remember that the British dispatched interventionist forces to Murmansk, Archangel and Vladivostok in 1917 in an effort to contain Lenin's revolution and support the anti-Bolshevik White armies.[9] Did some element of a shared crusade still linger in the minds and hearts of influential British officers?[10] Or was it a sense of "let bygones be bygones" that prompted the decision? The *Schützkorps* Cossacks were "old émigrés" who had not set foot in Russia for close to twenty-five years. Most carried Yugoslav papers or were listed as stateless and could hardly be regarded as Soviet citizens. Whatever the reason, the British chose not to return the White Russian *Schützkorps* to their original homeland. Instead, they disbanded them and permitted them to settle wherever they wished in the British zone of occupation.

Yalta and the Division

The British also decided not to return the members of the Halychyna Division. Unfortunately there is no clear record of who in the British command made that fateful decision or why. Certainly the Ukrainian Division was a prime candidate for repatriation given that its ancestral history included a record of close collaboration with the *Abwehr* prior to the war, the ruthless suppression of local revolts in Poland and Slovakia, and direct battle against the Red Army from Brody to Slovenia. If any formation was a likely candidate, it was the First Ukrainian Army. How did it happen then, that the 15th SS Cossack Cavalry Corps was forcibly delivered to their Bolshevik enemy and the Ukrainian Division was quietly "spirited away" to Italy out of the Russian's reach?

A variety of theories have been put forward including intervention by the Pope, intervention by General Wladyslaw Anders of the Polish 2nd Corps, confusion regarding the Division's citizenship and an appeal by General Shandruk to General Eisenhower. None of these theories are entirely satisfactory.

First, the Polish Corps.

According to Heike, Wächter did speak of transferring the Ukrainian, Cossack and Eastern Turkish armies to northern Italy where they could be handed over to the Allies. This done, he hoped to merge the Ukrainian Division with Anders' Polish army on the grounds that its members were former citizens of Poland. In order to make the Division more acceptable to the Poles, he recommended that the Division resume its original designation as "Galizien No. 1." But nothing came of Wächter's plan; the military situation didn't allow it. The Red Army was pressing too hard and Tito's partisan forces controlled the major passes to Italy.[11]

Even if circumstances had favored such a move, it is highly doubtful that Anders would have even considered it. Although bitterly anti-Communist, he was unlikely to extend the hand of friendship to a division that grew out of the Organization of Ukrainian Nationalists. The anti-Polish program of the OUN was too well known and their attacks on Polish villages too well recorded by the Polish National Army to allow him to come to the Division's rescue.

Next, the Catholic Church.

Without question there were Catholic churchmen who sought to prevent the repatriation of the Ukrainian Division. The bulk of the Division adhered to the Uniate Catholic Church, described as "a religious hybrid... Ukrainian in nationality, Orthodox in Slavic liturgy, but obedient to the Pope of Rome."[12] It would have been surprising if they had stood aside and refused to keep their faithful sons out of the hands of the Godless Bolsheviks.

Nikolai Tolstoy in his controversial book, *Victims of Yalta*, presents a scenario in which General Shandruk appealed to the Pontiff "who as early as 5 July, issued an appeal to the Allies against the forcible repatriation of the Ukrainians."[13]

In a lengthy footnote, Christopher Simpson, author of *Blowback*, dwells on the role played by Archbishop Ivan Buchko, the Pontiff's specialist on Ukrainian affairs. An American-born priest, Buchko served as Auxiliary Bishop of the Ukrainian Greek Catholic (Uniate) dioceses in the United States up to 1941. The Bishop was an ardent Ukrainian nationalist with great influence in Vatican circles. Buchko, who schemed and dreamed of delivering the Ukrainian Orthodox Church into the hands of Rome, was equally intent on saving the Ukrainian Division, "the flower of the Ukrainian nation," out of the Soviet's hands.[14]

Shandruk, in his autobiography, wrote that Buchko had a special audience with His Holiness Pope Pius XII in which the Pontiff promised to use his good offices on behalf of the Division. "I learned from the Archbishop that as a result of the intercession of his Holiness, the soldiers of the Division were reclassified as confinees rather than prisoners of war... and out of reach of Communist hands."[15]

Despite the Pope's willingness and Buchko's eagerness to keep the Ukrainian Division out of the Soviets' grasp, it is extremely doubtful that the Vatican had any influence on the decision of the British command to remove the Division from the list of units to be repatriated. Well before the Pope's July 5 message to the Allies, the decision had been taken and the Ukrainians were on their way to the prison camp at Riccione on the outskirts of Rimini.

Shandruk's letter to Eisenhower was also unlikely to have been effective. The General's claim that the Ukrainian Division never intended to do harm to the Allied cause could hardly have impressed the supreme commander of the Allied Expeditionary Forces. He is also unlikely to have given credence to Shandruk's claim that the Division planned from the start to desert the Germans and come over to the Allies at the first opportunity. In any event, the decision to preserve the Division seems to have been made hurriedly by local commanders out of view of Eisenhower's headquarters.

More plausible is the theory that the British officers on the scene accepted at face value the Division's claim that all of its 10,000 members were some kind of border Poles and therefore exempt from repatriation.

Initially raised in Galicia, the majority of the Division's original recruits could rightly claim Polish citizenship prior to September 1939 and therefore, ineligible for compulsory repatriation to Soviet dominated Poland—that is if one chose to ignore their fanatical hostility to the pre-war Polish State. But the Ukrainian military formation had undergone many changes since it first marched off to basic training at Debica. By the time the Division laid down its arms, it included almost as many recruits from the Soviet Ukraine as from the former Polish territory incorporated by the Soviet Union in 1939. The precise percentage is impossible to ascertain. Tolstoy, a defender of the Division and a fierce critic of the Yalta Agreement, nevertheless states: "In fact, a high proportion of the Ukrainians (in the Division) were Soviet citizens as specified in the Yalta Agreement. Mykola Wolynskyj, who was one of their number, gave a rough estimate of twenty percent; Dennis Hills the Russian-speaking British officer who had the task of screening them, puts it much higher—well over fifty percent."[16]

Whatever the count, no effort was made by 5th Corps to screen the men before the decision was taken to march them out to Italy. In fact, in the turmoil that followed the surrender, the precise criteria for repatriation and non-repatriation were still somewhat vague. It was not until May 21, 1945 that 5th Corps received a signal from Brigadier Low at 8th Army Headquarters clarifying the issue. Low ruled that the Russian *Schützkorps* would not be treated as Soviet nationals. However, the Ataman Cossacks, the 15th Cossack Cavalry Corps, the reserve unit and the Caucasians were to be classified as Soviet nationals and subject to repatriation. Once again, the Brigadier emphasized that any member of a German fighting unit that came from a territory that was part of the Soviet Union prior to 1939 would be treated as a Soviet national "for the purpose of transfer."

The dispatch is significant in three respects: first, it provides the local command with a definition of a Soviet citizen subject to repatriation. Second, the Russian *Schützkorps* has been exempted and third, *the Ukrainian Division has fallen entirely out of sight. It is no longer included in 5th Corps orders and disappears from 5th Corps records.*

Brigadier Anthony Cowgill, author of *The Repatriations from Austria; the Report of an Inquiry*, scoured the records of the London Public Record Office, the Imperial War Museum, the National Archives in Washington, the archives of the Red Cross and a number of prominent German archives, but could find no order, no memo, to explain the Division's sudden disappearance:

> There is no mention of the Halychyna Division in any movement order. We have
> found no documentary evidence at all to explain how such a large body of men
> came to leave the 5th Corps area, eventually to turn up in northern Italy... [The]
> Ukrainian Division was simply permitted to make its own way to Italy.[17]

Large bodies of men do not disappear inadvertently in military organizations. If the Division "disappeared," it was intended that it should disappear. If it was marched out to Rimini without having been fully disarmed, someone must have made the decision to march the men out and arranged to house them and guard them once they arrived. If there is no record of who made the decision and why it was made, it is because it was deemed best that no record should be kept.

What follows is admittedly speculative, yet it fits the situation that prevailed at the time and offers a better explanation of why the Division was spared than any of the others submitted.

Tito's Antics

The answer lies in the confrontation between the British and Yugoslav forces in southern Austria and Trieste, a confrontation that was far more than a local skirmish resolved by a show of force by a local commander. As a matter of fact, it was a major crisis, severe enough to merit a direct exchange of messages between Prime Minister Churchill and President Truman. In a top-secret message dated May 12, the President stated:

I have come to the conclusion that we must decide now whether we should up-hold the fundamental principles of territorial settlement by orderly process against force, intimidation or blackmail... The problem is essentially one of decid-ing whether our two countries are going to permit our Allies to engage in uncon-trolled land grabbing or tactics which are all too reminiscent of those of Hitler and Japan.[18]

Churchill replied that he agreed fully with the President and that he viewed the situation that had developed with the utmost gravity. "If it is handled firmly before our strength is dispersed, Europe may be saved another bloodbath," said the Prime Minister, adding that it would be wise to keep the American armies and airforces in place in Europe and North Africa for a few more weeks until the situation was resolved.

The implications were grave, indeed. If the Soviet Union chose to support Tito in his claim to Trieste (Venezia-Giulia) and portions of southern Austria, it could result in out-right war by the western Allies against the Yugoslavs and the Soviet Union. On May 11, 1945, Field Marshall Alexander advised the Combined Chiefs of Staff that force might be needed to prevent Tito from seizing Trieste. He warned the Chiefs that giving way to Tito and letting him take whatever he wanted, would lead to a serious lowering of British prestige, which, in turn, would create grave difficulties for the military government about to be installed in Germany, Austria and Italy.

If force did become necessary, Alexander estimated that he would require no less than eleven divisions to operate effectively, as well as the complete roster of naval and air forces stationed in the Mediterranean theatre.[19]

Alexander explained that his estimate of the forces needed was based on the assump-tion that they would display the same fighting spirit and high endeavor in battle as they had previously. However, the announcement of VE Day and the long publicity given to Tito's operations in aid of the Allies caused him to doubt whether this would, in fact, be the case. In his view, both U.S. and British troops would be very reluctant to engage at this stage of the war in a fresh conflict with the Yugoslavs.[20]

Alexander believed there weren't enough Allied troops in the theatre of operations to stop Tito if the Soviets came to his support either by attacking directly or supplying vol-unteer formations to serve under Yugoslav command: "The following troops are avail-able in this theatre—seven U.S. divisions, four Brit divisions, one N.Z. division, one S. African division, two Indian divisions, two Polish divisions, one Brazilian division, total EIGHTEEN divisions. Of these, four divisions are required for the occupation of North-West Italy, and two to control the large number of surrendered enemy personnel in the theatre. Further, the two Indian (divisions) are now concentrated for redeployment in the Far East. This reduces the number of divisions in North-East Italy and Austria to TEN divisions."[21] [Emphasis and spelling as in the original text.]

The Field Marshall goes on to advise the Combined Chiefs of Staff that before he could employ the New Zealand, South African, Indian, Polish and Brazilian troops in new fighting, he would have to obtain the consent of their respective governments. In addition, the Americans are eager to send their boys home, while the Navy and Air Force are working on re-deploying the bulk of their forces to the Far East.

As it happened, diplomacy resolved the crisis before it deteriorated into a shooting war; Belgrade withdrew its partisans from Austria and Trieste was internationalized. But while the crisis was brewing, short run decisions were made that undoubtedly affected the Ukrainian Division.

Under circumstances that appeared desperate at the time, it made sense to keep the Ukrainian Division intact and warehouse it nearby. Although the Allies did not yet consider employing German troops against the Russians—that would come later with NATO—the Ukrainians were a different case. At the moment, they were stateless, responsible only to themselves. They were somewhat Polish, yet not under Polish command, so there would be no necessity for lengthy diplomatic consultations should they be needed. Above all, they were bitterly anti-Soviet and had expressed themselves as eager to keep on fighting.[22]

The absence of records is puzzling unless one accepts that there was a great need for secrecy. If the Soviet commander in Austria, Marshall Feodor Tolbukhin, should learn that the hated, OUN-inspired Division was being held in reserve in the event of hostilities against Tito's forces, there would be a diplomatic explosion that could shatter the fragile Yalta Accord. So long as the war with Japan was still in progress, it was not wise to twist the tail of the Russian bear.

Favoured Enemies

There is no question that on its surrender, the Division received "favoured enemy" treatment from both the British and the Americans. Uncertain of the Halychyna Division's record and identity, British officers were both amused and impressed by the ragged unit's dash as it marched into camp to surrender. The Division's commander—now a Colonel Krat[23]—touched a sympathetic nerve when he announced that he and his men were "reporting for duty" and were prepared to join the victorious Allied Armies in driving the wicked Russians out of Europe. There was a "comic opera" quality about the Division as it arrived in "tattered shirts and torn shorts in a motley collection of vehicles" that amused the British officers who accepted their surrender at Tamsweg.

By the time the Division reached Rimini, the Ukrainian soldiers were well briefed on how to respond when questioned about their decision to join Hitler's crusade for a New Europe. Officers of the 80th Scottish Medium Artillery Regiment "adopted" the Division and advised them to destroy all documents that might prove that they were members of the SS or identify them as Soviet citizens.[24]

In daily conferences with his generous British captors, Colonel Krat offered his own version of the Division's history. He maintained that his men had fought for the freedom of the Ukraine and were in no way in conflict with the Allies. He left the impression that the Division had fought bravely and participated in many momentous actions against the Russians.

The Soviet Screening Mission

Soon after the Ukrainians went "behind the wire," word came down from Austria that two of the surrendered Cossack divisions had been handed over to the Soviets. It was also reported that "the Russians had lined up the officers and shot them in sight of our troops and carried off the rest to a fate none envied."[25] These reports caused the British officers of the 80th Scottish to fear for the fate of their prisoners. "We feared 'our' Ukrainians (for by this time we felt a certain responsibility) would suffer the same fate."[26] They urged Colonel Krat to have his men destroy any vestige of evidence that might prove they were Soviet citizens.

A Soviet screening mission, described as a "foxy-faced Colonel, a Captain and a rather jovial Lieutenant," arrived at the camp on July 15, 1945.[27] The British officers invited the Soviet officers to their mess for lunch and sought to persuade them that all the prisoners in their charge came from west of the Yalta Line. After lunch, they proceeded to the camp where the Division was lined up by regiment and company. Colonel Krat received the Soviet mission with obvious hate and loathing. The British officers stood aside as the Russians addressed the Division, regiment by regiment, inviting the men to step forward as a sign that they wished to return to their homeland.

Much to the disgust of their comrades, some 350 men volunteered to return to the USSR. Each time a man stepped forward, those standing near him attacked him. At one point, it seemed as if the whole division might break ranks and overwhelm the volunteers. "The situation was getting out of control and we had quickly to call in a large contingent of our Scottish Horsemen with fixed bayonets. Order was soon restored and we proceeded, the Russian Lieutenant booming in Russian and the Russian Colonel looking like Satan."[28]

Allied Forces Headquarters dispatched Major Denis Hills (author of *Tyrants and Mountains; A Reckless Life*) to Riccione in July 1945, to assess the men of the Galicia Division in terms of the Yalta Agreement. The British view of the agreement, he was told, was that citizens of pre-war Poland should be regarded as Polish nationals and were not to be repatriated without their consent. Hills writes:

> The Soviet authorities, on the other hand, were being difficult. They were still insisting that all citizens who originated from the territory lying east of the old Curzon line (including Polish Galicia and Lwow) were Soviet citizens and should be returned. The British military authorities, however, had become increasingly opposed to the use of force. The forcible surrender of the Cossacks and their dependents to the Red Army... had left an unpleasant taste, and a similar attempt to hand over thousands of Ukrainians would be a degrading and messy business involving bloodshed and damaging publicity.[29]

Hills found his task "a cartographer's nightmare" as he tried to distinguish the "border Poles" from the "genuine Soviet citizens." He recommended, therefore, "that the Ukrainian formation be treated as a cohesive whole and that all of them should be given the benefit of the doubt and classified as Polish citizens from Polish Galicia." In Hills' version of the encounter with the Soviet screening mission, the Soviet officers were greeted with total silence. Although the Soviet officers worked hard and long to interrogate the men individually, only a small number volunteered to return home. Most simply refused to answer the interrogator's questions. Hills was present at every interview to prevent any bullying by the Soviet mission's personnel. His presence assured the Ukrainians that the British favoured them against the Russians, that they could count on the British to protect them.

In effect, the Soviet representatives were stonewalled. The atmosphere in the camp was clearly hostile. There were no papers to examine and there was no need to give truthful answers. In frustration, the Soviet officers ranted and raved. One of them shouted: "You are a grey mass. You have nothing to offer but your hands. The world doesn't want you. For them, you are rubbish. Be warned. Sooner or later the Soviet Union will have you."[30] It should be noted that the screening commission's sole concern at the time was to persuade the men to return to the USSR. No effort was made to identify war criminals. Indeed, the question of war criminals was not on the Soviet's agenda as yet. That would come later.

Notes
1. Brigadier T.P.D. Scott, 38 Irish Brigade in southern Austria. Quoted in Anthony Cowgill, Thomas Brimelow and Christopher Booker, *The Reparations from Austria in 1945: The Report of an Inquiry*, (London: Sinclair-Stevenson Ltd., 1990), 1.
2. *Ibid.* 5.

3. Cowgill, 350.

4. J.C.B. Dear (ed), *The Oxford Companion to World War II,* Oxford: Oxford University Press, 1995, 54.

5. Eden's statement quoted in Cowgill, Brimelow and Booker, *The Reparations from Austria in 1945,* 53.

6. *Ibid.,* 52.

7. *Ibid.,* 5.

8. This account was assembled from various sources including Cowgill and Tolstoy (*Victims of Yalta*).

9. "Vladivostok was the gateway through which a wave of Allied men and weapons flowed into Russia...with eight hundred men of Britain's Middlesex Regiment, the city played host to the French contingent...and the Americans followed by men who wore the uniforms of Poland, Czechoslovakia, China, Serbia, Canada, and Italy." Lincoln, *Red Victory,* 184.

10. Field-Marshall Alan Brooke, Chief of the Imperial General Staff is said to have been "strongly sympathetic to the cause of the White Armies... He had fought on the same side as General Krasnov in 1919, when Krasnov had commanded the anti-Bolshevik *Landeswehr.*"

11. Heike, English edition, 120.

12. Mark Aarons and John Loftus, *Ratlines,* London: Heinemann, 1991, 173.

13. Tolstoy, *Victims of Yalta,* 324.

14. Aarons and Loftus, *Ratlines,* 179.

15. Christopher Simpson, *Blowback,* New York: Weidenfeld & Nicholson, 1988, 180.

16. Tolstoy, *Victims of Yalta,* 323.

17. Cowgill, Brimelow and Booker, 94.

18. PRO, FO 371/48815.

19. PRO, FO 1020/42.

20. *Ibid.*

21. *Ibid.*

22. Incredible as it may seem to speculate that the British would consider using the Ukrainian Division to help contain the Yugoslav Partisans, one must remember that the British rearmed surrendered Japanese troops to squelch an uprising of Burmese nationalists.

23. Colonel M. Krat was a longtime associate of General Shandruk. Both had served together in the Czar's army. Both were officers in Petliura's forces at the time of the civil war. Both became contract officers in the Polish army, were captured by the invading Germans in 1939 and volunteered to serve in the German-led Ukrainian Division. Shandruk had great confidence in Krat and intended to appoint him commander of the Division in place of General Freytag. Rapidly deteriorating circumstances in the last days of the war prevented the change. Krat's rank is hard to determine. He is sometimes referred to as "Colonel" and at other times as "General."

24. Technically, the 80th Scottish Horse Medium Regiment Royal Artillery.

25. Lieutenant Colonel Campbell-Preston, unpublished report to Cowgill Commission, 1990.

26. *Ibid.*

27. *Ibid.* See also Dennis Hills, *Tyrants and Mountains: A Reckless Life* (London: John Murray Publishers, 1982), 112. Hills offers a slightly different cast of characters. According to Hills, the Screening Commission consisted of General Basilov, Colonel Jakovliev and Major Federov.

28. *Ibid.*

29. Hills, *Tyrants and Mountains,* 111.

30. *Ibid.* 113.

CHAPTER 11

POSTWAR IRONIES

THE WAR WAS WON AT AN ENORMOUS SACRIFICE OF THE ALLIES' MEN, material and wealth and the peace that followed proved equally difficult. The Cold War set in well before the shooting ended, leaving the British and Americans face to face with the "Russkies"—an affinity that both sides found highly uncomfortable. The Soviets feared the Western Allies intended to continue Capitalism's war on the Communist system; the Allies, in turn, feared Soviet domination in Europe. Both sides lost no time probing each other for potential weaknesses. The Soviets suspected the British and Americans of recruiting collaborationist national groups to launch a sustained propaganda campaign against them. The Yugoslavs under Tito feared that their wartime Allies would give free reign to Chetnik, Ustasha and Nazi refugees to organize espionage and assassination teams to bomb their embassies and assassinate their leaders.

Their fears were not unrealistic. Yugoslav consulates *were* bombed and assassination attempts *were* made against Yugoslav leaders. Leaders of collaborationist states, quisling figures such as Karol Sidor and Ferdinand Durcansky of Slovakia, Yaroslav Stetsko of the Organization of Ukrainian Nationalists and Ante Pavelic of Croatia were protected and smuggled out of Europe to beat the drum for the Anti-Bolshevik Bloc of Nations.

The Soviets, in turn, heightened Western fears through diplomatic truculence and outright confiscation of Poland, Hungary, Czechoslovakia and East Germany through Moscow dominated Communist governments.

In addition to the mounting political dilemmas provoked by the Cold War, the collapse of the German armies presented the Allies with the enormous task of caring for an unexpected deluge of enemy prisoners of war. In addition, millions of refugees—displaced Slovaks, Romanians, Hungarians, Byelorussians, Latvians, Estonians and Ukrainians—wandered the German and Austrian countryside and crowded into hastily arranged Displaced Persons (DP) camps operated by the United Nations Relief and Rehabilitation Administration (UNRRA).

The shattered remnants of Hitler's foreign legions, the *freiwilligen legionen*, clambered over each other in their haste to surrender to the English and Americans. Brutal concentration camp guards whose camps had been overrun by the Allied forces joined the flow. Large contingents of auxiliary policemen, Latvian legionnaires, Lithuanian murder squads and Ukrainian *Schutzmänner*, no longer needed to round up Jews and Poles or burn down villages, retreated with their German masters. At their first opportunity they abandoned their uniforms and submerged themselves in the flood of refugees heading for the DP camps in Austria and Germany.

"At the end of September [1945], the Western Allies cared for nearly seven million displaced persons." Historian Michael Marrus, in his book on post-war European refugees recalls the,

> Endless processions of people trudged across the ruined Reich, sometimes with pathetic bundles of belongings... Western observers feared a complete breakdown of public order in Central Europe...the collapse of established authority and severe privation.[1]

The bulk of the refugees in Germany and Austria on VE Day were eager to return home and take up life again with their surviving neighbors and family. However, approximately one million of them adamantly refused to return to their countries of origin. They included Latvians, Estonians, Lithuanians, Hungarians and Ukrainians who loathed the Communist regimes that had seized power in their countries. Some had openly assisted the enemy and feared they would be met by a firing squad if they returned.[2] Equally unwilling to return were thousands of Jewish concentration camp survivors who could not face life in the towns and villages which held such tragic memories.

Among the refugees determined to stay in the west, were 300,000 Ukrainians thrown together from all parts of Ukraine. Included were former slave labourers and released prisoners-of-war as well as a small contingent of political refugees.[3] It is estimated that in the year 1946, some two hundred thousand Ukrainian refugees, who refused to return home, were housed in DP camps. But by 1950, that number had dwindled to 25,000 as a result of migration to the United States, Canada and Australia.[4]

While the rest of Europe was struggling to recover from the war's devastation, the Ukrainian Division was spared the hunger and turmoil that affected most dispossessed Europeans. For two years following their surrender, the Division remained comfortably ensconced out of harm's way in the Surrendered Enemy Personnel (SEP) Camp No. 374 in Riccione.

Life in the tents and orderly rows of Quonset huts may have been bare and simple, but the climate in the Italian Adriatic coast was benign, the people in the surrounding countryside friendly and forgiving. Within the camp, the formation remained intact; military discipline was maintained, orders issued, ranks recognized, officers saluted and parades regularly held. Meanwhile, Colonel Krat bent every effort to lessen the stigma of the SS on the Division. The straight-armed "Heil Hitler" salute was forbidden and the traditional fingers-to-the-forehead British salute substituted.[5] To maintain morale and ease the boredom of camp life, the Division organized choirs, orchestras and athletic teams. A number of the officers, graduates of Polish and German universities, gave courses in a variety of political and military subjects. Nationalist dogma dominated the curriculum.

Visiting British officers noted the that the camp's perimeter was lightly guarded, making it easy to slip through the wire to visit nearby towns, find work with local farmers, engage in black market activities and develop romantic relationships with Italian women. Many chose to escape entirely and join compatriots and kinfolk in Austrian Displaced Persons camps. In the two years of the Division's stay in Rimini, the camp population decreased from an initial nominal role of 9,500 to approximately 8,500.

The Division Accused

No matter how comfortable life in Rimini might be, the threat of repatriation still hung heavily over the Division. The Soviet authorities had neither forgotten the Halychyna Division nor forgiven its members for what they regarded as base treachery. Stalin himself made reference to the Division at the Potsdam Conference and demanded its return. General Basilov, head of the Soviet Repatriation Commission discussed the Division with Field Marshall Alexander, insisting it fell squarely within the Yalta criteria.[6] Unrelenting in their demand for the return of the Galicians, Soviet delegates to the newly formed United Nations made thundering speeches denouncing the Division as a gang of traitors and war criminals. In a note presented to the United Kingdom Foreign Office, they presented a list of 124 of the Division's officers whom they accused of war crimes and demanded their immediate surrender.

At the second session of the UN General Assembly in October 1947, the Ukrainian Socialist Republic's representative called again for the surrender of war criminals so they could be punished in accordance with the laws of the countries in which they had committed their crimes. Representative Kovalenko reminded the members that the General Assembly had unanimously adopted a resolution calling for immediate punishment of war criminals:

> The Ukrainian people are profoundly convinced that the Hitlerite war criminals
> and their henchmen, sidekicks, traitors, quislings and other war criminals ought
> not to enjoy sanctuary in any democratic country in the world. They have perpe-

trated the most monstrous crimes against mankind and they should be judged where they perpetrated their bloody deeds. They ought to be handed over for judgment by those countries whose people suffered that cruelty on their backs.[7]

Kovalenko chose not to mention the Division by name in his UN address but the men clustered in their Quonset huts in Rimini had no doubt that they were included in his definition of "Hitlerite henchmen, sidekicks, traitors, quislings and war criminals." Given the Soviet insistence that they be handed over, Italy no longer felt safe; they longed to put greater distance between the Russians and themselves.

The Central Ukrainian Relief Bureau also feared for the Division's safety. Headquartered in London, the Bureau represented a series of Ukrainian organizations and churches in Canada, Germany and the United States. Headed by former Royal Canadian Air Force (RCAF) officer Bohdan Panchuk, who had arranged to be discharged in London, the Bureau pleaded for the removal of the Division from Italy.

Panchuk, desperate to find a safe refuge for the Division, recommended that its members should become the nucleus of a British foreign legion along the lines of legendary French Foreign Legion. Failing the creation of a legion, Panchuk urged enlisting the Division in the British army for service wherever they might be required. If all else failed, he called on the British to transport the whole Division to England where they could be put to work as ordinary labourers.[8] In October 1946, this last suggestion seemed pure fantasy, however, before long it became official British policy.

Chetniks, Ustashas, and the Maclean Commission.

Despite Panchuk's efforts, it was not the Ukrainian Division that loomed large in the minds of England's policy makers. In the immediate post-war years, it was the Ustasha and Chetnik refugees that occupied the Allies attention and inspired a virtual flood of Foreign Office meetings and memoranda. While thousands of Yugoslavs had fought courageously against Hitler's invading armies, the Croatian Ustashas had collaborated with the Germans and actively fought on the German side. The Royalist Chetniks had temporized and lost British support. Now, with Tito and his Partisan forces victorious, the collaborators poured across the Austrian border to escape Tito's wrath.[9]

Unwilling to have several thousand vengeful enemies hovering on his border, Tito demanded that the fleeing Chetniks and Ustashas be returned to Yugoslavia for trial as traitors and war criminals.

For a week or so, following the German surrender, the British brass could see no reason to frustrate Tito. Angered by the heaps of corpses and the emaciated frames of the survivors at Buchenwald, Stuthoff, Natzweiler, Dachau and Bergen-Belsen, all ranks from generals to privates wanted no part of those who had done the Nazi's dirty work. It seemed only right to return Pavelic's Ustashas, the Slovenian Domobrans and Nedic's Serbia State Guard to meet their fate—execution by Tito's partisans.

But the first flush of anger soon dissipated and the Allies recalled that Tito, their Communist wartime ally with close ties to Moscow, might not prove to be their peacetime friend. Perhaps rank and file collaborators could be sacrificed, but the Ustasha and Chetnik leaders were passionately anti-Communist and claimed to possess valuable intelligence information previously unavailable to the British and Americans. They also persuaded the Allies that they still retained extensive networks of anti-Communist dissidents that continued to operate behind Russian lines.

Yet, under the rules of the Yalta Agreement, forged by Churchill, Roosevelt and Stalin in February 1945, the Allies were obliged to return war criminals for trial in the countries in which they had committed their crimes. To appear to be adhering to Yalta and still slow down repatriation, the British insisted that the Yugoslavs supply the name of each person they wanted returned, along with clear cut evidence of his guilt as a war criminal.

These names would be investigated by British Military Intelligence and placed in one of three categories, depending on the degree of their collaboration with the enemy. "Blacks," subject to automatic arrest, included traitors, quislings and outright war criminals. "Whites" were the innocent victims of Nazi brutality, concentration camp survivors, slave labourers and families displaced in Himmler's ethnic cleansing. The "greys" as expected, fell somewhere in between and included minor bureaucrats who had "gone along" with the Nazi occupiers but avoided taking part in atrocities. Of these, only the "Blacks" would be considered for repatriation.

The assignment of the proper classification was not intended to be a hit and miss process, but based on an individual interview and a careful examination of available records. "Screening sheets were made out for each person who gave information concerning his war-time activities. Each sheet was marked "Grey" or "White" as the situation required."[10] The British anticipated that the Yugoslav government might not agree in every case with the British classifiers. "Some whites may include persons who are regarded as innocent by the British or the United States government, but are not so regarded by their countries of origin."[11]

Churchill chose the ideal man for this excruciating task. Brigadier Fitzroy Maclean was commissioned to assemble a team of army officers and civilians to sort out the thousands of Chetniks, Slovenes and Ustashas detained in Surrendered Enemy Personnel camps in Austria and Italy. A distinguished diplomat and Conservative Member of Parliament, he had served as Churchill's personal envoy to Tito and the Partisans. He had parachuted into Yugoslavia while it was occupied by the Germans and was with Tito in the dark days of 1943 when the partisan movement was on the verge of being wiped out by a combination of German, Italian and Bulgarian forces. It was Maclean who persuaded Churchill to switch his support from Mihailovic to Tito when it became evident that the Communist-led Partisans constituted the only guerrilla force fighting hard against the Nazis. Tito was grateful to Maclean for his support at a critical time and trusted him to be fair in his judgments.[12]

Not everyone was enthusiastic over the choice of Maclean. There were those in the Foreign Office who felt he was too close to Tito to be trusted with the job. They feared that Maclean would be too eager to please his friend and would engage in wholesale condemnation of Chetniks and Ustashas.[13] His critic's fears were, however, illusory. Whatever sympathies or antipathies the Brigadier might have held, he was too disciplined a soldier and too responsible a diplomat to indulge them.[14]

Yet, despite his personal integrity, Maclean could manage only the most superficial of screenings. No sooner had he arrived in Italy than he signaled the Foreign Office that he was hampered by the complete absence of records upon which to base his decisions. "Before I left England," he complained, "I was assured that I should find all collated intelligence material of war years readily available in Italy, [instead] practically no material of the war period is available there, most War intelligence records having apparently been dispersed to Washington and elsewhere."[15]

The absence of records presented an even more insurmountable difficulty when the time came to screen the Halychyna Division. In the case of the Yugoslavs, the records had merely been misplaced; in the case of the Division, they had been deliberately destroyed. British officers, including Maclean, had served on military missions to Tito and had a grasp of the situation on the ground. But there were no British officers present in Warsaw and Galicia, so there was no one to gainsay the information supplied by Division members, no matter how misleading.

The Italian Dilemma

Initially, the Halychyna Division was not among the units scheduled for screening by the Maclean Commission but as events played out, some type of screening became necessary to keep the Soviets at bay and persuade Parliament and the British public that the decision to rescue the Division had been fully justified.

The British officers who had accepted the Ukrainian's surrender had been charmed by their magnificent choral singing and impressive church services. They also entertained the hope that these bitterly anti-Soviet, German-trained soldiers would be useful in the event the West set about liberating the "Captive Nations." But by 1947, the charm had worn off and the British government was left with the question of how to dispose of 8,500 Ukrainian Waffen-SS personnel who had fought on the German side. A whole regiment was tied down guarding them and they needed to be fed, clothed, housed and usefully employed.

Since they had served under German command, logically, they should have been transferred to a prison camp in Germany since they had served under German command. But given the fragility of the German economy and the extreme scarcity of food, fuel and housing in the battered country, the British authorities determined that no additions should be made to the population in the British zone.

No thought was given, at first, to bringing the Division to the United Kingdom. Thomas Brimelow (later Lord Brimelow) was among several Foreign Office officials who wrestled with the question of what should be done with the Ukrainian Division. In a letter to the author, written in 1992, Brimelow explained that the Foreign Office was eager to have the Division moved from Italy but had no intention of transferring it to the United Kingdom. For a time, Brimelow explained, the Cabinet hoped that the Division could be resettled in one of Britain's East African colonies, but the colonies refused to accept the burden of resettling them. The Cabinet then recommended that the Division should be transferred to Libya or Tripolitania where they could occupy the former *Afrika Korps* barracks, but the idea was vetoed on the grounds that it would be impossible for the men to sustain themselves in the African desert.[16]

While the Foreign Office and the War Office searched for a solution that would keep the Division far from Britain's shores, the situation in Italy was becoming increasingly complex. The Allies were preparing to sign a peace treaty with the Italians. Once signed, they would be required to withdraw their forces from the Italian peninsula by the end of 1947. The Foreign Office feared that the Italians, less willing to confront the Russians on behalf of an extraneous band of Ukrainian SS-men, would succumb to Soviet pressure and repatriate the Division once the British were gone.[17] Adding to the apprehension was the growing strength of the Italian Communist Party, which had earned increased respect among Italian voters for its willingness to engage the Germans in guerrilla warfare.

The solution, according to the Foreign Office was to act quickly before the Italian treaty came into effect. More and more Foreign Office minutes reflected a reluctant but growing acceptance of the necessity of transporting the Division to England and putting them to work on farms and in factories. There simply was nowhere else to put them now that the USSR claimed Galicia as Soviet territory.

The German Treaty and its Consequences

By 1947, the Western Allies had had enough of playing the occupier in Germany. The time had come to sign a peace treaty that would allow them to send their soldiers home and return Germany to its own civil authorities. But a peace treaty involved more than a handshake; it meant sending home the thousands of German war prisoners held in prison camps scattered throughout the British Isles.

To an England still on food rations, the release of the German POWs spelled disaster. In one of the many ironies precipitated by the war, the German prisoners of war held in Britain had been put to work on English farms and had shown themselves to be efficient, productive agriculturists. Indeed, with British farm workers still serving in the army and navy, the German POWs had become the backbone of British agriculture.

Meanwhile, British forces were still needed around the world. A considerable army was required to maintain the mandate in Palestine. India was a powder keg lurching towards independence. Greece and Burma were facing armed rebellion from the communist left and the nationalist right. Under the circumstances, the Home Office estimated it would be 1950 at best before the British army could be sufficiently demobilized to allow its personnel to return to jobs on farm and factory. If rationing was not to be depressingly extended, substitutes would have to be found for the homeward bound Germans.

Faced with this dilemma, it occurred to Britain's policy makers that the Ukrainian Division, rusting and molting in Riccione, would make admirable replacements. A War Office memorandum describes them as "stout hearted and reliable men" but warns that there will be "some political opposition" if they are brought to Britain:

> It is believed that these Ukrainians are for the most part stout hearted and reliable men whose only crime is that they opposed Communism during the War. As they fought at one time against Allied forces in German units, it does not seem that we should be incorrect in treating them as Prisoners of War instead of Enemy Surrendered Personnel as they are classed at present... On the other hand there would certainly be some political opposition to the proposal to bring more PW (Prisoners of War) to this country at a time when there is considerable pressure to send them all home as soon as possible.[18]

But if the opposition could be diverted and the Division transported to Britain, two problems could be solved simultaneously: the Division could be removed before the Italian Treaty took effect and its personnel could substitute for the departing Germans.

While this scheme clearly had the support of the Foreign Office and the War Office, the Home Office and the Ministry of Labour were much less enthusiastic. The latter feared that once the Ukrainians were admitted, they might decide to stay, thereby occupying the jobs and homes the government felt obliged to reserve for the returning Tommies.

Eventually, a compromise was reached between the conflicting concerns of the various government departments. The Division would be brought to England late in 1947 and housed in barracks previously occupied by the German POWs. They would be put to work on the land and in Britain's mines and factories—but they must be gone again by 1950 when it was estimated the British soldiers would come marching home again.

History Re-written

Before this plan could be seriously considered, however, the Ukrainian Waffen-SS Division had to be made more palatable to the British and American public; a new rational had to be supplied to explain away the Division's motives for rushing to the banner of Himmler's SS legions. It was left to General Shandruk, ensconced among friends in Munich, to make the case. In a memo addressed to the British Foreign Office, Shandruk wrote: "The 1st Ukrainian Division must be considered as [part] of continuous struggle for the re-establishment of an independent Ukrainian state."[19] Ukrainians had hoped to achieve their independence peacefully, he wrote, but lost all hope when it became clear that "the Germans wished to oppress the whole of Europe and occupy Ukraine as their Lebensraum."[20] The Germans, he pointed out began to annihilate the Ukrainians and colonize the Ukrainian territory.

By 1942, Shandruk wrote, it was also becoming evident that the Germans were losing the war. He cited the severe losses suffered by the Nazis at Stalingrad, the defeat of the Afrika Korps at El Alamein and the loss of Tripoli. Ukrainian nationalist leaders feared that chaos would descend on Europe in the wake of a German defeat. In that event, he stated, a Ukrainian military force formed under German auspices would serve as an embryo national army to protect the Ukrainian people from revolutionary chaos and establish a democratic, independent Ukraine. It would also protect Ukrainian citizens from the rampages of demoralized German soldiers.

This line of thought, Shandruk insisted, was proof that in organizing the Division, the Ukrainian people had not intended to collaborate with Hitler or help him conquer Europe and thereby turn Ukraine into a German colony. The Division was only "formally" joined to the German army, he claimed, and could not be genuine SS-men since only people of Germanic racial origin such as Norwegians, Dutchmen and natives of Flanders were allowed to serve in Himmler's SS. Enlistment in the Division, he claimed, was merely a convenient way of receiving military training for young Ukrainians who would later desert and join UPA and other resistance groups. By joining the Division they also avoided being drafted for forced labour in Germany where they risked dying from exposure, starvation and Allied bombs.

The Division's volunteers were ardent patriots, Shandruk proclaimed, who demanded nothing from the Germans except arms which they anticipated using in a proper time for the creation of the Ukrainian national army.

In his final summary, Shandruk proclaimed: "The Ukrainian volunteers had nothing in common with the programme of the Nazi Party, and they did not commit a single crime during their service in the Ukrainian Division which would dishonour their national dignity or violate international law."[21]

The Shandruk's manifesto is contradictory and illogical, suggesting that the Ukrainian nationalist leadership was either unrealistically optimistic, incredibly naïve or insidiously deceitful. Certainly they were overly optimistic if they if they believed a small military force attached to a defeated army would metamorphose into a mighty national army capable of wresting control from a victorious Russian army, no matter how exhausted.

Given the arrest of Bandera and Stetsko following their 1941 declaration of independence in Lviv, they were tragically naïve if, in 1943 when the Division was organized, they believed that Nazi Germany would allow them a generous measure of independence in return for wartime service. Shandruk confesses that the Germans regarded Ukrainians as *Untermenschen,* fit only to serve as *Knechte* or slaves to German settlers. He had observed the beginning of Himmler's efforts to clear out Ukrainian villagers and replace them with members of the super race. Shandruk himself cites the death and destruction inflicted on innocent Ukrainian civilians. He admits that Hitler had no intention of withdrawing from Ukraine but planned to occupy it forever.

In his appeal to the Foreign Office, Shandruk deplores the deportation of young men and women as slave labourers in Germany, yet he fails to mention that the Halychyna Division participated in rounding up the unwilling draftees and escorting them to the trains that would deliver them to their brutal taskmasters.

According to Shandruk the Ukrainian leadership recognized that the tide was running against the Nazis after Stalingrad. Yet despite his recitation of German ravages, cruelty, subterfuge and contempt, the Ukrainian general continued to justify the raising an armed force of young Ukrainians to fight and die on the losing side.

Nevertheless, Shandruk's plea for understanding provided British officials with the rationalizations they sorely needed to justify their own actions.

Notes

1. Michael Marrus, *Unwanted: European Refugees in the Twentieth Century* (Oxford: Oxford University Press, 1985), 299-300.

2. Report of a Special Subcommittee on the Judiciary, House of Representatives, pursuant to H. Res. 238, January 20, 1950, *Displaced Persons in Europe and their Resettlement in the United States*.

3. Ukraine, *A Concise Encyclopaedia*, Vol. 2, 1210

4. *Ibid.*

5. Styrkul, 291.

6. Tolstoy, *Victims of Yalta*, 258-268.

7. PRO, FO 371/64722.

8. PRO, FO 371/156791 - Disposal of Ukrainians in Italy.

9. The details of Yugoslav resistance, German invasion, the Serb rebellion under Mihailovic, the cruelties of the Ustasha puppet state in Croatia, the rise of Tito are too complicated to describe in this book which focuses primarily on a Galician Division. For a full treatment, see: Jozo Tomasevich, *The Chetniks: War and Revolution in Yugoslavia, 1941-1945* (Stanford University Press, 1975) and David Martin, *The Web of Disinformation; Churchill's Yugoslav Blunder* (New York: Harcourt Brace Jovanovich, 1990).

10. PRO, FO 371/66605, Cabinet distribution from Foreign Office to Washington.

11. *Ibid.*

12. See Sir Fitzroy Maclean's obituary in the New York Times; page A14, August 2, 1996: "During the Second World War, he parachuted into Yugoslavia while it was occupied by the Germans. He went to work for Tito and he has been widely credited with a substantial role in Winston Churchill's decision during the war, to back Tito instead of a rival partisan leader in Yugoslavia."

13. PRO, FO 371/67370.

14. Sir Fitzroy Maclean of Dunconnel died on June 15, 1996 at the age of 85 in his family home in the Scottish county of Argyll.

15. PRO, WO 204/10444, LCAB Refugee Screening Commission, February 8, 1947. In the end, no more than three percent of those fleeing Tito, of any political stripe, were detained and returned to Yugoslavia.

16. Personal correspondence between Lord Brimelow and the author, December 4, 1992.

17. *Ibid.*

18. PRO, WO 32/13749.

19. PRO, FO 371/1/56791.

20. *Ibid.*

21. *Ibid.*

CHAPTER 12

THE HALDANE PORTER REPORT

JUDGING FROM THE HIGH VOLUME OF MEMORANDA AND argumentative notes appended to letters and proposed drafts of public statements composed by high-ranking civil servants, the British civil service was in a genuine stew over what was to be done with the Ukrainian Division. Within the ranks of the Foreign Office's Refugee Committee a fierce battle was being fought—with all necessary British decorum—between those on the Refugee Committee who favoured bringing the Division to the United Kingdom and those who thought the idea ridiculous and immoral. Thomas Brimelow, who held the somewhat lowly rank of Second Secretary at the time, vigorously opposed the transfer. It was his opinion that the Division should be abandoned to whatever fate befell it in Italy:

> It seems out of the question that [the Ukrainian Division] should be transferred to territories under British control... [Our] first obligation is to provide homes for the Poles who fought for us, and the Chetniks who fought against the Germans. The Ukrainians who fought for the enemy should surely come last. We have no obligation towards them... I see no special reason why we should have qualms about leaving them to their fate in Italy, or why we should object if the Italians ultimately decide to repatriate them.[1]

Refugee Committee colleagues E. Basil Boothby and A.W.H. Wilkinson strenuously opposed him, however. Boothby, a former secretary to Winston Churchill and a powerful figure in the Foreign Office, had the ear of Prime Minister Clement Attlee and Foreign Secretary Ernest Bevin. A colorful, contradictory, manipulative bureaucrat, he was a virtual prototype for the role of the fast-talking, duplicitous, senior civil servant in the British television series, "Yes, Minister."[2] Wilkinson, a younger man, served as Boothby's protégé and stalking-horse.

A tiger in defence of his Minister, Boothby was determined to bring the Division to Britain because that was what Foreign Secretary Ernest Bevin wanted. Bevin, an old Socialist trade unionist who had engaged in bitter feuds with his Marxist union rivals, was fond of sticking his thumb in the Soviets' eye. To preserve the Division and still claim to be adhering to the Yalta Agreement was an excellent way to frustrate the Communists.[3]

Boothby, in a handwritten note on Refugee Committee letterhead, stated: "If we cannot find places for them in Africa or recruit men for work in this country, we shall have to abandon them. But this would be a shocking way of winding up a dear military responsibility..."[4] The War Office was also adamantly opposed to abandoning the Division, both as a matter of military honour and because they might prove militarily useful.

Brimelow responded in a lengthy memorandum, stressing repeatedly that all the Ukrainians in SEP Camp 374 were captured wearing German uniforms and were still liable to forcible repatriation since their true citizenship had never been adequately established. "There clearly must be a proper screening of all these men if the Cabinet ruling and the undertakings given by Field Marshal Alexander [to Soviet General Basilov] are to be carried out... The discovery that the inmates of No. 374 SEP Camp have not been properly screened has an embarrassing bearing on Sunday's Soviet complaint that we are harbouring several thousand Soviet citizens in Italy."[5]

Boothby thanked Brimelow for his "very lucid explanation," but brushed aside his objections. Brigadier Maclean would be ordered to screen the men, Boothby said, thereby silencing all possible objections. That done, the War Department would change their status from "Surrendered Enemy Personnel" to "Prisoners of War" so that they could be put to work at whatever task they were assigned in Britain so long as it was consistent with the Geneva Convention.[6]

Belatedly, and without consulting the Foreign Office, the British Chiefs of Staff began to make plans to screen the Ukrainians and Yugoslavs in their charge. In May 1947, they issued a long and complicated directive to Lieutenant-General Sir Frederick Morgan, the Deputy Chief of Staff of the Supreme Headquarters Allied Expeditionary Force (SHAEF) which controlled Allied forces in north-west Europe, ordering him to set up a screening process that would search out those who had committed "atrocious crimes" and "war crimes against the Allies." The scheme called for numerous sub-categories that would require a large, experienced, joint U.K. and U.S. screening team.

Brimelow, an active member of the Foreign Office Refugee Committee until 1948 when he took up a diplomatic post in Havana, recalls: "It would have been reasonable to assume from this document that the War Office was serious about comprehensive screening. The assumption would have been erroneous... The War Office telegraphed to [the British ambassador in Rome] that the Division would be screened on its arrival (in the UK). It was not."[7]

Almost simultaneously, Maclean reported from Rome that he had made a quick visit to No. 374 SEP Camp near Rimini where a team under the direction of David Haldane Porter worked to distinguish the lambs from the wolves. The camp, he discovered "is organized on political-military lines under a fanatical Ukrainian nationalist leader who formerly served Skoropadsky. Ultra nationalist badges and flags are freely displayed."[8]

The screening of the Ukrainians was taking much longer than originally anticipated, Maclean explained. With no records available, it had taken two weeks to interview two hundred men: "Really careful screening of the whole camp would take many months."[9]

"It must, of course be borne in mind that we have only their word for it that they come from Polish as opposed to Soviet Ukraine and that they have not committed atrocities or war crimes; on the other hand we have no means of disproving their statements and those interrogated give a general impression of telling the truth," Maclean concluded.[10]

The Foreign Office recognized the difficulties faced by Maclean. In a telegram marked "of particular secrecy" the FO agreed that it would be impossible to screen the men properly in the time available and that few of the camp's inmates would be eligible for international aid. The FO further agreed that a substantial proportion of the Division's personnel were, in all probability, Soviet citizens resident within Soviet territory on September 1, 1939 and therefore eligible for repatriation. Yet, whatever the difficulties, Maclean was ordered to get on with the job; everything possible must be done to prevent the problem being left in the hands of the left-leaning Italians.[11]

Haldane Porter, a member of Maclean's Refugee Screening Commission, was hurriedly seconded to Rimini to determine the status of the Ukrainian Division detained in Surrendered Enemy Personnel 374 and report back to Whitehall. Porter was keenly aware of what his government expected of him. His task was to clear the Division of war crimes charges and provide evidence that none—or at least very few of them—were Soviet citizens prior to September 1939. At the same time, he must not appear naive or easily deceived since the vigilant British press and the outspoken Russians were peering over his shoulder.

Porter submitted his report on February 21, 1947.[12] In the first part of his report he grappled with the number of inmates in the camp, explaining that it varied from time to time due to escapes and transfers to hospitals and other camps. He made no count of his own but arrived at the figure of 8,272 men, a number confirmed by the British camp authorities. The camp population had shrunk from its original 9,500 members, but he concluded that the bulk of the Division was intact.

Given the limited time assigned for the task, Porter stated that he found it impossible to undertake individual screening. The best that he and his small staff could manage was to question a small cross-section of 200 men drawn from each of the "Wehrmacht" formations. (Porter consistently employed the term "Wehrmacht," indicating that he was either ignorant of the difference between the German regular army and the Waffen-SS or was determined to ignore it.)

Major Jaskewycz—who was not further identified—provided Haldane Porter with the camps nominal role and his version of the history of the 1st Ukrainian Division. "It should be emphasized," Porter warned, "that all these nominal rolls and the short history of the Division were supplied entirely by the Ukrainians and that we had no information of any kind which could be checked, and virtually none of the men had any identifying documents of any use, such as German army pay books." Porter, nevertheless, stated he was satisfied that Major Jaskewycz had done his best to provide accurate and complete information.[13]

The Commission's ability to get at the facts was also handicapped by the lack of independent interpreters. "Except in the case of Mr. Brown, who was able to question the men in Russian, Ukrainian speaking interpreters who were actually inmates in the camp, had to be used," Porter confided. Although he did his best to check for discrepancies in Jaskewycz's account, Porter stated he was unable to identify any.[14]

Porter accepted the myth that the Division ceased to exist after its defeat at the Battle of Brody and assumed that an entirely new unit sprang into being in 1944 with only tenuous connections to the Waffen-SS formation organized a year earlier. He failed to realize that the Division was never disbanded and the 14th Galician Waffen-SS Division and the 1st Ukrainian Division were one and the same military formations. Jaskewycz failed to inform him that General Shandruk was a mere figurehead and that General Freytag continued to be the commander of the Division until the moment of his suicide. He made no mention of the fact that the Division's German officers and non-commissioned officers continued to serve until the front dissolved and it became every man for himself.

Jaskewycz's "short history" utterly confused the English investigator. According to the Ukrainian major, the Division "appears to have been formed about September 1944 and actually to have fought for only a month in the late stages of the campaign in Austria (April 1945); the rest of its time was occupied in training and guard duties in Austria and Yugoslavia." Yet some of the men interviewed reported that "they had volunteered for armed service with the Germans as early as July 1943, whereas the 1st Ukrainian Division does not appear to have been formed until the late summer of 1944."[15]

> One of the officers of the 14th Galician Waffen Grenadier Division has stated that
> it was originally called by the Germans a Waffen-SS but the SS was dropped from
> its title, on the Ukrainians protesting, and that it subsequently became an ordi-
> nary German army division. It seems, however, to have had some SS training,
> which would account for some of its officers having given their ranks as
> 'Untersturmfeuhrer,' which is an SS rank and not an ordinary German rank.[16]

On the crucial issue of the men' citizenship and eligibility for repatriation, Porter throws up his hands and confesses he has no information other than that supplied by the men themselves. "Many of the places they have given us as their place of birth and/or their habitual residence are small villages and hamlets which are not likely to be marked on any but the largest maps; but I think we can safely assume that the great majority of those born after 1919 were born in Poland, and were resident in Poland on 1st September 1939."

Porter gained the impression that the men in the camp were "decent, simple-minded sort of people... [who] do not seem conscious of having done any wrong." Despite their seeming simplicity, he admitted that he may have been misled. "We have... obtained a reasonably consistent picture so far as it goes, and as far as one can go within the limits of our time and resources. The men may be all or in part lying, and even their names may be false. No attempt at cross-examination was made except where some glaring discrepancy was revealed during the course of the interrogation."[17]

Porter confessed that the screeners had done little more than take down the men's answers to a limited number of set questions. Although he clearly understood the inadequacy of this form of interrogation, Porter concluded that, by and large, the men were who they said they were and had done what they said they did. Nevertheless, he recommended further screening by checking the names on the Division's nominal role against the lists compiled by UNWCC (United Nations War Crimes Commission) and CROWCASS (Central Registry of War Criminals and Security Suspects) or specifically accused of war crimes by the Russians.[18] "It might (also) be possible to locate some of the German officers of the Division and have them questioned," he added.[19]

None of these measures were ever undertaken.

Porter also wrestled mightily with the definition of treason. Were the members of the Division traitors unworthy of our concern, or were they victims of Stalin's terror deserving our warmest sympathy. Porter concluded: "The great majority of them voluntarily enlisted in the German armed forces and fought against our allies, Soviet Russia and Yugoslavia... Allowing for intimidation, dislike of forced labour, the majority for our purpose must be regarded as volunteers. There are, therefore, prima facie grounds for classifying them as traitors."[20]

However, the writer of the report extended a merciful hand and called for an examination of the men's motives: "[We must] take into account their motives for having voluntarily offered their services to the enemy...[since] they probably were not, and certainly do not seem to be at heart pro-German."[21] He lists the possible motives as:

- The hope of obtaining a genuinely independent Ukraine.
- Without knowing exactly what they were doing, e.g., because other Ukrainians whom they knew had already volunteered.
- As a preferable alternative to forced labour, etc. or to living in Soviet controlled territory.

- To have a smack at the Russians, whom they always refer to as 'Bolsheviks.'[22]

In the end, Haldane Porter set aside his misgivings and recommended that the Ukrainians be reclassified as Displaced Persons and placed under the protection of the International Refugee Organization (IRO) on humanitarian grounds. This would effectively prevent the Italian government from handing them over to the Soviets. Failing that, he advised removing them "lock, stock and barrel from Italy before the Italian Treaty comes into force."[23]

In retrospect one recognizes that Porter's report is a masterpiece of bureaucratic report writing in which he confesses all of the report's shortcomings yet manages to provide the government with the conclusion it wants. He underlines the fact that there wasn't enough time and enough staff to do more than a superficial survey. He also wants it known that he had to do his work without the necessary supportive documents: nominal rolls, rosters, war diaries and Division history. All have been lost or destroyed. He is frank to say that he can't tell whether Jaskewycz and his officers are lying or not. He does not conceal his lack of independent translators, or that he was compelled to accept whatever he was told without the possibility of cross-examination.

Above all, Haldane Porter missed the fact that the vast majority of the men in SEP Camp No. 374 had served in various auxiliary police units prior to enlisting in the Waffen-SS. He accepted all too readily their claim that they had begun their careers under German command as late as the spring of 1944. He betrayed no knowledge of *Roland* and *Nachtigall*, or of Battalion 201. He was seemingly unaware of the Division's participation in so-called anti-partisan warfare, the destruction of countless Polish villages and the Ukrainian Division's role in suppressing the Slovak Rebellion. He knew nothing of the 31st SD and its part in the brutal repression of the 1944 Warsaw Uprising.

Despite its limitations, the report was received enthusiastically in Whitehall. Boothby, who had largely engineered the report—not out of love for the Ukrainian soldiers but to protect his Minister from criticism—was particularly exuberant. "This is a very good report which grapples manfully with the questions in which we are most interested and seems to bring out the human side of the question without exaggerations," he wrote in a memorandum to his colleagues.[24]

Brimelow disagreed with Boothby but was unable to prevail against his more experienced, better-connected colleagues.[25] Years later (1992), Brimelow wrote: "The Division was never comprehensively screened by any British authority to establish either the national status (Soviet or Polish) of its members or for war crimes... Haldane Porter's screening of some 200 members of the Division seems to have been the only serious attempt at screening ever conducted by a British authority and his team paid more attention to national status than criminality... When Haldane Porter did his screening, he only had their word to go on and it was in their interest not to disclose anything which might suggest that they were Soviet citizens or had committed crimes... [and] once all relevant documents disappeared, concealment of the truth became easy."[26]

Yet, it was Haldane Porter's report, with all its failings, that was trotted out by the Foreign Office whenever someone had the temerity to question the wisdom of bringing the Division to the United Kingdom. And thirty-five years later, a Canadian judge heading a Royal Commission of Inquiry into War Criminals in Canada relied almost entirely on the same report to conclude: "Charges of War Crimes against members of the Galicia Division have never been substantiated."[27]

Notes

1. PRO, FO 371/1/56791.
2. "Queer of the Realm," *Time Out* (London) June 19, 1997.
3. *Ibid.*
4. PRO, old classification WR 630, 24 Feb. 1947.
5. *Ibid.*
6. *Ibid.*
7. Lord Thomas Brimelow to Sol Littman, private correspondence, December 4, 1992.
8. PRO, FO 371/66605.
9. *Ibid.*
10. *Ibid.*
11. PRO, HO 213/1881.
12. PRO, FO 371/66605.
13. *Ibid.*
14. *Ibid.*
15. *Ibid.*
16. *Ibid.*
17. *Ibid.*
18. UNWCC: United Nations War Crimes Commission; CROWCASS: Central Registry of War Criminals and Security Suspects of the Allied Control Council in Berlin assisted in the apprehension of war criminals.
19. Haldane Porter Report.
20. *Ibid.*
21. *Ibid.*
22. *Ibid.*
23. *Ibid.*
24. FO 371/66605, Boothby's hand-written note, 10 March 1947 appended to Haldane Porter Report.
25. Lord Thomas Brimelow did not remain a lowly servant of the Foreign Office for long. In the course of a long career he served as Ambassador to Poland, 1966-69; Deputy Under-Secretary of State, Foreign Office, 1969-73; Permanent Under-Secretary of State and Head of Diplomatic Service, 1973-75. As Second Secretary in the Foreign Office, Brimelow was concerned with the execution of the Yalta Repatriation Agreement. Following his retirement in 1975, he devoted considerable time to compiling a comprehensive history of the Allied policy of repatriation to the Soviet Union.
26. *Supra*, private correspondence, December 4, 1992.
27. Commission of Inquiry on War Criminals Report, Part I, page 261, paragraph 60.

CHAPTER 13

FROM ITALY TO THE UNITED KINGDOM

THE TRANSPORTATION OF MORE THAN SEVEN THOUSAND Ukrainian Waffen-SS men from Italy to England in the spring of 1947 did not pass without comment. Felix Wirth, a prominent member of the Foreign Press Association, addressed a letter to Labour Party Member of Parliament Tom Driberg in which he asked whether careful investigation wouldn't reveal that many members of the Division could be classified as war criminals:

> Little is known...of the Ukrainians terrible role as Germany's active henchmen in the slaughter of the Jews in Lwow and other towns in that part of the world as well as in the murder factories throughout Eastern Europe. The notorious Ukrainian SS division 'Galizien' and other Ukrainian formations bear full responsibility for a good deal of the monstrous outrages there.
>
> Whatever our quarrel with the Russians, surely the conscience of civilization could not permit to classify these people as innocent political refugees unless we establish that they are definitely not guilty of crimes which cry to heaven unretributed.[1]

Driberg passed on Wirth's letter to Minister of State, the Right Honourable Hector McNeil. A letter penned by a member of the Foreign Press Association and forwarded by Driberg to a Minister of State could not be safely ignored. The Foreign Office's Northern Department set to work to design an acceptable answer to Wirth's accusatory letter. The task of drafting the reply fell to A.W.H. Wilkinson and was vetted by Boothby. It read:

> Cross-sections of these men have already been screened in Italy. In August 1945, a Soviet Mission examined a number of them, and last February a further group were subjected to a very exhaustive screening process at the hands of our own Screening Mission. Neither of these interrogations revealed any persons guilty of crimes against humanity. They will, however, be subjected to still further screening in this country and you may rest assured that we shall do our best to see that any war criminals who may be among their number are brought to book.[2]

The statement, designed to justify importing the Division to England, relied again on the supposed screening by the Soviets and the wholly inadequate Haldane Porter Report. The promise of further screening once the Division landed in Britain came close to being an outright lie. The Foreign Office had no intention of doing any further screening because the last thing it wanted to learn was that a significant number of the Ukrainians were war criminals or Soviet citizens or both.

Lord Brimelow, retired after a long distinguished diplomatic career, commented on the Wilkinson draft in a 1992 letter: "In general, the duty of the civil servants who draft letters for Ministers to sign in reply to criticisms of the Government's policy is to defend that policy. It is traditional wisdom that one should expose as little surface as possible. This involves being economical with the truth; but one should not actively mislead." It was his cautious judgment that several of the Wilkinson letters he had reviewed were "ill-judged and regrettable."[3]

Among the letters Brimelow judged "misleading" was a communication offered in response to an angry letter by Oxford graduate Leslie W. Carruthers, who wrote: "It is well to know that the members of the blood covered 1st Galician Division are not to be let loose and pampered on our farms and in our industries and that honest British folk will not be insulted by an invitation to work beside these perambulating depravities... That any who fought against Britain and her Allies should in any circumstances receive British protection is a total enormity."[4]

The Foreign Office replied: "These prisoners of war were members of the 1st Ukrainian Division of the Wehrmacht which was not an SS unit and whose record appears to be free from atrocities. It is possible, however, that some of its members were survivors of the 1st Galician Division which was for a while designated as an SS unit and which, it is alleged, did not have such a clean record. Nevertheless, the screening of groups of these men by Soviet and British teams has failed to reveal any war criminals although further screening will take place in this country to make certain that such is the case."[5]

The statement, drafted by Wilkinson and signed by McNeil, was sharply challenged by an English language newspaper published in Rome: "The statement has occasioned considerable surprise in Rome press circles since the 'Galician Division' was notorious for its cruelty and belonged to an SS formation. No Soviet representatives took part in any check-up of these 8,000 men, as the British military authorities invariably replied with a refusal when approached by Soviet representatives on the subject. Mr. McNeil's statement is clearly intended to mislead public opinion."[6]

Even more scathing was the letter addressed to Member of Parliament Richard Crossman by H.L. Hyams, one of his Coventry constituents:

While denying asylum to thousands of displaced persons and having no compassion on these poor, homeless, starving creatures, the British government brought into the country 8,000 bloodthirsty cut-throats, part of a German force which was guilty of the most brutal atrocities against defenceless people during the war. One can't help feeling there is something wrong with the mentality of a government, especially a Socialist government, which on the one hand refuses to give succor to so many helpless creatures whose only 'crime' was they were either Jews or defied the Nazi hordes, and on the other hand opens the doors of this country to scoundrels whose entry is an insult to every decent British subject.[7]

The civil servants in the Foreign Office scurried to find a convincing response to Hyam's bitter letter. Several versions were drafted, each of them evasive and confusing. Generally, they played with the same themes: "There is no evidence that any of these Ukrainians are 'bloodthirsty cut-throats.' Cross-sections of them have been screened... by British and Soviet missions without any war criminals revealed... We have no record of the 1st Ukrainian Division... having ever been involved in acts of barbarity in the service of the enemy. An earlier Ukrainian formation, which, it is alleged did participate in such activities, was annihilated on the Russian Front in July 1944."[8]

Another version stressed "screening by Soviet and British teams" and denied that the Division had been an SS unit or that it had participated in atrocities. Both versions promised that "further screening will take place [once the unit arrives in England] to make certain such is the case."[9]

Not all the correspondence addressed to the government was hostile to the Division. The Tolstoy Foundation, representing the Countess Alexandra Tolstoy, daughter of the famous Russian writer, Leo Tolstoy, dispatched lengthy letters to members of parliament extolling the religiosity and anti-Bolshevik virtues of the Division's members.

The Manchester *Guardian* published a lengthy letter composed by Tracy Philipps, the former British secret agent who played a major role in the organization of the Ukrainian Canadian Committee—a role that will be fully described in a later chapter. Philipps claimed: "The Division was organized from Ukrainian patriotic and religious reasons, primarily to in order to save Ukrainian youth from being...forcibly conscripted into German regular forces which would be used anywhere by the Germans at will, and also in order that as far as humanly possible, these boys of Christian ethic and Western tradition should not be used against the Western Allies." Philipps takes pains to mention that Ukrainians in Canada had "intermarried with 'Anglo-Saxon' stock," and that their "sturdy womenfolk are in value and habit the equal of the Baltic girls who have made themselves such welcome workers here..." A firm believer in the call of blood and soil,

Philipps adds: "Love of farming is in these men's blood and they are itching to get their hands into the soil to see it bring forth fruit in due season."[10]

Compromise and Cover Up

Meanwhile, the Foreign Office, the Home Office and the Ministry of Labour were engaged in numerous, heated discussions regarding the Ukrainian Division. British manpower was in short supply because Britain's army was not due to be fully demobilized until 1950. As we have previously noted, British forces were needed to police Palestine and to retain a grip on anachronistic vestiges of Empire in faraway places such as Burma and India. The point was made at these inter-departmental meetings that it would be extremely embarrassing to Attlee's Labour Government if the British army veterans were to come home and find their jobs occupied by foreigners who had fought alongside their former enemies. A guarantee was, therefore, exacted by the Ministry of Labour that when the British army was fully demobilized—probably by 1950—the Ukrainians would be gone and the jobs would be freely available to the returning servicemen.

This pragmatic approach meant that another home would have to be found for the Ukrainians once their services were no longer needed. Meanwhile, the Foreign Office worked diligently to prevent any close examination of the members of the 1st Division of the Ukrainian Army. In February 1948, Bohdan Panchuk, the former Royal Canadian Airforce Officer who headed the London-based Ukrainian Relief Bureau, sought to enlist the aid of A.W.H. Wilkinson to prevent the impending deportation from Belgium of a Division member, Jaroslav Petriw. According to Panchuk, Petriw had chosen to join his family in Belgium rather than come to England with the rest of the Division. The Belgian authorities had arrested Petriw and charged him with being "a member of a criminal organization" and handed him over to British military authorities. They, in turn, were proposing to send Petriw to Germany for trial.

Petriw should be freed, Panchuk insisted, because "Petriw's case was no different from that of all the other Ukrainians in this country." Wilkinson agreed to look into the matter but discovered after investigation that Petriw was "undoubtedly a most objectionable individual" who had served as a sergeant in the SS and participated in the fighting against the British forces in North Africa. Given Petriw's record, Wilkinson advised Panchuk, that this was hardly the kind of case in which either the Foreign Office or Panchuk should intervene. Panchuk, fearful of losing credibility with the best friend he had in the Foreign Office, agreed to drop the case instantly.

Despite the best efforts of McNeil and Wilkinson to smooth the Ukrainian's entry, the issue remained troublesome. In March 1948, the Soviet government again named 124 of the Division's Ukrainian officers as war criminals and demanded the British turn them over. The Home Office grew nervous and declared itself opposed to the admission of the 124 so long as the Soviet government insisted they were war criminals. Rather than bring them to England, the Home Office recommended that the Ukrainian officers be shipped to Germany where the War Office could do a thorough investigation and determine whether or not they should be handed over to the Russians.[11]

Wilkinson countered with the recently received Haldane Porter Report:

From this report it seems unlikely that more than a handful, if any, of these Ukrainian officers are Soviet nationals by our definition. It also seems that the "SS" part of the description of the Galician Division was largely a misnomer and that it could certainly not be held to apply to the bulk of the Ukrainian POW in this country.[12]

Meanwhile, British and American right-wing voices, which had campaigned to keep their respective countries from entering the war against Hitler, were now organizing to rescue as many of the Nazi's henchmen as possible. Loud cries were heard denouncing the Nuremberg Trials as "revanchist," "contrary to international law" and "victor's justice." Articles and books accused the Allies of atrocities equal to those committed by the Nazis.[13]

In the years prior to Pearl Harbor, the pro-Nazi German-American Bund held mass meetings in Manhattan and paraded through the streets of American cities with large German populations. Isolationist groups, some believing genuinely in the evil of war, others using isolationism as camouflage for their pro-fascist sentiments, sought to deny Britain arms and delay America's entry into the war. Powerful British and American economic interests lobbied behind the scenes to protect their German investments.

British journalist Tom Bower in his *Blind Eye to Murder*, remarks: "Ethnic German communities were unwilling to believe stories about gas chambers in Poland...Jewish refugees...were members of the Zionist conspiracy still intent on destroying Germany... remnants of the bacillus which was even infecting America."[14] Silenced temporarily while the war was still being fought, they came out of the shadows again in the post-war period to take up the defence of quislings, collaborators and war criminals. They attacked the Nuremberg Trials as an abuse of justice, proclaimed the innocence of Nazi officials who were "merely following orders" and condemned the repatriation of Cossack, Chetnik and Ustasha troops under the Yalta Agreement.

Stonewalling

Caught between those who were shocked by the government's willingness to import Ukrainian Waffen-SS men to the United Kingdom and those who demanded that Britain open the gates even wider to enemy collaborators, the Foreign Office replied testily to its critics. In a letter to an opposition Member of Parliament who was calling for increased employment opportunities for the Ukrainian veterans, Minister of State Hector McNeil argued uncharacteristically that "the Ukrainians have already been allowed to volunteer for civilian employment in this country without any quota restrictions such as we have applied in the cases of German prisoners." McNeil reminded the M.P. that members of the 1st Ukrainian Division "are believed to have served voluntarily in a Waffen-SS Division on the Eastern Front" and therefore "it is hard to see that they have any greater claim than the numerous ex-enemy soldiers of non-German nationality."[15] In this letter, as in many Foreign Office, War Office and Home Office communications preserved in the London Public Record Office, it is clear that McNeil and his subordinates held no illusions regarding the nature of the Halychyna Division. Yet the Secretary of State and his colleagues were ready to distort the truth for what they considered reasons of state.

In June 1948, the Soviet Ambassador to the United Kingdom, M. Zaroubin, once again raised the question of the 124 officers of the "S.S. Galichina [sic] accused of war crimes." Once again the ambassador demanded their surrender to Soviet authorities and once again the Foreign Office dismissed the Soviet request as "specious." In his draft reply to the ambassador C.R.A. Rae, of the Northern Department, argued: "Of course we know that the SS...committed war crimes, but my impression is that the Galichina Division [sic] was neither long nor actively engaged on the Russian Front."[16]

Some days later, the Refugee Department asked whether the Nuremberg Tribunal's decision to declare the whole of the SS a criminal organization didn't obligate the United Kingdom to hand over the 124 Division officers demanded by the Russians. Determined to head off any such notions, Wilkinson drafted another of the many memoranda in which he skillfully misstated facts and sowed confusion:

> While there is reason to believe that at least some of the officers concerned were voluntary members of a unit which for a while was given the title of a Waffen SS Division, there is reason to believe they did not join it when it was given that title, but before. In any case, the title was subsequently dropped and the origin al division ceased to exist after being cut to pieces at the battle of Brody. In the absence of clear evidence that these officers knowingly joined a <u>Waffen S.S. Division,</u> [underlined in the original] I do not think there are anygrounds for them to be indictable under the Nuremberg decisions as members of a criminal organization.[17]

Regardless of the individual guilt or innocence of the 124 Halychyna officers that were the subject of so much correspondence, the arguments offered up by McNeil, Boothby, Wilkinson and Rae were less than honest. Even if they were not cognizant of the truth, they made strenuous efforts to avoid learning it.

None of this was inadvertent or due to bureaucratic fumbling. "Whitehall knew what it was doing," Bower stated in a series of articles in the London *Times* describing how the Ukrainian Division arrived in England."[18]

Professor David Cesarani, former Director of Studies at London's Institute of Contemporary History and Principal Researcher for the All-Party Parliamentary War Crimes Group, comes to a similar conclusion. He accuses the Foreign Office in particular of sanitizing the Ukrainian Division's history and deliberately deflecting questions raised in Parliament:

> Protests from other departments of state were neutralized by use of misleading and selective information. Even if the Soviet claims that the unit contained war criminals were flimsy, no great effort was made to check them. The caveats in the various screening reports were overlooked, while the reservations of the Home Office were brushed aside. The frequently expressed suspicions concerning the Division and the men in it were not followed up.[19]

The men of the Division were scattered over the United Kingdom in former German prisoner of war camps located in the vicinity of Sheffield, Lincoln, Norwich, Cambridge, Willesden, Edinburgh, and Glasgow. One hundred and twenty-seven officers were concentrated in a camp at Allington in the Midlands. The largest number of enlisted men were held in camps at Hampton Green Camp in Norfolk (1,593) and Camp Victoria at Bury St. Edmunds (1,196). All in all, some 8,250 members of the Division were present and accounted for in Britain by July, 1948.[20]

As 1950 approached, the year in which the Division was to leave England and settle elsewhere, British bureaucrats cast about desperately to find a new destination for the Ukrainian SS men. At the heart of what had once been a great empire, British civil servants still tended to think in colonial terms. Just as intractable second sons of the English aristocracy who made an embarrassing nuisance of themselves at home were traditionally sent off to make a career in the colonies, troublesome problems, incapable of resolution in Britain, were passed on to the Commonwealth. If Britain wanted to rid itself of the bulk of the Galician Division, what better solution than to ship them off to Canada, Australia and other British territories.

However, Canada's immigration regulations forbade the entry of anyone still classified as a prisoner of war. Other countries had similar restrictions. Obviously, if their departure was to be expedited, the Galician Division would have to be "civilianized" as quickly as possible. Beginning in 1948, the first contingents of the Division were briefly interviewed by British immigration officials. With few exceptions, the officials were unable to speak Ukrainian and, as a result, they learned nothing from the interviews.

Although the Home Office would have preferred to clear out all of the Ukrainians brought to Britain in 1947, about 1,500 decided to remain in England and augment the small pre-war Ukrainian community centered on Bradford.

Emboldened by the knowledge that they had cultivated powerful friends in government, the members of the Division who remained in England took to representing themselves as "freedom fighters" and holding annual regimental church parades. They prevailed on the Provost of Bradford Cathedral to allow them to erect a plaque in honour of their political and spiritual mentors in the OUN. To this day, Bradford remains a major centre of Ukrainian culture in the Ukrainian Diaspora and a hotbed of Ukrainian nationalist propaganda.

Notes

1. PRO, FO 371/66712, Felix Wirth to Tom Driberg, June 7, 1947.

2. PRO, FO 371/66712.

3. Private correspondence, Brimelow to Littman, December 4, 1992.

4. PRO, FO 371/66712 ,Carruthers letter, date indistinct.

5. PRO, FO 371/66712, Letter to Carruthers signed by P. Gore-Booth, July 9, 1947.

6. PRO, FO 371/66712, The article quoted is reproduced in its original in the FO file but there is no identification of the newspaper in which it was published or the date on which it appeared. Very sloppy of the Foreign Office.

7. PRO, FO 371/66712, M.L. Hyams to R.H. S. Crossman, Esq., June 128, 1947.

8. PRO, FO 371/66712, Wilkinson to Crossman.

9. *Ibid.* Unsigned to L.W. Carruthers, Esq. July 9, 1947.

10. PRO, FO 371/66712, Extract from the *Manchester Guardian* of June 12, 1947, "UKRAINIANS IN ENGLAND."

11. PRO, FO 371/71662/136950.

12. PRO, FO 371/71662/136950.

13. Among others, see: Montgomery Belgion, *Victor's Justice* (Hinsdale, Illinois: Henry Regnery Co., 1949).

14. Bower, *Blind Eye to Murder*, 313.

15. PRO, FO 371/72078/136531, Minister of State Hector McNeil to The Right Honourable Oliver Stanley, M.C., M.P., June 18, 1948.

16. PRO, FO 371/71663/136950, Draft memorandum N 7500/70/38, June 30, 1948.

17. PRO, FO 371/71663/136950, A.W. H. Wilkinson to Refugee Department, July 30, 1948.

18. Tom Bower, "How the SS came to Britain," The *Times* (London), August 20, 1987, 8.

19. David Cesarani, *Justice Delayed*, 132.

20. PRO, WO/321/13190, Association of Ukrainians in Great Britain to War Office, July 19, 1948.

CHAPTER 14

LOYALTIES IN DOUBT

BETWEEN THE TWO GREAT WARS, ENGLISH CANADA SAW ITSELF as an Anglo-Saxon country, British to the core. The United Kingdom was referred to as "the Mother Country" and there was strong pressure to conform in language and custom to the British model. Yet, almost half the population outside French-speaking Quebec was of non-British origin with large contingents of Germans, Slavs, Italians and Japanese. As the threat of war loomed larger in 1938 and 1939, the inevitable question arose: "How loyal will these people be in the event of war? What shall we do in the event they prove troublesome?"

In World War I, the Canadian government, doubting the loyalty of German and Austrian citizens, had thrown large numbers of them into internment camps as "enemy aliens." The bulk of the 180,000 Ukrainian settlers who arrived in Canada before World War I—largely Carpatho-Ukrainian in origin—had taken root in Canadian soil and "discarded whatever attachments they may have had to their Austro-Hungarian Fatherland."[1] However, few of the 70,000 who arrived between 1910 and 1914 had managed to apply for their citizenship papers and, therefore, remained Austrian citizens.[2] When war broke out, they fell under the same suspicion as other enemy aliens.

Those suspicions were aggravated when Bishop Nykyta Budka of the Ukrainian Greek Orthodox church and Dr. Alexander Sushko, editor of the Catholic *Kanadyiskyi rusyn* proclaimed their loyalty to Austria and the Hapsburg dynasty and issued a call for Ukrainians in Canada to return to return home in order to "defend the Fatherland" and their beloved Emperor Franz Josef.[3] Several days later, Bishop Budka, made aware of the serious damage his sermons and pastoral letters were imposing on his parishioners, changed tack and urged his followers "to join the colours of our new fatherland...which has taken us to its bosom and given us protection under the banner of Liberty of the British Empire."[4]

But the damage was done and as a result, thousands of Ukrainians in Canada were interned, abused by their neighbors and fired from their jobs. In addition, the Canadian government of the time utilized the War Times Election Act to disenfranchise the detainees for ten years after the war had ended.[5]

For those interned or put "behind the wire" for the war's duration, the experience was physically punishing and psychologically demeaning. The men were separated from their families and confined in remote lumber camps where they were compelled to do heavy work in all kinds of weather. They felt victimized for deeds and events that were not of their doing. Above all, they saw their internment as further proof of the prevalent Anglo-Canadian attitude that Ukrainian immigrants were too socially and economically backward to take part in building a great nation.[6] Although more than 10,000 Ukrainian Canadians voluntarily joined the armed forces, many Ukrainians, including priests were deported after World War I.[7]

Between the wars, the Ukrainian population in Canada continued to grow, augmented by a relatively high birth rate and continued immigration. By 1939, Ukrainians had grown to be the fourth largest ethnic group in Canada. After the British and the French, only the Germans were more numerous. In the three Prairie Provinces, Manitoba, Saskatchewan and Alberta, they comprised ten percent of the population. Politically, they ranged from the centre to the extremes of left and right. Canadian historian Lita-Rose Betcherman, in her analysis of pro-fascist movements in Canada, saw the Ukrainian community of the time as divided into "left" and "right" wings:

> Those who had emigrated during the Tsarist regime tended to be pro-communist, while those who came over during the twenties were mainly anti-communist because the Bolshevik Revolution had failed to produce an independent Ukraine. Among the latter were right-wing nationalists who continued their struggle for the liberation of their homeland, principally by fighting their pro-communist compatriots. Their militant anti-communism combined with a [culturally inherited] dislike of the Jews, made them ready recruits for a fascist movement.[8]

The same sentiment was expressed by Deputy Minister of External Affairs, O.D. Skelton who described the Ukrainian community as sharply "divided on political lines between Communists and irredentist nationalists."[9]

As the possibility of war increased in 1938 and 1939, the Canadian government was far from sure it could count on the loyalty of Canada's Ukrainians. As far as Ottawa could tell, one third of the community was communist, one third broadly democratic and another third distinctly pro-fascist. Ottawa's best information concerned the communist third, since Canada's federal police force, the Royal Canadian Mounted Police (RCMP), had long ago infiltrated the Communist Party of Canada. In a crisis, it needed only to reach out to arrest its leaders, followers and sympathizers. As it happened, Ukrainian Canadians were an important part of the Communist Party of Canada; indeed, the largest

krainian section.[10] However, the RCMP—pre-occupied
own "Commies"—had neglected to develop equally reli-
far right.

ome on September 1, 1939, the bulk of the Ukrainian community did,
The communist wing opposed the war because Stalin had concluded a
pact with Hitler earlier in the year. Communist movements world-wide
red to support the Comintern, by condemning the war as "imperialist" and ag-
against it. The Canadian government declared the Communist Party illegal and
rested its leaders. By Order-in-Council the leftist Ukrainian Labour Temples, meeting halls, libraries, musical instruments and newspapers were seized by the Crown and sold at giveaway prices to their right-wing opponents.

Operation Barbarossa, the German invasion of the Soviet Union in June 1941, brought a rapid change of heart in the communist ranks. Overnight, the war changed from a reactionary imperialist conflict to a holy war against fascism. Communist leaders, released from internment camps, urged their members to join the armed forces, buy Victory Bonds and work hard to produce food and munitions.

The Ukrainian nationalists on the right opposed the war on other grounds. They welcomed the Nazi destruction of their traditional Polish enemies and trusted that the Germans would recognize an independent Ukraine, free of Jews and Poles, reaching from the Carpathians to the Caucasus.

Three organizations on the Ukrainian right could fairly be described as fascist in outlook at the time: The United Hetmen, the *Sichovi Stril'tsi* (Sich Sharpshooters) and the Ukrainian Nationalist Federation (UNF). The Hetman organization dreamed of restoring the monarchy in Ukraine and establish a military dictatorship modelled on Mussolini and Italian Fascism. The *Sichovi Stril'tsi* operated under the leadership of Colonel Konovalets who, as we have seen, maintained close ties with the *Abwehr*.

The Ukrainian Nationalist Federation, the largest and most powerful of the three, was described in a confidential 1940 report to the Department of War Services as "rabid admirers of the Nazi system:"[11]

> They see the only salvation of the Ukraine in the adaptation and imitation of Nazi methods. Till the outbreak of the present war, their official organ, *The New Pathway* of Saskatoon, roundly berated the other Ukrainian groups in Canada for their democratic leanings, even so far as to call them traitors... However, the outbreak of the war in 1939 has toned down their ardent admiration of Hitler...to the extent of declaring themselves willing to support the Canadian war effort. Yet this sudden and too obviously advertised loyalty to the British cause is taken by many

Ukrainians with a proverbial pinch of salt [beca
nounced or rejected those of their European leaders
now serve in the German army.[12]

The UNF was, of course, the Canadian branch of the OUN (Organiz
Nationalists). The Canadian president was Wladimir Kossar and its exe
was W. Swystun. At UNF banquets in the thirties, the German Consul Ge
his swastika emblem on his lapel, was honoured with a seat at the head table.

At the same time, a U.S. congressional committee was investigating Fascist and C
munist connections in the United States. Evidence offered to the Dies Committee re
vealed that the UNF's counterpart in the United States, The Organization for the Rebirth
of Ukraine (ODVU), had been in touch with agents in Italy "who were working for the
Nazi and Italian regime." The committee counsel accused the ODVU of printing material
"which struck at the very heart of American democratic institutions and was distinctly
pro-Nazi and pro-Fascist."[13] Professor Alexander Granovsky, president of the ODVU,
admitted "that part of the funds for the upkeep of [ODVU's] New York and Washington
offices were supplied by Germany."[14]

The Canadian and U.S. Ukrainian nationalist organizations were closely linked. On
July 18, 1939, Canada's High Commissioner in London advised the Minister of External
Affairs that "Mr. Wladimir Kossar (President of the Ukrainian National federation of
Canada) called at this office yesterday along with one Alexander Granovsky of Minne-
sota." The two Ukrainian nationalist leaders asked the Commissioner's assistance in
meeting with representatives of Britain's Foreign Office.[15]

The nationalists' support of Hitler's Germany was not exclusively a matter of ideology and rhetoric; it was also expressed by force of arms. "In Poland we have a
well-developed secret military organization which works both among the civilian population and the Ukrainian ranks of the Polish army," wrote a well-informed Ukrainian-Canadian in a secret report to his Member of Parliament.[16]

Kirkconnell, Philipps, Simpson and the Founding of the UCC

Canadian Professor of English Literature, Watson Kirkconnell, dabbled in many fields. A
skilled linguist he was capable of reviewing works in Icelandic, Ukrainian, Russian and
Lithuanian. In his 1939 book, *Canada, Europe and Hitler*, he described the UNF as a "modi-
fied branch of the OUN" and the latter as "perverted patriots... Ukrainian Nazis,
anti-Semitic, markedly military, authoritarian and anti-democratic."[17] Ironically, scarcely
a year later Kirkconnell was appointed an "honorary advisor" to the same organization
he had so forthrightly condemned.[18]

"section" of the Party ... *Tribune* photo shows Kirkconnell flanked by a covey of
over the years with hund... U... ...le under the photograph reads: "Leading Ukrainians met
able information on th... ...nd formed a committee to co-ordinate work in Canada for Ukrai-

When war ...a...pendence... Prof. Watson Kirkconnell, member honorary advisory
in fact, oppose it

non-aggressio... ...bout Kirkconnell's remarkable transformation? Part of the explana-
were requi...ctivities of a British secret agent named Tracy Philipps.

itating ...ce of war quickened, the Canadian government grew increasingly anxious
ar... ...ome means to encourage the Ukrainian community to support the war effort.
...nable to find the solution on its own, Ottawa imported a "Ukrainian expert" to survey
the situation and formulate a "game plan." The "expert" was British secret agent Tracy
Philipps, who described himself as a soldier, anthropologist, administrator and diplomatic correspondent who had seen service in Arabia with the legendary T.E. Lawrence.
His other assignments took him to Italy, Africa, Palestine, Greece, Bulgaria, Turkey, and
of course, Ukraine.

Philipps travelled to the Soviet Ukraine in 1924 in the guise of a famine relief worker
and became emotionally enmeshed in the nationalist's campaign for Ukrainian independence. On his return to England, he began to deluge the Foreign Office with long,
complicated memoranda in which he sought to convince the government that the ultimate fate of the British Empire depended on the restoration of an independent Ukraine.
His flaming enthusiasm on the subject was greeted with considerable amusement by the
Foreign Office civil servants who were the targets of his frequent communications.

Philipps arrived in Canada early in 1940 as the guest of the Department for External
Affairs. His first assignment, arranged by the Department of National War Services, required him to set out on a cross-country tour to test the temper of the Canadian Ukrainian community. His survey confirmed what had long been suspected—there was,
indeed, danger on the right. Although there was a sizeable, moderate, middle group such
as the Ukrainian Self-Reliance Organization that saw Canada as its homeland and supported its democratic institutions, the three major right-wing organizations were not inclined to be supportive of the war effort.

On his return from his tour, Philipps announced that a new Ukrainian umbrella organization was needed to rally the community to King and Country. His plan was to dilute
the influence of the pro-Nazi UNF by including them in a coalition with more moderate
groups with more democratic leanings. The honey in the trap was the promise of Canada's support for an independent Ukraine after the war was won.

His report received the full approval of the Department of External Affairs, the Department of National War Services and Canada's federal police force, the Royal Canadian Mounted Police (RCMP). Philipps went to work at once to forge his broad gauge committee, but despite his official position, found the going heavy. The UNF had only recently insisted that all other Ukrainian organizations renounce their democratic convictions and accept the UNF ideology as their own while the democratic Self-Reliance League resolved it did not want "to belong to any central committee which would include representatives of the (UNF) because we don't want to have anything to cover up in Canada, we want to keep ourselves in the open."[20]

Finally, in a forceful confrontation, Philipps told Wasyl Swystun, a Winnipeg lawyer and Executive Secretary of the UNF, that he was "doing criminal work by splitting the Ukrainians in Canada wide open... He told the Kushnir-Swystun gang there must be one committee or else, and this got the ball rolling." While Philipps didn't specify what he meant by "or else" his meaning was clear. "It is general knowledge that members of the Ukrainian National Federation seem to be very much afraid of the 'wire fence', the internment camp," a Vancouver member of the UCC confided to an RCMP officer.[21]

Philipps played the role of the secret agent to the hilt, implying mysterious connections and vast powers. By November 19, 1940, he had succeeded by intimidation, promises and persuasion in uniting all the nationalist groups in a "united Canadian front." The Winnipeg *Free Press* reported: "The Ukrainian Canadians have decided to bury the hatchet of differences and dissensions which for years have kept them divided into rival groups. After a series of conferences and meetings they have decided to unite their groups and parties into one Canadian front."[22]

Thus was born the Representative Committee of Ukrainian Canadians, forerunner to the Ukrainian Canadian Committee, brainchild of a British secret agent hired to advise the Canadian government on how to persuade Ukrainian Canadians to support the war effort.

Who paid Philipps? Even men of mystery must earn money to support families. According to Philipps, he worked for the RCMP, External Affairs and the Department of National War Services in turn. The record shows that on May 2, 1941, RCMP Commissioner S. T. Wood wrote to Philipps offering him "employment for a period of three months, at $12.20 per diem," and the title "Director General, European Department." Philipps accepted the appointment but wrote back to convey his disappointment at the smallness of his proposed salary.[23]

The "Kushnir-Swystun gang" lost no time taking control of the new organization. The Rev. Dr. William Kushnir, an ardent nationalist and Chancellor of the Ukrainian

Catholic Bishop was elected president and W. Swystun, the vice-president. Whether Philipps wished it or not, the UNF became the dominant force in the coalition.

Organizational unity did not, however, solve all problems. Despite ardent public declarations of loyalty to Canada, democracy and the British Empire, UNF members remained "pro-Nazi in their hearts."[24]

Informants within the Ukrainian community reported to the RCMP that UNF leaders had learned to dance to a different tune but had not changed their ideological stripes. "You cannot change a man with a pro-totalitarian mentality into a champion of democracy in a fortnight," a moderate Ukrainian confided to an RCMP officer. Aware that the transition might not come easily, the government arranged the appointment of two eminent advisors, Professors George W. Simpson and Watson Kirkconnell.

Simpson, who taught at the University of Saskatchewan, boasted a long association with the Ukrainian nationalist community. In 1937, he had visited Hetman Skoropadsky in Berlin and greeted Skoropadsky's son when the latter visited Saskatoon.[25]

Kirkconnell, who taught at McMaster University in Hamilton, Ontario, joined Simpson in coaching the Canadian branch of the UNF and defending it against all comers. It became their task to teach the old gang the new words and music; to instruct them on how to make democratic noises in public no matter what their private convictions.[26]

"As I promised last night," Kirkconnell wrote Swystun, "I am enclosing herewith my suggested draft of a memorandum for the Representative Committee. I think it will be most effective to prepare it as Canadians and British subjects...and while stating the Ukrainian case clearly and positively, to avoid provocative references to countries with which the Allies are not at war." Kirkconnell recommended the issuance of a lengthy statement, replete with fulsome pledges of loyalty to the Crown and unswerving dedication to democracy for the use of the same groups he had denounced as totalitarian the previous year.

Simpson, Kirkconnell and Philipps came "to be looked upon by UNF members as their 'patron saints' and 'protective shields' insofar as the security of the organization was concerned in wartime," says a secret report to the RCMP found in the Public Archives of Canada.[27] They also joined in the clamor for an independent Ukraine in their own name, giving newspaper interviews, delivering radio addresses, and swamping government agencies with memoranda advocating the nationalist position.

At some point, External Affairs became disillusioned with the trio. The civil servants at External Affairs appreciated that the trio had converted the nationalist Ukrainian community into loyal Canadian citizens but they didn't appreciate the constant deluge of notes and memoranda calling on the government to announce its support for an independent Ukraine. The Department found their efforts particularly embarrassing since the Ukrainian state visualized by the OUN and the UNF would have to be carved from the territories of Canada's hard-fighting allies, Poland, Czechoslovakia and the USSR.[28]

"It is essential that Tracy Philipps should cease to have any connection with the Canadian government... and should be sent back to the United Kingdom where he can do less harm," the Canadian Secretary of State for External Affairs confided to Canada's ambassador to the USSR in a "most secret" dispatch on May 17, 1943.[29]

"I presume there is nothing we can do to persuade Kirkconnell to leave his hobby alone," George de T. Glazebrook of External Affairs wrote in a note to his colleague Norman Robertson.[30]

But Philipps, Kirkconnell and Simpson were not readily retired. They had embedded themselves deeply in the Committee on Cooperation in Canadian Citizenship sponsored by the Department of War Services—another of Philipps brain waves. The Committee, established on October 30, 1941, was intended to serve as a "permanent Government agency... for work amongst foreign language groups." Not only were Philipps and Simpson founding members, they were also on the Committee's payroll.[31]

Philipps continued his practice of deluging government officials with lengthy memoranda denouncing the Soviet's call for a second military front and inveighing against Pan-Slavism as a Russian plot. In response, Philipps was mocked and criticized in a widely-circulated inter-departmental memorandum: "[Philipps] is so perturbed about 'Communism' that he has little energy to devise ways and means of enlisting the cooperation of foreign-born persons of European origin in the common fight."[32] Unable to find a sympathetic audience in Ottawa, Philipps visited the U.S. State Department in Washington to lecture them on the dangers of Pan-Slavism. Without clearing his comments with anyone in Ottawa, he boasted that his views coincided with those of the Canadian government. External Affairs was incensed by this unauthorized visit and it was not long before Philipps was dismissed. He hung about for a while, hoping for other employment, but when none was forthcoming he returned to England.[33]

Although the Canadian Citizenship Committee was later disbanded and its duties assigned to other departments, it nevertheless gave the Representative Committee intimate access to the RCMP, External Affairs and the Department of War Services. With Philipps organizing and maneuvering from within and Kirkconnell and Simpson coaching on the field, organizations once feared subversive, gained easy access to Ottawa decision makers. But as the trio lost influence, their Ukrainian pupils began to feel that they could do better without their intercession and a feeling of coldness increasingly separated the Ukrainian organizations from their mentors.

Panchuk and the Central Ukrainian Relief Bureau

As the war drew to a close, the Ukrainian Canadian Committee shifted its focus from winning the war against fascism to preserving the fascist-inspired Galician Division. Long before civilian visitors received permission to visit their camp at Rimini, Royal Canadian Air Force officers of Ukrainian origin extended their travel orders to visit with Bishop Buchko and through him with the Ukrainian Division's camp in Riccione. The information they gained from Buchko was reported to the Committee's headquarters in London and Winnipeg.[34]

Heading the effort in England was Pilot Officer Gordon Richard Bohdan Panchuk of the Royal Canadian Air Force. A former school teacher and son of Ukrainian pioneers to Canada, Panchuk was a born organizer who spent all of his free time searching out Ukrainian communities in the United Kingdom once he arrived overseas. He founded the Ukrainian Canadian Servicemen's Association (UCSA) which served as a much needed canteen for Ukrainian-Canadian and Ukrainian-American soldiers in London. Panchuk used the experience and contacts he had made organizing the UCSA to create the Central Ukrainian Relief Bureau (CURB), which by late 1945 had begun refugee relief operations on the continent. In the name of the latter organization, Panchuk deluged the British Foreign Office with voluminous memoranda calling for the rescue of the Galician Division and its transfer first to England and subsequently to Canada. The Ukrainian Canadian Committee and its American counterpart, the United Ukrainian American Relief Committee recognized Panchuk's organization as their European agent.

Panchuk, who confessed that he knew nothing of the Division until their surrender in Austria in the last days of the war, began an incessant campaign to whitewash the Division. "We did all we could to familiarize the West with the background of the Division, who they were, where they were, and so on," he stated. "We wanted to make certain that they were not unjustly treated as war criminals or Nazis, since we knew quite a bit about them."[35] What Panchuk knew of the Division he learned primarily from Ukrainian Catholic Bishop Ivan Buchko who resided in Rome, Professor Kubijovyc who had fled to Munich and Genèral Shandruk who was under American protection in Germany. Ukrainian Canadian airmen flying post-war missions to major European cities became his emissaries.[36]

According to Panchuk, the War Office called him in and asked him to serve as their Consultant on Ukrainian Affairs, a task he welcomed and readily undertook. In return, he requested that the War Office do nothing affecting Ukrainians, particularly the Galicia Division, without seeking his advice.[37]

The Central Ukrainian Relief Bureau (CURB) lost no time in applying for permission to visit the Rimini camp. As early as November 27, 1945, CURB requested visas for Rev. Kushnir and a half-dozen additional Ukrainian representatives to visit a number of Uniate Ukrainian communities in Germany. Among the representatives listed was the ubiquitous Dmitri Dontsov, the OUN ideologue, whose name appeared as CURB's delegate from France.

Kushnir visited the Ukrainian Division in March 1946. His visit caused considerable anxiety on the part of the British Military Government which was trying to keep the lid on tensions between the Soviets and the Western Allies. British Foreign Secretary Ernest Bevin had assured Soviet Foreign Minister Molotov that the British and American governments would take steps to prevent any action which was hostile to the Soviet Union in the British and American sectors in Germany. Therefore, they would have preferred to bar Kushnir entirely, but the Foreign Office was uncertain "whether it is better to face possible protests from the Russians for allowing Dr. Kushnir to visit Germany or possible protests from the Ukrainians for preventing him from doing so."[38] It was felt necessary to instruct Kushnir that "he should abstain from political activities to which the Soviets might take objection and you would be well advised to caution him about the undertaking we made at Potsdam not to tolerate any anti-Soviet activities in our zone.[39]

Kushnir apparently ignored the Foreign Office's admonitions to avoid inflammatory political statements. In his homily to the troops, he prophesied the early start of a third world war in which the Division would play a major role.[40]

The leaflets and pamphlets supplied to the Division for "educational purposes" by the Ukrainian Relief Bureau were at times so inflammatory that the Political Branch of the British Military Government ordered them censored. Among the items considered excessive was a tirade by Kirkconnell, titled "The Ukrainian Agony" in which the McMaster University political scientist denounced the Yalta Agreement and denounced the Atlantic Charter as a "mockery marked by the blood of murdered millions."[41] Similarly, a booklet by Lancelot Lawton accused the Jews of grinding the Ukrainian peasants "into misery and destruction." In the same booklet, Lawton proclaimed the people of Ukraine as racially superior to the Russians and praised the Black Hundreds, the pogromists who murdered thousands of Ukrainian Jews.[42]

Panchuk and Kushnir were seen as "pains in the neck" by the civil servants in the Foreign Office.[43] Repeatedly, British Foreign Office memoranda remind the recipient that Panchuk has "no official status whatsoever" in Canadian eyes, even if he is behaving as if he were Canada's ambassador to Great Britain.[44] The attitude of the Canadian government, they reported, "is one of reserve" and that they are to be given "normal assistance and no more."[45] Nevertheless, Panchuk and Kushnir were never turned away because the possibility existed that they could be instrumental in persuading the Canadian government to allow the settlement of large numbers of the Division members in the Dominion when the time was ripe. The UCC representatives boasted of their influence with Canadian politicians and the eagerness of Canadian Ukrainians to welcome and assist their countrymen once the roadblocks to their immigration had been cleared away. For Cabinet Ministers who would have to answer to Parliament if the Ukrainians were still hanging about after the British troops came marching home, Panchuk and Kushnir's influence—no matter how minimal—could not be lightly dismissed.

Early indications from Canada were far from promising. On February 13, 1946, Brimelow noted, "Mr. Holmes of Canada House thinks, but cannot state categorically, that the Government of Canada is opposed to immigration of Ukrainians in any numbers."[46] The matter was still far from resolved a year later when O.D.O Robinson of the Home Office asked Boothby what consideration the Cabinet had given to the ultimate disposal of the Division: "You refer to the prospect of some of these individuals being accepted into Ukrainian communities in Canada, but I do not gather that the Canadian Government have as yet been approached on this point..." In a subsequent letter, Robinson underlines the absolute necessity of disposing of the Ukrainians by reminding Boothby "that there are already in this country 76,000 Poles 'eating their heads off at our expense.' "[47]

Among the Poles supposedly eating their heads off in the United Kingdom was a large contingent of veterans of Anders Polish Army that had fought bravely side by side with the British and Americans in North Africa, Italy and Normandy. These men were also determinedly anti-Communist and resolved not to return to Poland now that it was under the Soviet's thumb. Despite their proud war record, the British were just as eager to see them leave the United Kingdom as the Ukrainians. In the summer of 1947, the British Foreign Office persuaded a reluctant Canadian government to accept a block of 4,500 Polish veterans as agricultural workers. However, C. Costley-White of the Commonwealth Relations Office warned the Home Office that such arrangements were "altogether exceptional" on Canada's part and were not likely to be repeated.[48]

Since the ultimate fate of the men of the Division could not yet be determined, the debate turned to whether the men could be "civilianized" and permitted to determine their own future. The Ministry of Agriculture, while agreeing that the agricultural work of the Ukrainians was satisfactory, saw problems ahead if an effort were made to absorb them as civilians. "Such a proposal... could be expected to be strongly resisted by the Agricultural Workers' Unions, and by the workers themselves, on political and social grounds."[49]

The answer, provided in a variety of memoranda in 1947 and 1948, was that the Division would continue to be classified as prisoners of war, so long as their labour was required. They would remain prisoners of war until the day, when their labour was no longer required and they were put on board ship for Canada, United States, Australia and Argentina.

In June 1948, Panchuk produced another of his lengthy memoranda outlining the Association of Ukrainians in Great Britain's version of the Division's history. Its contents is so remote from the truth that one has to assume either that Panchuk deliberately misrepresented the facts, or that he knew nothing of what took place in Galicia from the 1920s through to the end of World War II. He claimed, for example, that Ukrainian nationalist leaders were reluctant to see the Division formed and lent their efforts only after the Germans announced their firm intention to organize it. He made no mention of the voluminous correspondence and personal interviews in which Melnyk and Kubijovyc pleaded for the recruitment of a Ukrainian Waffen-SS Division. He minimized the role of the *Roland* and *Nachtigall* Battalions and makes no mention of the pogroms that coincided with their arrival in Lviv.

Despite the fact that the enlistees were all volunteers, Panchuk implies that they were coerced and did not serve the Germans gladly. He is totally confused about the Division's stay in Slovakia and the part it played in suppressing the Slovak Rebellion. In Panchuk's version, the Division's task was to do a spot of training in Slovakia and help recruit Slovak partisans for the Wehrmacht.

There is no mention of the Division's anti-partisan activities, of the Beyersdorff Battalion or of the attacks on Polish villages such as Huta Pieniacka. There is also no mention of any actions against the Red Army. Mention of the Battle of Brody is studiously avoided. All in all, Panchuk gives the impression that the Division spent the bulk of its time, not in Poland and the western Ukraine, but in Slovakia on training missions. Its chief preoccupation throughout the war, according to Panchuk, was to find a means of surrendering to the British and adopt a democratic way of life:

"All of the men are strongly and permanently Western minded...and developed in the democratic way of life as understood in the West." He praises the 8,500 Division members in the United Kingdom as "the most disciplined, most honourable, most loyal to their unit and to the traditions of solidarity which they have always displayed."[50] He might have added that they were also the most fanatical and the most committed to the ideology that motivated them to join the Division in the first place.

Panchuk's final shot is to recommend that the Division be "civilianized" forthwith and that all those who wish to take up employment in the United Kingdom be encouraged to do so. He urges that more sympathetic consideration should be given to permitting entry to the wives and children of those who volunteer to remain in England.[51]

The British government preferred, however, to place its hopes on shipping the Division to Canada. Foreign Minister Bevin urged further discussions with Ottawa and pointed out that "there is a great deal of interest in the fate of these men among Canadians of Ukrainian origin."[52] However, if the British were eager to rid themselves of the large body of Ukrainians they had almost inadvertently collected, the Canadians were even more reluctant to receive them. The Canadians cited strict immigration regulations which barred former Waffen-SS personnel. "The question is how are we most likely to be able to put the idea in an acceptable form to the Canadian Government?" the Foreign Office pondered.

Norman A. Robertson, the External Affairs veteran who was serving his first term as Canadian High Commissioner to London, helped provide the answer. Robertson thought it might be possible to persuade the Canadian government to relax their immigration requirements in order to take a number of these men. However, he anticipated many difficulties and would need information on their qualifications for civilian employment, their ages and "a brief statement of the war record of the Division generally, *without much detail as to individuals.*"[53] (Emphasis added by the author.) Robertson also requested information regarding the status of the Division, pointing out that for security reasons "it would be much easier for the Canadians to consider individuals in this group if the division of the Wehrmacht to which they belonged were regarded as disbanded and they were no longer treated...as prisoners of war."[54]

In preparation for further talks between the Commonwealth Office and Canada House, Boothby offered the following description of the Division to persuade the Canadians:

> These Ukrainians were members of the 1st Ukrainian Division of the Wehrmacht which appears to have been formed in the year 1944 around the remnants of what appears to have been for a short time a Waffen-SS Division which was cut to pieces at the Battle of Brody. Its members appear to have joined the Wehrmacht in the belief that the Germans would honour their promises to create an independent Ukraine. As the members of this Division all appear to hail from the former Polish Ukraine which was subsequently annexed by the Union of Socialist Soviet Republics, they are not regarded by us as Soviet nationals or Quislings, since they did not owe allegiance to any Allied power and did not collaborate with the Germans during the latter's invasion of Poland. They did not bear arms

against the Western Allies and promptly surrendered when they encountered our forces in Austria as the war ended.[55]

Boothby was too clever and too well informed not to know better. Again we have the omission of relevant facts, the use of the term "Wehrmacht" to lessen the significance of the SS affiliation and the shortening of the time frame in which the Division operated to make it appear that the Division arrived on the scene much too late to be have been involved in atrocities. Boothby makes a virtue of the Division's peaceful surrender on the last day of the war, as if there was any other possibility open to them except capture by the Russians. He also makes a virtue of the fact that they did not bear arms against any western forces, as if this was anything more than an accident of war. There is no reason to believe that the Galician Division would have failed to fire on Allied troops, if they had encountered them in the course of a campaign. Certainly, the vicious anti-western propaganda published in the Division newspaper and the contempt for democracy embedded in their ideology does not suggest that they would have laid down their arms rather than fire on British and American troops.

As for the oft repeated claim that the organizers of the Division had agreed that the Ukrainian formation would never be used against the Western Allies, there is no recorded evidence of such an agreement in any of Himmler's papers. It would have been totally out of character for the Nazis to make such an agreement even in the face of their desperate manpower shortage. The SS made no allowance for partial support; you were either with them all the way or you were against them. One can hardly imagine General Freitag and the other German Division officers tolerating such ambivalence. Boothby, as an astute, high-ranking civil servant familiar with all the evasive ploys employed by bureaucrats, must have known there was no truth to this claim, but truth was not his goal in this case.

Finally, it is shamefully dishonest to suggest that the Division sat on its hands for the greater part of the war and ignore the fact that it fought actively against the Red Army which included millions of Ukrainians. The Galician Division may not have been the bravest or the most successful of Himmler's legions but they were, nevertheless, a significant factor in the German onslaught that cost the USSR millions of lives.

The Shifting Tide in Ottawa

The Bevin/Boothby campaign to persuade Canada to take at least a portion of the Ukrainian Division did not meet with immediate success despite voluminous exchanges of correspondence. In October 1948, the High Commissioner's office reported that the Canadians remained adamant in their refusal. Canada's Cabinet level Committee on Immigration had "considered the proposal in all its aspects" and decided "that these Ukrainians would not be admitted to Canada as immigrants." The decision had been unanimous and it was unlikely to be changed.[56]

Yet, eight months later, Panchuk was able to report that the Canadian government had relented and was now willing to accept members of the Division. "After a long period of pressure," Panchuk explained, "[the Canadians] have removed the ban on the immigration...of Ukrainians who fought with the enemy... [Not] only would they consider these men who have families or relatives in Canada, but would also welcome fit young men willing to undertake agricultural employment."[57] Panchuk believed that 5,000 to 6,000 men would jump at the chance to come to Canada, especially since they would have to spend only one year as agricultural workers and then be free to take up residence anywhere in Canada they chose and move to whatever occupation they preferred.

Panchuk frequently reminded British officials of Canada's large Ukrainian population and the intense concern Ukrainian organizations expressed over the fate of its Galician SS compatriots.[58] Now, he could honestly boast that pressure, in the form of intense lobbying by the Ukrainian Canadian Committee, had persuaded the Canadian Cabinet to abandon its official immigration policy to accommodate the Halychyna Division. A cabinet directive issued October 28, 1949 stated:

> Displaced persons and certain classes of prospective immigrants desiring to enter Canada are investigated under established procedures by the [Royal Canadian Mounted] Police. Persons in specified categories (i.e., Communists, members of the Nazi or Fascist Parties or any revolutionary organization, "collaborators," and users of false or fictitious names or documents) are regarded as inadmissible under the Immigration Act and are refused a visa.[59]

If nothing else, the members of the Division, their ideologues and political advisers qualified as "collaborators" and the OUN as a fascist party. Nevertheless, all such considerations were swept aside and the road to admission cleared.

To advise the Cabinet on security matters, the Canadian government had created a secret Security Panel consisting of high ranking civil servants, police and military personnel. Their recommendations were generally accepted as gospel by the Cabinet. It is, therefore, interesting to note that as late as April 30, 1952, the following regulations were still in effect:

- Non-German members of the Waffen-SS who joined that organization prior to 1st January, 1943, will remain blanket rejects. Non-German members of the Waffen-SS who joined after 1ˢᵗ January 1943, will be required to satisfy the Security Officer that they were drafted and did not enlist voluntarily.

- The following were listed as "major collaborators" whose entry should be denied:
  (a) Those convicted of fighting against, or engaging in activities harmful to the safety and well-being of the Allied forces;
  (b) Those convicted of implications in the taking of life, or engaging in activities connected with forced labour and concentration camps;
  (c) Those who were employed by German police or security organizations and who acted as informers against loyal citizens and resistance groups;
  (d) Those charged and found guilty of treason.[60]

A subsequent meeting of the Security panel in May of that year recommended that members of the SS, the *Sicherheitsdienst*, the *Abwehr*, the *Gestapo* and former members of the Waffen-SS should be denied entry. An exception was made for German nationals who joined the Waffen-SS before the age of 18 and where there were reasonable grounds for believing they were conscripted or joined under coercion.[61]

Several of the categories listed above closely fit the veterans of the Halychyna Division. There was, for example, no question that the vast majority had enlisted voluntarily and that very few could claim that they were drafted or coerced. There was also no question that they had participated in the killing of innocent civilians and acted against resistance groups as well as rounding up young Ukrainians for slave labour in Germany. Yet, exceptions were made and Canadian regulations ignored to make the entry of Division members possible.

How did this come about?

Notes

1. Orest Martynowych, *Ukrainians in Canada: The Formative Years* (Edmonton: Canadian Institute of Ukrainian Studies Press, 1991), 309.

2. *Ibid.* 309.

3. Flier published by Association of United Ukrainian Canadians, 593 Pritchard St., Winnipeg, Manitoba, 1959.

4. Martynowych, 318.

5. Paul Yuzyk, "The Political Achievements of Ukrainians in Canada, 1891-1981," *New Soil-Old Roots: The Ukrainian Experience in Canada,* editor, Jaroslav Rozumnyj (Winnipeg: Ukrainian Academy of Arts and Science in Canada, 1983), 305.

6. Peter Melnycky, "Political Reaction to Ukrainian Immigrants: The 1899 Election in Manitoba" in *New Soil—Old Roots: The Ukrainian Experience in Canada,* Edited Jaroslav Rozumnyj (Winnipeg: Ukrainian Academy of Arts and Sciences in Canada, 1983), 18.

7. Raymond Arthur Davies, *This is Our Land; Ukrainian Canadians against Hitler* (Toronto: Progress Books, 1943), 16.

8. Lita-Rose Betcherman, *The Swastika and the Maple Leaf* (Toronto: Fitzhenry and Whiteside, 1975), 62.

9. Public Archives of Canada (PAC), RG 25, Vol. 1896, File 165, pt. 1.

10. Interview with Joseph Salsberg, once a leading member of the Communist Party of Canada.

11. Public Archives of Canada (PAC) RG25, Gl Volume 1896, File 165, Part II.

12. *Ibid.*

13. Public Archives of Canada (PAC), RG 25 Vol. 1896, File 165, pt.1.

14. *Ibid.*

15. *Ibid.*

16. *Ibid.*

17. Watson Kirkconnell, *Canada, Europe and Hitler* (Toronto: University of Toronto Press, 1939).

18. Kirkconnell, who ended his career as President of Acadia University in Wolfville, Nova Scotia, was an ardent anti-Zionist. In an article published in a 1956 edition of *The University of Toronto Quarterly*, titled "Publications in Other Languages," he includes the following in a review of a book on Mennonite colonies in Russia and Israel: "Those (Mennonites) in Palestine were driven out in 1946-8 by Israeli invaders along with a million other victims of Zionist violence... The author of this present history is ninety-six years old and belongs to the group that was settled in Palestine until the Israelis usurped the land."

19. *Ibid.*

20. *Ibid.*

21. Public Archives of Canada (PAC), MG 30, E350, vol. 1.

22. Public Archives of Canada (PAC), RG 25, Gl rol 1896, file 165, part II.

23. Public Archives of Canada (PAC), MG 30, File 350, File 350, Vol. 1, "Tracy Philipps, Personal Dossier."

24. Public Archives of Canada (PAC), RG 30 E 350, Vol. 1.

25. Davies, 68.

26. Public Archives of Canada (PAC), RG 25, Gl, rol 1896, File 165, Part II.

27. Public Archives of Canada (PAC), MG 30, File 350, Vol. 1, "Tracy Philipps, Personal Dossier."

28. PAC, RG 25, Gl, Vol. 1896, File 165, Part III.

29. *Ibid.*

30. *Ibid.*

31. *Ibid.*

32. Quoted in Bohdan S. Kordan, "Disunity and Duality: Ukrainian Canadians and the Second World War," unpublished manuscript, January 15, 1981. Kordan's reference is Canadian External Affairs Archives, File: 4174-40.

33. Philipps' dismissal was effective March 31, 1944.

34. Bohdan Panchuk, *Heroes of Their Day: The Reminiscences of Bohdan Panchuk,* trans. Lubomyr Luciuk (Toronto: The Multicultural History Society, 1993), 75.

35. *Ibid.* 75-76.

36. *Ibid.* 75-76.

37. *Ibid.* 77.

38. PRO, FO 371/57828, February 7, 1946.

39. PRO, FO 371/57828.

40. Styrkul, 294.

41. PRO, FO 371/57828.

42. *Ibid.*

43. PRO, FO 371/71636, Memorandum on Ukrainians and Ukrainian Nationality, dated August 10, 1948. "I cannot help thinking that the main purpose of this memo is to request that Mr. Panchuk himself be appointed Ukrainian Ambassador... In fact, Mr. Panchuk fulfils (not to everybody's satisfaction) the function already quite unofficially, and the Home Office would, I think, throw a fit if it ever became more than that. I am sure this proposal need not go any further."

44. PRO, FO 371/71636/195328.

45. *Ibid.* From Foreign Office to Office of Political Adviser to Commander-in-Chief Germany, February 18, 1946. Also, HO 213/1851 "Ukrainian Surrendered Personnel and their Dependents."

46. *Ibid.* Brimelow, Northern Department, February 13, 1946.

47. PRO, HO 213/1851 Robinson to Boothby, April 11 and May 2, 1947.

48. PRO, FO 371/3362.

49. *Ibid.*

50. PRO, FO 371/71636.

51. *Ibid.*

52. PRO, WO 32/13190 Bevin to Shinwell, July 5, 1948.

53. PRO, FO 371/3362.

54. PRO, WO 32/13190.

55. PRO, DO 35/3362.

56. PRO, DO 35/3362 and FO 371/3362.

57. *Ibid.* Hanson to Goldberg, June 19, 1950.

58. PRO, DO 35/3362.

59. Privy Council Office, Cabinet Directive, October 28, 1949, Circular No. 14, "Rejection of Immigrants on Security Grounds." (Obtained through Access to Information, Employment and Immigration Canada.)

60. Security Panel Document SP-119, "Immigration Security Policy, Nazis Fascists and Collaborators, April 30, 1952. Obtained through Access to Information.

61. Security Panel, 42nd Meeting, May 15, 1952. Obtained through Access to Information.

CHAPTER 15

PRESSURE, PRESSURE, PRESSURE

IN 1948, THE BRITISH COMMONWEALTH SECRETARY ADDRESSED a letter calling on Britain's "White Dominions," Canada, Australia, and New Zealand—and ironically—the Union of South Africa, to provide shelter to a fair portion of the Ukrainian Waffen-SS men. Looking back, it is hard to realize the extent to which Canadian public servants admired and respected their British colleagues. Although Canada was no longer a subservient British colony, Canadian political leaders still suffered, nonetheless, from a colonial mentality. England had called on Canada to help solve a pressing problem. Canada might pout and stamp its feet but it could not ignore the wishes of the "mother country." Therefore, when the Canadian government received the Commonwealth Secretary's letter suggesting it take a share of the Ukrainian Division members, the Canadian government found it difficult to respond with a blunt and irrevocable "No!"

By 1948 it had become obvious to the External Affairs Department of Canada that their British colleagues had lost interest in punishing Nazi war criminals, no matter how atrocious their crimes. In a secret dispatch dated July 13, 1948, The British Commonwealth office advised all Commonwealth countries that all war crimes cases trials were to end by August 31st even if the alleged war criminals were already in custody. "In our view punishment of war criminals is more a matter of discouraging future generations than of meeting out retribution to every guilty individual," the Commonwealth Secretary stated. Even more significant was the sentence that followed: "Moreover, in view of future political developments in Germany envisaged by recent tripartite talks, we are convinced it is now necessary to dispose of the past as soon as possible."[1]

The Cold War tocsin had sounded. The new foe was the Soviet Union. The past, with all its horrors, needed to be buried and Germany welcomed back into the community of nations. The United Nations War Crimes Commission (UNWCC) was to be closed down and the West Germans given the responsibility for any further war crimes cases.[2]

Canada replied that it was in full "agreement with the conclusions reached by the Government of the United Kingdom" and the Canadian representative to the UNWCC would be instructed to support this decision when the matter came up at the Commission's meeting in November. The response was signed, "Lester B. Pearson, Secretary of State for External Affairs."

The Ukrainian community, sensing a softening in attitude, became increasingly aggressive in its efforts to bring Division members to Canada. The Canadian Relief Commission for the Relief of Ukrainian Refugees had confidently addressed the Honourable Walter Harris, Minister of Mines and Resources in 1947 to request the admission of the 8,000 men held in eight camps in the United Kingdom.[3] The Commission's letter regurgitated the usual litany of rationalizations; the eight thousand were members of the First Ukrainian Division which had been organized in late 1944, they had joined the Wehrmacht in the belief that the Germans would help them achieve an independent Ukrainian state, they were not Soviet nationals and had not collaborated with the Germans in the invasion of Poland. They added that the Division had surrendered promptly to the British forces and were withdrawn first to Italy and then to the United Kingdom.[4] Their note stressed that at least half of them were agricultural workers and the rest skilled workers, labourers and assorted "others"—statistics sure to please a Minister of Mines and Resources seeking strong backed immigrants in a period of labour shortage.

However, the Canadian decision *not* to admit the Division's members seemed firm at the time. The Cabinet Committee on Immigration, meeting in April 1948, reiterated its decision to refuse admission to "members of this group to migrate to Canada because they had served in the German armed forces." But in the summer of 1948, the British began to push harder, calling on Canada to take several hundred of the Division members, preferably those for whom no work had been found in England.

While the British nudged the Canadian government from one side, the Ukrainian Canadian Committee pushed harder from its side. It stepped up the pace of its representations to have the ban withdrawn, pointing to the large number of Division members who had Canadian relatives eager to receive them. To underline its numbers and influence, the UCC pointed out that it was representative of a long list of chartered Ukrainian organizations such as the Ukrainian Catholic Brotherhood, Ukrainian Self-Reliance League, Ukrainian National Federation, Ukrainian Workers League, and Ukrainian Canadian Veterans Association.

The only dissenting Ukrainian voice was that of the battered Ukrainian left-wing represented by the Association of United Ukrainian Canadians. Much diminished in numbers and influence in the post-war, Cold War era, the Association continued to be closely scrutinized by the RCMP. Meetings at the Labour Temple in Winnipeg, Manitoba and a union hall in Timmins, Ontario were disrupted and the participants beaten up. A bomb was detonated one Sunday afternoon in the Labour Temple on Toronto's Bathurst Street. Fortunately, it went off well before the children's concert scheduled for that afternoon.[5]

The assailants were never identified. In 1949, the Association of United Ukrainian Canadians wrote to the Prime Minister to denounce the Halychyna Division as "part and parcel of Hitler's Army" and to endorse the Cabinet's earlier decision not to admit members of the Division. However, since the Association was affiliated with the communist left, their protest was given little standing.

Panchuk and his coterie had learned the effectiveness of employing a variety of letterheads and committee names to inflate their influence and numbers. They responded to the decision to bar the Division members with a steady stream of letters and memoranda from their headquarters at 49 Linden Gardens, Notting Hill Gate, London, addressed to the Prime Minister, External Affairs and Mines and Resources. Theodore Danyliw, Secretary General of the Central Coordinating Committee of Ukrainian Organizations in London, wrote persuasively:

> The Germans, who fought against the Western Allies from the first day to the last...are being increasingly admitted to other countries and are being granted more and more privileges, whilst former members of the Ukrainian Division who never fought against the Western Allies, are barred from immigration to the Dominion... (As) the Germans are more freely admitted to the Family of Nations, we would ask you to give our application for the removal of the bar to immigration of former members of the "Halychyna" Division your favourable consideration.

Dr. Osyp Fundak, President of the Association of Ukrainians in Great Britain, wrote to Lester Pearson, then the Secretary of State for External Affairs, to argue that, "Any of these vigorous and willing workers would be an asset to a country that admitted them as immigrants. All are however barred from immigration on the grounds that they fought against Russia with the German army. We submit this is only technically correct."

The Canadian Christian Council for the Resettlement of Refugees.

The Ukrainian community was not alone in urging the government to abandon the ban on Waffen-SS personnel. The Canadian Christian Council for Resettlement of Refugees lobbied strenuously for a change in regulations that would make it easier for their co-religionists to be admitted for permanent settlement.[6] A coalition of German Lutherans, German Catholics, Mennonites and German Baptists, they had as their principal interest the rescue of fellow Germans inhabiting seventy-five refugee reception centres established by the West German authorities.

The Council's chief concern was the rescue of the ethnic Germans, known as *Volksdeutsche,* who had settled generations ago in a number of non-German European countries such as Ukraine, Yugoslavia, Hungary, Poland, Russia and Czechoslovakia.

Classified by Hitler as biological Germans, they were proclaimed German citizens who were liable to be drafted into the German armed forces. In many cases, particularly in the Sudeten territory of Czechoslovakia, they had served as the advance guard of Nazism and welcomed the opportunity to reunite with their Aryan brethren. Many of the young men did not wait to be drafted but volunteered to serve in the *Sicherheitsdienst* and the Waffen-SS.[7] As Waffen-SS members they were denied entry to Canada under the regulations existing at the time.

The Canadian Christian Council lobbied hard to remove the prohibition against their admission. Headquartered in Winnipeg, the Council stationed emissaries throughout Germany and Austria. As representatives of Canadian organizations, they were in a position to develop close, quasi-formal relationships with Canadian immigration officials and engage in special pleading for those of their co-religionists whom they considered worth saving. In many cases, they were able to persuade the Canadian officials to rubber stamp their requests or stretch the rules of eligibility on behalf of their clients.[8]

Unfortunately, not all those saved by the Council were worthy of being saved. Helmut Rauca, the SS master sergeant who personally selected 9,200 Lithuanian Jews for extermination and supervised their killing was among those whose good character was vouched for by the Council.[9] Similarly, Hermine Braunsteiner, the Maidanek concentration camp guard who tore infants out of their mother's arms and savagely whipped their protesting mothers, was another of those "rescued" by the Council.[10] Both their names appear on Canadian immigrant ships' lists and both were provided with Canadian sponsors through the good offices of the Christian Council.[11] Between 1947 and 1950, some 15,000 *Volksdeutsche* and 6,500 Mennonites arrived in Canada under Council auspices.[12]

Nevertheless, armed with the credentials of respectable church organizations, Council representatives were seen as doing God's work and received sympathetic attention from Canadian officials, including the new Prime Minister, the Honourable Louis St. Laurent.[13] When a large percentage of those applying for admission were rejected on security grounds, the Council appealed to the Prime Minister for greater leeway by the examining officers. Their pleas were successful. In 1950, three quarters of the *Volksdeutsche* applications were rejected because of German citizenship and only one quarter were approved. A few months later, the Council was able to report that the percentage had been reversed.[14]

With pressure applied from all sides, the Cabinet Committee on Immigration reviewed the Waffen-SS issue again in April of 1950 and concluded: "That aliens...who served with the Enemy Forces during the war are not admitted to Canada, unless they can definitely establish that such service was rendered under compulsion. The group under consideration served voluntarily in the German armed forces." But, the Committee added, there had been a significant change in the regulations governing the immigration of *Volksdeutsche* and German citizens the previous month. Those who had close relatives in Canada and were prepared to do farm work had become admissible even if they had served in the German armed forces. Surely then, the Ukrainians who were in the United Kingdom as prisoners of war should be admissible under the same conditions.

The switch in policy was officially announced in a brief June 6, 1950 memorandum signed by Deputy Minister Laval Fortier. It read:

> At its meeting on Wednesday May 31st, the Cabinet has agreed that Ukrainians, presently residing in the United Kingdom, be admitted to Canada notwithstanding their service in the German army provided they are otherwise admissible. These Ukrainians should be subject to special security screening, but should not be rejected on the grounds of their service in the German army.[15]

Further correspondence between the RCMP and the newly formed Department of Citizenship and Immigration called for "full security screening of both the applicant in Canada (sponsor) and the proposed immigrant will be required in these cases, and instructions to this effect are being sent out to our staff in Canada and overseas."[16] The procedure outlined by the Immigration Branch required applications for entry to be submitted by their relatives in Canada. The application was not to go ahead, however, until the RCMP had cleared both the relative and the Division veteran.

On its face, it would appear that the Division members accepted as immigrants to Canada must have been thoroughly screened before they left England. In fact, the screening was at best superficial and incomplete. The RCMP, stationed in Europe as Visa Control Officers, served as the investigators. However, the record shows that they maintained a minimal staff in the United Kingdom and were ill-prepared to handle a large flow of Ukrainian immigrants.[17] The same problems that impeded Haldane Porter were still present; the men had no identification papers, the Division's key records had been destroyed and sources of valid information were extremely limited. Having no information of their own, the RCMP relied heavily on the records of the U.S. Counter Intelligence Corps and the CIC's access to the Berlin Document Centre.[18] Unfortunately, these sources, rich in information regarding individuals and events in the West, contained almost no information bearing on atrocities in the East. A further complication was the huge increase in immigration applicants in the 1950s which made it impossible for the American and British security agencies to speedily process Canadian cases. When the backlog of investigations began to slow the immigration stream and ships were leaving European ports half empty, the RCMP stopped approaching the Americans and the British for background information and relied on hurried personal interviews to screen the immigrants.[19]

The Soviets had volumes of information gathered by Extraordinary Commissions of Investigation that followed on the heels of the retreating Germans into every liberated town and village to interview witnesses and disinter the buried bodies. Teams of forensic scientists examined the corpses while KGB investigators compiled lists of those who had participated in the slaughter of innocent civilians. However, the Americans and the British did not deign to request this information from the Soviet authorities. The Cold War chill had deepened in the wake of the Gouzenko case—the Russian file clerk in the Soviet embassy in Ottawa who defected in September 1945, with evidence that the USSR maintained an extensive spy network in Canada and the USA. Gouzenko's revelations discouraged communication with any agency of the USSR, let alone the wicked KGB.[20]

Curiously, the RCMP was also reluctant to make use of unimpeachable "Western" sources such as the vast accumulation of the names of suspects and witnesses compiled by the United Nations War Crimes Commission. Although readily available to the Canadians, there is no record that the RCMP made any use of the UNWCC files.[21] In any event, war crimes and crimes against humanity were of no interest to the RCMP in the post war period.[22] Now that membership in the Waffen-SS was no longer an issue, their sole focus was "security," defined as rooting out Communists.[23] Since the men of the Division were unequivocally anti-Communist, there wasn't much left to be investigated. However, they did keep a lookout for "bad apples," men who may have misbehaved while in England, committed minor crimes or proven to be chronic drunkards. Checks were made, therefore, with local English police units only to determine whether individual Division members were likely to cause trouble or become a burden on the community if they immigrated to Canada.

For a third time, the promised screening was no screening!

There is in fact, no substance to the claim made by some Ukrainian Canadian scholars that the Division members were admitted only after "carefully ascertaining that no war criminals were among those wishing to come to Canada" and that they had been subjected to "many screenings and much vetting of the Division's history and membership."[24]

In the following months, news of the dramatic change in Canadian policy was spread throughout the Galician prisoner of war camps in England and proclaimed in the Displaced Persons camps in Germany and Austria. In the following years, thousands of European refugees boarded ship in Cuxhaven and Liverpool and disembarked in Halifax. Although no accurate count is available, it is estimated that between 1200 and 2,000 Division veterans settled in Canada in the years between 1950 and 1955. Most farmed for the obligatory year and then headed for the city. While some settled in the west and added to the Ukrainian population of Winnipeg, Edmonton, Calgary and Vegreville, most of the Ukrainian "Third Wave" chose to make their homes in the industrial cities of the eastern provinces.[25] In spite of the British government's efforts to encourage the veterans of the Division to settle elsewhere, a sizeable contingent remained in England and added to the Ukrainian population in the Bradford area. Others chose to live in Australia, New Zealand and Argentina while a good number made their homes in the United States.

The Canadian Jewish Congress (CJC) vs. The Ukrainian Canadian Committee

The decision to admit members of the Halychyna SS Division was greeted with great concern by the Canadian Jewish community. Samuel Bronfman, National President of the Canadian Jewish Congress (CJC)[26] telegraphed Walter Harris, Minister of Immigration and Citizenship on July 4, 1950, to express his organization's stern disapproval of Harris' announcement in Parliament that the Halychyna Division was now free to apply for admission on the same basis as other immigrants:

> The Executive Committee of the Canadian Jewish Congress is dismayed at the intention expressed in your speech in the House of Commons about two weeks ago of remitting the entry to Canada of the Halychyna Division of Ukrainians... Information in our files discloses that this group enlisted as volunteers in the German SS... We believe that the Nuremberg Tribunal in declaring the SS a criminal organization, encompassed all voluntary groups such as the Halychyna Division. We urge upon you the necessity of a careful and complete investigation of the alleged Halychyna association with the SS... Its history would suggest need of extraordinary close scrutiny and an examination into the political creed of its members. We further submit that a delay of this movement be imposed for such clearance and investigation until we can obtain evidence which we think is forthcoming for your later consideration. Assurances from you would go a long way to remove our feeling that a serious error would be perpetrated without such full and complete investigation.[27]

Harris was taken aback by the fervor of Samuel Bronfman's protest. He wrote the next day to assure the prominent Jewish businessman and philanthropist that "we have no intention of admitting anyone who cannot pass the most rigid screening." The Minister of Citizenship and Immigration explained that enormous pressure was being exerted by the "non-Communist Ukrainian organizations in Canada" to permit "close relatives and sponsored personnel of this group to come to Canada." He cited letters from the Central Coordinating Committee of Ukrainian Organizations in the United Kingdom and representations from Members of Parliament and Legislative Assemblies, all calling for the admission of the Halychyna Division members. Harris advised Bronfman that special investigations had been made "into the reasons for the Division being raised" and that special care had been taken to make sure that "we also had the means to do a good screening on each application."[28]

Nevertheless, Harris added: "In view of what you have said, I am quite prepared to delay approval of applications for a reasonable time, in order to give you an opportunity to send me any pertinent material." The Minister had put the ball in Bronfman's court.

On Harris' instruction, no further approvals were to be granted to Ukrainian Surrendered Personnel in the United Kingdom until further notice from his office. Screenings already underway could, nevertheless, continue.

The Anglo-Jewish press joined the battle. *The Daily Jewish Forward* published a scathing article by Jewish Telegraphic Agency correspondent Boris Smoliar on July 23, 1950:

Jewish leaders in Canada can of course not object to the fact that the Government wishes to admit more Ukrainians as immigrants, but what kind of Ukrainians? It is no secret that the Ukrainians, who are at present in Europe as refugees, were all on the side of the Nazis. Moreover, a large number of them actually took part in helping the Nazis to exterminate the Jews when the German army occupied Ukrainian towns. The pogroms on the Jews of Galicia and throughout the Ukraine were carried out through special Gestapo units, but with the direct participation of the local Ukrainian population. Ukrainians also played not a small role as guards, in whom the Gestapo had the fullest confidence, in the gas chambers and extermination camps. Particularly did the so-called Galician Division of Ukraine distinguish itself. This Division was formed by the Nazi army for the purpose of helping to free the Ukraine from the communist regime, but every member of this Division had to take an oath that he will help exterminate the Jews. The text of this oath is now printed in Canadian newspapers which protest why the Government wishes to admit pogrom immigrants to Canada.

As part of the Nazi army the Galician Division of Ukraine marched with the Gestapo units from town to town through Nazi occupied Ukraine and drove thousands of Jews to their destruction. In many cities they compelled Jews to march to the outskirts of town and dig their own mass graves. In other towns they participated in the mass murder of Jews in other horrible ways.[29]

Ottawa was evidently taken off guard by this dust up between the Jewish and Ukrainian communities. It is clear from the correspondence that Canada's bureaucrats knew next to nothing of the Division. The Acting Deputy Minister of Immigration and Citizenship,

A.L. Joliffe, hurriedly called on External Affairs to "obtain information regarding the record of the Halychyna Division" from the appropriate department of the United Kingdom:

> It would be helpful if we knew when and where the Division was recruited, what war service the Division engaged in and where; if they were employed in combat against the 'Western Allies'. Further, is there any justification for the intimation that this Division was actively engaged in the elimination of the Jewish population of the Ukraine.[30]

The reply forwarded by the London High Commissioner, L.D. Wilgress offered the familiar litany reiterated by the United Kingdom Foreign Office; there was no evidence of the Division fighting against the Allies or engaging in crimes against humanity; there was no indication that they were infected with the Nazi ideology; the Division was a Wehrmacht unit formed late in 1944 which had participated in only one action against the Russians. The Germans had wanted to make it into a Waffen-SS unit but this had been resisted by the Ukrainians themselves. A Cold War note was added, not seen in previous evaluations of the Division: "Although Communist propaganda has consistently attempted to depict these, like so many other refugees, as 'quislings' and 'war criminals' it is interesting to note that no specific charges of war crimes have been made by the Soviet or any other government against any member of this group."[31]

Meanwhile, the Canadian Jewish Congress was scrambling to locate the evidence needed to convince the government to reverse its decision and support its claim that it had incriminating material in its files. Until now, the CJC had devoted all its energies to opening the immigration gates to the Jews living in desperate circumstances in European refugee camps. The government which had closed its doors to Jews fleeing Hitler before the war, made it equally difficult for Jews to gain admission to Canada after the war. It required great ingenuity and persistent lobbying to persuade the government to admit a block of Jewish tailors badly needed by the clothing industry. It took equal persistence and ingenuity to gain the admission of a thousand Jewish children orphaned by Hitler. Too busy rescuing the living to devote itself to avenging the dead, Congress found itself ill prepared for the challenge suddenly thrust upon it.

At the time, the only Jewish agency with an extensive list of East European war criminals was the World Jewish Congress, with headquarters in New York. But even that prestigious organization had little hard information concerning the activities of the Halychyna SS Division. The Division's reputation as Nazi collaborators was well-known in the Jewish community, but specific details were lacking. The best that the World Jewish Congress could provide was a list of ninety-four names of informers, policemen, po-

166 /   PURE SOLDIERS OR SINISTER LEGION

lice chiefs, militiamen, mayors, district chiefs and OUN leaders who had persecuted Jews in the Lviv area. Although the list is headed "Ukrainian Surrendered Enemy Personnel, Halychyna Division", it is not clear from an examination of the names on the list that these were actually Division members. Some, such as Mrs. Babiuk who is alleged to have handed over hidden Jews to the Gestapo, and Dimitri Dontsov, the OUN ideologue who was serving as a professor of Ukrainian Literature at the University of Montreal by then, were clearly *not* Division veterans.[32] The remainder of the descriptions was extremely brief and many of the Christian names of those listed were missing. However, this was the best that the World Jewish Congress could assemble in a hurry on an under-reported Division that took great pains to conceal its record and rewrite its history.

The Canadian Jewish Congress was aware that the information it had on hand was far from convincing. Information on individual members of the Division was hard to come by since men in uniform who appear at dawn firing their rifles, seldom introduce themselves to their victims by name, rank, number and birth date. The Congress argued, however, that even if "it is impossible to find files or documents on every single member, or even a large proportion of members of the Division...that one ought to be guided by certain generalities." In a letter addressed to Harris by Bronfman, Congress insisted:

a) That millions of Poles, Ukrainians, Hungarians, Romanians, though equally anti-Communist, did not voluntarily join the SS;

b) That the SS, a notorious arm of the Nazi machine...was recognized by world opinion as one of the foulest manifestations of the Nazi creation. Its crimes against humanity were heinous;

c) That for a person voluntarily to have joined the SS was a confession of his attitude and political philosophy;

d) That each individual who was a member of the Halychyna Division ought to be stamped with the stigma that is attached to the entire body of the SS.

Bronfman, who had experienced numerous tussles with a discriminatory Ottawa bureaucracy over the years, was aware that he was fighting a losing battle. He called on Harris to delay his decision until Congress could gather irrefutable evidence that "the Halychyna Division was an SS auxiliary and that the Halychyna Division was not impressed into service but voluntarily offered to serve." However, Bronfman added, if evidence on the Division as a whole would not suffice, "(then) I fear that the pith and substance of our submission is not being regarded."[33]

There was some further skirmishing. Although several of the names on the list of alleged war criminals supplied by Congress corresponded to the names of persons applying for admission, each of the cases was airily dismissed without further investigation.[34]

Harris was not inclined to wait further. On September 15 he advised Bronfman that he had waited "a reasonable time and that he now intended to give approval to the applications on hand and to continue with the screening process for any future applications. He assured the CJC President that "our screening facilities are adequate and we can in all probability exclude anyone's entry into Canada who is prohibited for security reasons."[35]

The representatives of the Ukrainian Canadian Committee were jubilant. They had bested the Canadian Jewish Congress and out-lobbied the Jewish lobby. Henceforth, the members of the Division could hold their heads high in Canada; the Cabinet itself had confirmed their right to take up residence in Canada. In effect, they had been legitimized and could no longer be regarded as traitors, quislings and war criminals. The Cabinet's judgment could be thrown into the teeth of anyone who dared challenge their presence. Fresh accusations could be dismissed as "communist propaganda that was indiscriminately circulated...by the communists against anybody who disagreed with them."[36]

In the years since, members of the Division have attended numerous reunions with German and Baltic Waffen-SS units. On occasion, they have held church parades in which they have donned the blue blazers and berets worn by Canadian veterans of World War II. "Membership in the Division has never been regarded by its veterans as a cause for shame," explained Ukrainian Canadian Civil Liberties Association spokesman Lubomyr Luciuk. "Veterans living in Canada, the United States and Western Europe belong to a public organization, the Brotherhood of Veterans of the 1st Ukrainian Division of the Ukrainian National Army. The Brotherhood publishes a journal, *Visti Kombatanta* (Veterans' News) and holds regular membership meetings."[37]

The arrival of the veterans galvanized life in the Ukrainian community and moved its political centre considerably further right. Intense in their hatred of Communism in all its aspects, they were suspicious of much of the social legislation enacted in the post war years. Lubomyr Luciuk, who regrets that the Banderist ideology was not fully embraced by the previous generation of Ukrainians in Canada, summarizes the effect of the veterans' arrival in the following terms:

> The influence of the post-war immigrants exerted on Ukrainian-Canadians came from their strong political convictions... They viewed Canada as a temporary refuge where support could be gained for the destruction of the Soviet Union and the liberation of Ukraine. Towards that end they set up a network of political organizations and institutions that replicated the ones they had established in Europe.[38]

As individuals, the veterans of the Division were generally better educated than the peasant farmers who were Canada's original Ukrainian settlers. Their Ukrainian speech was fresher, their knowledge of Ukrainian literature better and their choral and dance skills greater than those of the partially assimilated Ukrainian Canadians who greeted them on their arrival. As a result, they were appointed the editors of Ukrainian language newspapers, secretaries of Ukrainian Nationalist Federation branches, teachers in the Ukrainian language schools and instructors in their choirs and dance groups. Ambitious, they enrolled in high schools and universities and strove for professional careers. Some became priests, others doctors, lawyers, engineers and university professors.

In effect, they became the sum and substance of Canada's organized Ukrainian community, its political spokesmen, its social conscience and its ethnic memory.

Notes

1. PAC, RG 18, Volume 120, Privy Council of Canada, Subject: War Criminals.

2. PAC, RG 25, Volume 2108 AR 405/4.

3. Canada has always maintained a close relationship between the needs of its farms and industries and its immigration policies. It made sense, therefore, that the Minister of Mines and Resources should be in charge of immigration This was changed in 1950 when a Ministry of Immigration and Citizenship was created.

4. The material in the following pages is drawn almost entirely from Public Archives of Canada (PAC) Immigration Branch Records, R.G. 76 Volume 656, file #B53802, part 2. In order to avoid endless "*Ibids*" only references to other sources will be listed.

5. Flier published by Association of Ukrainian Canadians, Winnipeg, 1959.

6. PAC, RG 26, Volume 115, File I-20-20, June 28, 1949. The organizations comprising the Canadian Christian Council for Resettlement of Refugees included: Catholic Immigrant Aid Society, Canadian Lutheran World Relief, Canadian Mennonite Board of Colonization, German Baptist Immigration and Colonization Society, and Sudeten Relief Committee.

7. See Rodal, 243.

8. *Ibid*. 204.

9. See: Sol Littman, *War Criminal on Trial; The Rauca Case* (Toronto: Lester Orpen and Dennys, 1983).

10. See: Alan A. Ryan, Jr., *Quiet Neighbors*, (New York: Harcourt Brace Jovanovich, 1984), 46-52.

11. Rauca was arrested in Toronto and extradited to West Germany where he died in prison awaiting trial. Braunsteiner, after a brief stay in Halifax, married an American G.I. named Ryan and took up housekeeping in Queens. She was identified, returned to Germany, tried and sentenced to life imprisonment.

12. Rodal, 243.

13. PAC, RG 26, Volume 115, File I-20-20, December 22, 1949, Letter from Prime Minister to T.O.F. Herzer, Chairman, Canadian Christian Council for Resettlement of Refugees.

14. William J.H. Sturhahn, D.D., *They Came from East and West; A History of Immigration to Canada* (Winnipeg: North American Baptist Immigration and Colonization Society, 1976), 85.

15. RG 76, Volume 656, file #B53802, part 2. Laval Fortier, Deputy Minister, Citizenship and Immigration to C.E.S. Smith, June 6, 1950.

16. *Ibid*. J.D. McFarlane, Deputy Commissioner Citizenship and Immigration to G.R. Benoit, June 13, 1950.

17. Rodal, 180.

18. *Ibid.* 200.

19. *Ibid.* 232.

20. Igor Gouzenko, a cipher clerk in the Soviet Embassy in Ottawa, defected and revealed that the Soviet Union had organized an extensive espionage network in Canada.

21. Rodal, 196.

22. Between 1945 and 1962, the RCMP had no mandate to investigate or arrest war criminals since the Canadian criminal code did not include crimes committed beyond Canada's borders. In 1962, in response to an inquiry by the RCMP to the Solicitor General and the Justice Minister, the RCMP was given specific instructions not to involve themselves in war crimes issues. It was not until Justice Jules Deschênes report was accepted in 1982 that the hunt for war criminals became a part of their duties. See: Sol Littman, *War Criminal on Trial; Rauca of Kaunas* (Toronto: Key Porter Books, 1998). 200.

23. Rodal, 175.

24. Roman Serbyn, "Alleged War Criminals, the Canadian Media, and the Ukrainian Community", in Yury Boshyk, *Ukraine during World War II* (Edmonton: Canadian Institute of Ukrainian Studies, 1986), 129.

25. The first two waves of Ukrainian immigration to Canada are described as economic, poor peasants and industrial workers seeking a better life for their families. The "Third Wave" following World War II is seen as politically motivated, i.e., a flight from Communism.

26. Samuel Bronfman was President of Seagrams and father to Edgar Bronfman who currently heads the World Jewish Congress.

27. PAC, RG 76, Volume 656, file #B53802, part 2. Bronfman to Harris, July 4, 1950.

28. *Ibid.* Harris to Bronfman, July 5, 1950.

29. The Smoliar letter is contained in a communication between A.L. Joliffe, Acting Deputy Minister, Department of Citizenship and Immigration to A. Heeney, Under-Secretary of State for External Affairs, August 8, 1950. Obtained through Access to Information.

30. *Ibid.*

31. PAC, RG 76, Volume 656, file # B53802, part 2. High Commissioner for Canada in the United Kingdom to Secretary of State for External Affairs, Canada, September 5, 1950.

32. The Director, Department of Citizenship and Immigration to the Deputy Minister, "Ukrainian surrendered Personnel (Halychyna Division)" December 6, 1950.

33. *Supra.* Bronfman to Harris, September 25, 1950.

34. *Ibid.* District Superintendent to Commissioner, November 16, 1950.

35. *Ibid.* Harris to Bronfman, September 15, 1950.

36. *Ibid.* Letter of the Ukrainian Canadian Committee (UCC) to the Israelite Press and the Canadian Jewish Congress, Winnipeg, Manitoba, August 26, 1950.

37. Letter by Lubomyr Luciuk, Research Assistant, Canadian Institute of Ukrainian Studies, to Mark Starowicz, CBC Television, April 12, 1983.

38. Lubomyr Luciuk, "This Should Never Be Spoken or Quoted Publicly: Canada's Ukrainians and their Encounter with the DPs," in *Canada's Ukrainians: Negotiating and Identity* (Toronto: University of Toronto Press, 1991), 147.

CHAPTER 16

GUILT AND INNOCENCE

Although Communist propaganda has constantly attempted to depict these, like so many other refugees, as 'quislings' and 'war criminals' it is interesting to note that no specific charges of war crimes have been made by the Soviet or any other Government against any member of this group. —*L.D. Wilgress, High Commissioner for Canada in the United Kingdom, September 5, 1950*

This group has commonly been referred to as 'Divisia Halychyna' (Galician Division) of the German Wehrmacht. The Communists have chosen to insist on branding this Division as an SS Division because of its strong anti-Communist character. —*G.R.B. Panchuk, Canadian Relief Mission for Ukrainian Victims of War and Central Ukrainian Relief Bureau, August 4, 1947*

IN ITS ANXIETY TO BE RID OF THE MEMBERS OF THE UKRAINIAN DIVISION once they were no longer needed for work on British farms and factories, the Foreign Office tried various stratagems to convince the reluctant Canadians that the Division was free of sin. British officials claimed that "no specific charges of war crimes had been made by the Soviets" while Ukrainian organizations emphasized the "anti-Communist character" of the Halychyna veterans.

"124 Officers of the Division"
Neither of them made mention of the 124 officers of the Division specifically named by the Soviets. Neither of them spoke publicly of the repeated requests by the USSR for their extradition from the United Kingdom.

The 124 became the subject of a difficult correspondence between the United Kingdom Foreign Office and Soviet Ambassador Zaroubin throughout the spring and summer of 1948. Zaroubin served notice that he would press for the extradition of the former officers of the SS-Galician Division, "which as is well known to everyone, engaged in the destruction of population on Soviet territory occupied by the Germans."[1]

Zaroubin insisted that all the persons mentioned were Soviet citizens and, according to the judgment handed down at the Nuremberg trial of Major War Criminals, deserved to be repatriated to the USSR.[2] The 124 officers, Zaroubin stated, had voluntarily joined the Galician Waffen-SS Division, knowing full well that they would be expected to conduct punitive operations against civilians. They were, therefore, precisely in the category recognized as criminal by the Nuremberg Tribunal and indictable for war crimes committed on Soviet territory. Decisions made by the Allies at Yalta and Potsdam supported the Soviet interpretation, the Ambassador claimed. "Therefore, the Embassy, once again requests the Foreign Office to take measures without delay to surrender the 124 aforesaid war criminals to the Soviet authorities."[3]

C.R.A. Rae of the Foreign Office dismissed Zaroubin's invocation of the Nuremberg judgment as "specious" and accused Zaroubin of being unable to distinguish between treachery and war crimes, Potsdam and Yalta. "Of course we know that the SS...committed war crimes, but my impression is that the Galichina [sic] Division was neither long nor actively engaged on the Russian front," Rae minuted his colleagues. "My understanding is that all non-Germans called up or volunteering for service with the German forces were automatically enrolled with the SS. I do not know if the criminality of the SS organization was intended to extend to such people, nor whether the Nuremberg decision gives the Russians any ground to demand that they be tried on Russian territory."[4]

Not everyone accepted Rae's impressions and understandings. The Home Office would have preferred to return all 124 of the men to Germany "willy-nilly" where they could be properly tried.[5] The Home office feared embarrassment if it civilianized the 124 Ukrainian officers and it later became known that they were war criminals or had "unpleasant" SS records.[6] But Rae felt he must keep his finger in the dike or the whole web of rationalizations that had been assembled to justify bringing the Division to Britain would fall apart. The 124, being officers, made the matter especially sensitive. If the officers were guilty of war crimes, then the men who followed their orders must certainly be guilty of the same crimes. He appealed to the Foreign Office's Legal Department to provide some legal basis to counter Zaroubin's demands. The legal department was more than happy to oblige the Foreign Office by providing their analysis of the obligations imposed on the United Kingdom by Yalta, Potsdam and the dicta of the Nuremberg Tribunal:

- If the Russians claimed the officers under the understanding reached at *Yalta* that citizens should be returned to their country of origin, the Russians would have to prove that the men had been Soviet citizens prior to September 1, 1939.
- If they claimed them under the *Potsdam Agreement* calling for war criminals to be punished, the Russians would have to provide *prima facie* evidence of crimes committed on Soviet soil.

- If the Russians relied on the *Nuremberg Judgement*, which declared the whole of the SS a criminal organization, the situation became complicated. Special German courts were doing a good job of trying German nationals who were members of criminal organizations, but they were not allowed to try non-Germans. If the 124 were to be tried as members of a criminal organization, they would have to be turned over to Control Commission Courts operated by the Military Government in Germany. But the Control Commission courts were overcrowded and unable to handle any more non-German criminal organization cases. This would mean handing the 124 over to the Russians and that would deeply embarrass the Allied Control Commission in its dealings with the USSR.[7]

The Foreign Office had no wish to embarrass the Control Commission, which was having a rough time administering its zone in Germany. "There can be no doubt it would be embarrassing to the Military Governor to have to offer these people to the Russians for trial...at this stage, assuming that the Russians had proved they were Soviet citizens on the 1st September, 1939."[8] The Foreign Office was grateful to the Legal Department's advice that "there is no possible reason for [the Ukrainians] being handed over to the Russians by anyone on the strength of the Nuremberg Judgment."[9]

Yet, a separate branch of the United Kingdom's legal services, the Legal Division of the Control Commission for Germany, was offering exactly the opposite advice to its prosecutorial staff in Germany. In an address to the assembled prosecutors in June 1974, the Chief of the Commission's Legal Division reminded the gathering that the International Military Tribunal, meeting at Nuremberg, had ruled the whole of the Waffen-SS a criminal organization.[10] The judgement had been based on the old, well-established concept of *conspiracy* in British and American law requiring that two or more persons agree to commit a criminal act. "Proof of individual guilt rests on a demonstration that the defendant knowingly and voluntarily participated in a plan to commit a recognized crime."[11] Conspiracy laws had been used in the United States against organized crime with great effectiveness. By declaring a Mafia family a "criminal organization" the police could lay charges not only against those who committed murder, but also against the Dons who ordered it and the "soldiers" who engaged in intimidation and shakedowns.

In the case of the SS—and this included the whole of the Waffen-SS—the court needed only to prove that participation was voluntary and that the accused had knowledge of the unit's criminal purpose. Only those who were drafted or otherwise forcibly compelled to serve, or who had no knowledge of the criminal nature of the organization, were exempted. It was, however, the opinion of the Tribunal that the activities of the SS were so well known that it would be hard to believe that anyone in its ranks was not aware that the SS engaged in shooting Russian prisoners, exterminating Jews, operating concentration camps, rounding up slave labourers and destroying civilian populations.[12]

In his address to the assembled prosecutors, the Chief of the Legal Department made it plain that the prosecution, "in dealing with any member of the SS, is entitled to ask the Court to infer, in the absence of clear proof to the contrary adduced by the accused, that in virtue of his membership he must have had knowledge of some of the appalling criminal acts and purposes of the SS provided that any of the following acts can be proved against him:

(I) That he held a rank or position at some time between the 1st September, 1939, and the 8th May, 1945, which was likely to give him the opportunity to acquire some knowledge of these criminal acts and purposes, or

(II) That irrespective of his rank or position, he remained a member of the organization for a year or more during that period, or

(III) That he served for a shorter period where such criminal acts and purposes were perpetrated.[13]

These criteria, which fit the Halychyna Division so neatly, were patently ignored by the Foreign Office. No effort was made to determine the actual guilt or innocence of the men involved. No effort was made to learn from the Soviets what they knew of the Division's history, despite numerous indications in the correspondence and minutes on file at the London Public Records Office that the Foreign Office, Home Office and War Office were well aware that there were significant numbers of war criminals in the Ukrainian Division's ranks. Beryl Hughes, the tough-minded director of the Home Office's Alien's Department openly voiced her suspicions to Rae of the Foreign Office:

I don't know what progress you have been able to make in your researches into the Soviet claims but a report which I have received from our Immigration Officer at Munster D.P. Transit Camp, a copy of which I enclose, leads me to believe that at any rate some of these officers may be war criminals. You will note that on the evidence provided by the United States authorities...which was substantiated by [an intercepted] letter sent from Officers of the Division, now in the United Kingdom, HARASSOWSKI was promptly arrested in Germany as a war criminal. I cannot think that the officers with whom he was corresponding in the United Kingdom can have had careers, which differed very greatly, from his and it would be patently unfair to allow them to escape because they happen to be in the United Kingdom.[14]

Panchuk too, before he learned the strategy of absolute denial, conceded that "there may be a few 'blacks' in this group." In a typically lengthy memorandum addressed to the

War Office and the Foreign Office, he hastened to explain that while the history of these men "might date further back than the history of the unit, the great majority by far of these men and particularly other ranks, could be made 'white' and the character of the group changed from P.O.W. to D.P. voluntary labour."[15]

Surprisingly, there is no mention in the voluminous correspondence accumulated in the London Public Record Office, of the Division's German officers who took to their heels in the last days of the war. [See Appendix: Order of Battle, 14. Waffen-Gren. Div. Der-SS (ukrain. Nr. 1)] Nor is there any exploration of the intimate relationship between Wächter and the Division. Nor is any attention paid to the records of Beyersdorff, Bissell, Blankenhorn and Bristot whose crimes were well documented by the United Nations War Crimes Commission. Had their records been explored the realization would inevitably have dawned that they did not commit their crimes single-handedly, that they must have employed the Galician Ukrainians who served under them.

The avoidance of embarrassment rather than a thirst for justice seems to have motivated the British civil servants and their political masters. Time and time again, we see them trivializing or denying the connection between the Division and the Waffen-SS. The wholesale transfer of Ukrainian police units into the Division is either unknown or misinterpreted by the British authorities. The losses at the Battle of Brody are used to camouflage the Division's sad record as a ruthless anti-partisan force prior to 1944.

The guilt of the Division was never honestly evaluated by the British and its innocence never genuinely established. Instead, the problem was handed on to the Canadians to resolve.

Justice Jules Deschênes and The Commission of Inquiry on War Criminals in Canada
Unfortunately, the Canadians did no better. Once the Canadian government signaled on September 25, 1950 that the ban on the Division had been lifted, little was heard of the Division in the Canadian news media. But, if the rest of the world was prepared to forget the Division, one man could not put his memories aside—that man was Simon Wiesenthal. In the first days of the German occupation of Lviv, Wiesenthal was taken into custody by Ukrainian police auxiliaries and witnessed the promiscuous cruelty imposed on the city's Jews and Poles. In the months that followed, he lost his whole family to the Nazi terror and he himself barely escaped death on several occasions. Sick and emaciated when liberated by American troops he determined to seek justice for those who were brutally murdered. He organized an information centre that collected the statements of surviving witnesses and sought out the hiding places of Nazi war criminals.

Working out of his cramped, cluttered headquarters in Vienna, Wiesenthal was keenly aware that most of the killing of civilians on Soviet territory was done by police battalions. His research showed that these police units had graduated into the ranks of the Waffen-SS as the war progressed.[16] As a former resident of Lviv, he was particularly interested in the Halychyna Division. In 1984, he forwarded a list of 217 Division officers whose names he had gathered from a variety of sources to the then Solicitor General of Canada, Robert Kaplan. Canada, he suggested to Kaplan, was a good place to search for them because so many veterans of the Division had chosen to settle there. "Enclosed please find the list of Ukrainian-SS officers, who survived the war and are not living in Europe," he wrote. "According to our experience a great number of them should live in Canada."[17]

Kaplan, unfortunately, had no opportunity to investigate Wiesenthal's list. Although the Solicitor General was nominally the cabinet minister in charge of the Royal Canadian Mounted Police, Kaplan was aware that the RCMP had no mandate at the time to search for war criminals. In addition, the Liberal Party government of Pierre Trudeau in which he served gave way in 1983 to the Conservative Party government of Prime Minister Brian Mulroney and Kaplan was relegated to the Opposition benches.

However, the new government sensed that the interest in war criminals was quickening. The whole civilized world was engaged in a highly publicized search for Doctor Death of Auschwitz, the charming, handsome, sadistic Josef Mengele. The heroic actions of Raul Wallenberg, who saved thousands of Hungarian Jews from incineration at Auschwitz, helped throw the spotlight on the Central-European nations that collaborated willingly with Hitler. Closer to home, SS Master Sergeant Helmut Rauca, responsible for the death of 9,200 Lithuanian Jews in one twenty-four hour period, had been discovered living in Toronto. After a lengthy hearing, in which it was revealed that he had been granted Canadian citizenship, travelled regularly on a Canadian passport and received a Canadian government pension, Rauca was extradited to Germany where he died in prison awaiting trial.

Word of the success of the U.S. Justice Department's Office of Special Investigations in stripping Nazi war criminals of their American citizenship and deporting them from the United States began to drift across the Canadian border. Booklets and pamphlets published in the Soviet Union and distributed by the Soviet Embassy in Ottawa were finding their way into the hands of reporters. The Soviets named names and described the criminal actions of Latvian, Lithuanian, Byelorussian, Ukrainian and Georgian SS units. Most of the booklets were badly written and full of overblown rhetoric, nevertheless, each contained some element of truth that merited further investigation. Organizations such as the Canadian Holocaust Remembrance Association, Canadian Jewish

Congress, B'nai Brith and the newly arrived Simon Wiesenthal Center (named after the famous Nazi-hunter) sent delegations to Ottawa to demand government action against the hundreds of war criminals they alleged had found shelter in Canada.

At the same time, a number of East European organizations forged a clamorous counter-lobby. Concerned that the growing interest in identifying and prosecuting Nazi war criminals might put some of their own members in jeopardy and stain the reputations of their communities, they talked heatedly of Soviet imperialism, KGB plots and the Jewish lust for vengeance. They called for assurances that no one would be arrested, that no one would be sent back to an Iron Curtain country. They visited their Members of Parliament and reminded them that there were at least two million non-Jewish, Canadian citizens of eastern European descent in Canada, as opposed to, perhaps, five hundred thousand Jews.

Finding itself between the proverbial "rock and a hard place" in its efforts to do justice to both sides, the Progressive-Conservative Mulroney government did what all Canadian governments have done—it appointed a Royal Commission of Inquiry. Those familiar with Canadian Commissions of Inquiry know that they usually take several years to hold hearings and write their reports. The reports, in turn, are long and their recommendations numerous. The Cabinet can choose to implement some of the recommendations, all of them or none of them as suits its political purpose. In many cases, by the time the report is filed with the Governor General, the public has lost interest in the issue or no longer recalls what precipitated the inquiry.

Canada's Commission of Inquiry on War Criminals began its work on February 7, 1985 and delivered its 965-page report on December 30, 1986. As Commissioner, the government appointed Justice Jules Deschênes, an experienced judge of the Quebec bench who had earned a reputation for independence by striking down a separatist French language law. Deschênes' report was not received warmly by the Canadian branch of the Simon Wiesenthal Center, the only Canadian agency at the time with a detailed knowledge of World War II Nazi war crimes:

In our judgment, the report—while it does offer some positives—is, nevertheless, seriously flawed and is bound to create confusion and impede the process of prosecuting war criminals. We sense that it will increase the tensions bared between the Jewish community and a number of right-wing East-European communities that appeared at the Commission's hearings. We reject the low estimate of the number of war criminals in Canada announced by the Commission and regard the wholesale clearance of the Galician Waffen-SS Division as illogical, hasty and naive... *In all likelihood, Canada will try no more than two or three war criminals in the next ten years.* By then, most of the alleged war criminals will be able to claim—with some justice—that they are no longer fit to stand trial.[18]

These 1986 predictions have been largely borne out. In the fifteen years since Deschênes tabled his report, the Special Unit established by the Canadian Justice Department in co-operation with Canada's immigration ministry has brought only seventeen persons before the courts on War Crimes charges. As of July 1, 2001, the Special Unit succeeded in gaining convictions in only six cases and lost three. Six of the accused died during the proceedings and two left Canada voluntarily rather than risking a trial. All in all, Canada has succeeded in deporting only three alleged Nazi war criminals.[19]

Much of the difficulty encountered in identifying and prosecuting the numerous World War II war criminals who found a safe haven in Canada can be traced back to Deschênes' report. Looking back, the judge's report smacks more of a political document than a strict judicial review of cases and their historic setting. In an absolutely unprecedented action, Deschênes rewrote sections of his completed report at the request of the government in order to obliterate all signs of where the crimes were committed, when they were committed and by whom they were committed. This was a highly unusual circumstance; there is no other instance in which a Commissioner changed any part of his report at the government's bidding. While it was entirely proper to keep the names of alleged war criminals names confidential, the report is a no-man's land denuded of all landmarks. One can't tell what town, what country, what military unit, or even which war was involved. Although the Quebec judge insisted that nothing vital was changed or obliterated, one cannot help wondering why a highly experienced jurist would acquiesce to making changes to the text of a Royal Commission report.

In Part I of the report—Part 2 was classified as confidential and has not been released—Deschênes presented a master list of 774 persons who had been alleged to be war criminals and collaborators, an addendum of 38 additional names and a list of 71 German scientists who may have settled in Canada. Each name is accompanied by a brief, featureless summary of the Commission's findings. Most of the cases were dismissed for lack of clear-cut *prima facie* evidence.

Judging from the case descriptions, Commission research was amateurish, hasty and incomplete. In many cases, the commission either didn't know where to find information or was reluctant to do so. In one case, the commission reported that it had made inquiries at the Berlin Document Centre, the Central Office of Land Judicial Authorities for the Investigation of National Socialist Crimes located in Ludwigsburg, the Central Information Office of the Federal Archives in Aachen-Kornelimunster, the German Military Service Office for notifying next-of-kin of members of the former German *Wehrmacht* (WASt) in

Berlin and the Berlin Sick Book Depository, none of which had a record of the subject. "On the basis of the foregoing, it is recommended that the file on the subject be closed," the report concluded. There is no consideration of the possibility that the subject came to Canada under an assumed name or that small changes in spelling and transliteration of Slavic names may have caused difficulty. There is no realization that the West German archives, like the case records of the United Nations War Crimes Commission, were basically collections of western names and incidents. Yet, at least seventy-five percent of the names in Deschênes' data bank consisted of East and Central-European names that never made it into West German archives.

The East Germans had much better information than the West Germans on eastern SS units, but as a matter of policy, Deschênes made "a conscious decision...that it would not forward names on its master list to any East European country." The reason offered by the commission was that it feared that for "ideological or political reasons, the recipient country might wish to publicize the names of the individuals and attempt to give the impression that the Commission or the Government of Canada had somehow conceded that these individuals were war criminals." This reason would be sound if there were any experience to suggest that the USSR or Poland had previously taken advantage of such inquiries in its dealings with the United States, West Germany, Holland or any other country. But there is no evidence that the USSR or Poland chose to make political capital out of inquiries from any of the agencies engaged in prosecuting war criminals.

Arnold Fradkin, a veteran Canadian Justice Department litigator and a former member of the Special Unit on War Crimes organized in the wake of the Deschênes Commission Report to prosecute war criminals, puts the matter tersely in an article he wrote in 1997 for *The Canadian Jewish News*:

> A review of these [individual] summaries [in the Commission Report] reveals a dependence upon what is characterized as "external checks," namely inquiries made at German archives that specialized in German nationals and membership in the German Nazi Party, the German police and military organizations. Often the commission recommended closing a suspect's file if his name was not located in these archives. This approach may have foreclosed further consideration of other war criminals or collaborators in Canada since, as the commission explained elsewhere in its report, "a substantial proportion of its master list was comprised of Russians, Ukrainians or Balts." Persons of these nationalities being Eastern European rather than German might therefore not have been recorded in the German archives upon which the commission relied, although they may have participated or collaborated in war crimes.[20]

The least comprehensible part of the Commission's report was Deschênes' decision to exonerate the whole of the Galician Division while refusing to hear any evidence on the unit except that provided by the lawyer hired to defend the Division before the Commission. The same litany of rationalizations and lies offered by members of the Division and its supporters were apparently accepted as gospel by the learned judge. The same Haldane Porter Report was waved before the learned judge who, in defiance of all logic, quotes generously from it without noting its inadequacies. As a judge accustomed to the close examination of documents, Deschênes should have noted the lack of reliable evidence available to Porter and resisted Porter's convenient conclusions. Instead of demonstrating the same skepticism he exhibited in other sections of his report, Deschênes seems to accept uncritically whatever statements were put before him by the Division's defendants.

No better example could be found of the naiveté of the Commission and its inability to distinguish between self-serving claim and historical fact than the following statement issued by the Ukrainian-Canadian Servicemen's Association, which Deschênes quotes with considerable approval:

> In accordance with general policy for all non-German "foreign" units, the unit was termed Waffen-SS. This should not be mistaken, however, for the actual German SS in which only "pure bred" Germans could serve. The Ukrainians were permitted to have priests in their units, they were not given any SS identity marks whatsoever and the terminology of their ranks and titles were those of the Wehrmacht.[21]

Deschênes was also under the illusion that "The members of the Galicia Division were individually screened for security purposes before admission to Canada."[22] The report offers no evidence to support this conclusion and, ironically, Deschênes' conclusion was totally contradicted by the carefully researched supplementary report composed by Alti Rodal the Commission's official historian. An Oxford University doctoral graduate, Rodal devotes considerable space in her report to a discussion of the inadequate screening methods employed by the RCMP and the British security services. Rodal states bluntly: "There is therefore little basis for current statements suggesting that the Canadian government admitted members of the Galician Division only 'after carefully ascertaining that no war criminals were among those wishing to come to Canada', and after many screenings and much vetting of the Division's history and membership."[23] Her report, incidentally, is an official Commission of Inquiry document, approved paradoxically by Deschênes himself.

Evidence given by the RCMP at Commission hearings also revealed that information gathered in the immediate post-war years from British and American sources—the Canadians had few sources of their own—proved to be highly unreliable. It has, for example, been widely recognized that Canadian, British and American authorities deliberately rewrote the histories of Nazi scientists in order to make them more eligible for entry into the USA and Britain.[24] Is there any reason to believe that members of the British security forces who cleared the veterans of the Galician Division were any more punctilious in examining the backgrounds of individuals their government was eager to be rid of, than they had been in dealing with those their government was determined to recruit?

Witnesses before the Deschênes Commission also testified that Canadian Visa Control Officers working in Europe, refused, as a matter of policy, to seek information behind the Iron Curtain.

How and why Deschênes chose to ignore Rodal's findings and the evidence of reliable witnesses before the Commission is difficult to comprehend. The answer may lie in his anxiety lest he arouse the wrath of several of the militant East European organizations with a record of collaboration under Nazi occupation. In refusing to review the Canadian government's 1950 decision to admit the Division, Deschênes stated: "The Commission has not been created to revive old hatreds that once existed abroad between communities which should now live in peace in Canada."[25] Laudable as this sentiment may be, the Commission was created to determine the truth about war criminals in Canada and not to referee inter-ethnic relationships.

Even more puzzling is Deschênes' assertion that: "The Commission has not been created to review government decisions taken by previous generations of public officials."

Why not? One would expect that such a review would have been a priority for the Commission. Otherwise why examine questions such as "How did war criminals enter Canada?" Why review post-war immigration regulations or the whole question of war crimes itself if not to throw light on previous government decisions?

Deschênes claimed: "No case can be made against members of the Galicia Division for revocation of citizenship or deportation since the Canadian authorities were fully aware of the relevant facts in 1950 and admission to Canada was not granted them because of any false representation, or fraud, or concealment of material circumstances."[26] This claim is contradicted by scores of documents in the British and Canadian archives that reveal that Division spokesmen lied to the British, and the British, in turn, lied to the Canadians. Relevant facts *were* concealed from the Canadian authorities and further distorted by the briefs offered by Panchuk and his cronies. If ever there was cause for suspicion of fraud, misrepresentation and concealment of relevant facts that deserved intense investigation rather than easy dismissal, it was the self-serving claims of the Galician Division.

Distinctly troubling was the total lack of moral perspective in the Commission's report. There is no sign that Deschênes disapproved of those who guarded concentration camps and served as willing executioners in *Einsatzgruppe* police battalions. Family court judges have been known to express more disapproval of an erring husband's failure to keep up his alimony payments than the Deschênes Report expresses for those alleged to have committed mass murder. There is not a single mention of the victims of Nazi war criminals in his 965 page report, no word of sympathy for those that suffered in Nazi camps and no expression of indignation for the atrocities committed by the Nazi collaborators who fled to Canada.

The question has been raised whether Deschênes was the most appropriate judge to undertake Canada's first and only full-scale war crimes investigation.[27] In 1979, full of years and experience, Deschênes published a book, *The Sword and the Scales,* in which he expressed his strong disapproval of the post-war trial of Vichy president Marshall Philippe Pétain. "I am very much afraid that the rule of law has known more glorious days," Deschênes wrote.[28] In a subsequent paragraph he stated that he agreed with Field Marshal Hermann Goering that the "Nuremberg [Trials] represented the justice of the victors."[29]

In the same book, Deschênes also questioned the Allies' moral right to try Nazi war criminals after World War II. He claimed: "The German forces could not have monopolized all the wrongdoings in Europe and Africa as well as the Mediterranean and the Atlantic."[30] One despairs of a judge who cannot distinguish between the behaviour of the Allies and that of the Nazis. And, under the circumstances, one cannot help wondering about the judge's commitment to the prosecution of war criminals. Unfortunately, nothing in his voluminous report serves to dispel such doubts.

Deschênes went on to serve on the United Nations International Court of Justice established to try the host of Serbian, Croatian and Bosnian war criminals that emerged in that tragic effort at "ethnic cleansing." His experience on the Canadian war criminals inquiry was seen as a prime qualification for the task. The eleven-member tribunal issued arrest warrants for more than 75 people accused of war crimes in that savage conflict. To date, few of them have been arrested and fewer tried. Illness cut short the career of the judge once regarded as a likely candidate for the position of Chief Justice of the Canada Supreme Court. Deschênes resigned from the International Court in 1997 and full of honours and expressions of appreciation, retired to his home in Montreal.[31]

Deschênes' report had much to do with the failure of the Canadian effort to prosecute war criminals. The absence of a clear call to justice, the failure to place any impera-
tive on the government to proceed with prosecutions, his eagerness to close cases rather
than explore them fully, his trivialization of the number of war criminals who had found
a safe haven in Canada—all sent a clear signal to the Canadian government that the pursuit and punishment of war criminals was not a clear necessity. It suggested that if undertaken, it could be handled with a minimum of effort and a pedestrian amount of
commitment. The report's hasty, unjustified clearance of the Galician Division served as
warrants of protection for what may well be the largest pool of alleged war criminals in
Canada.

War Aims of the Ukrainian Nationalists

The 1943 war aims of the Ukrainian nationalists are hard to discern because they were
formulated at a time when they themselves recognized that "the imminent defeat of the
Germans was obvious."[32] What then prompted the Ukrainian nationalist leadership to
"make a pact with the devil" at such an inappropriate time.

In an appendix to the English edition of Heike's *The Ukrainian Division 1943-1945*, political geographer Volodymyr Kubijovyc, the leading Ukrainian member of the Military
Committee, struggles to justify the nationalist leadership's decision to throw in their lot
with the Germans. Quoting from a paper he delivered at an April 18, 1943 conference,
Kubijovyc states: "We live in the midst of the cruelest war...in which only might, physical
might has any value." But, deprived of an army of its own, the Ukrainian nationalists remain impotent, "the object and not the subject of events unfolding around us."[33] To
strengthen its hand, "the establishment of the Ukrainian Armed Forces is our desire, because then we will become an allied fighting force recognized for having sacrificed our
blood for our cause. In this way we will become an active force in politics..."[34]

In his view, a Ukrainian Waffen-SS Division would provide the visibility needed to
impress the Germans and prove to Berlin that Ukrainians are worthy of being granted a
major role in the eastern empire Hitler would establish after the war. Meanwhile,
Kubijovyc anticipated that cooperation with the Germans would bring a number of short
run advantages:(1) "instead of an anonymous force we become a recognized part of the
struggle against Bolshevism; (2) we enter the political arena (no matter how humbly) of
Europe and the world: (3) we take measures to preserve our physical well-being and we
establish the nucleus of an army; (4) this can be the starting point for the development of
future plans; (5) only in this fashion can we establish a military academy for our youth,
run by a Ukrainian officer corps. This academy will be able to instill discipline, obedience,

sincerity, honesty, resoluteness, a sense of responsibility, and other military virtues. Our war with Moscow will take on official form."[35]

The chief advantage, as Kubijovyc analyzed the situation, would be a softening of the German position, a relaxation of the strict discipline imposed on the region and an increase in the number of administrative posts available to Ukrainians. Kubijovyc and his colleagues hoped that Wächter, more sympathetic to their cause than other Nazi officials, could arrange an amnesty for all OUN political prisoners, return control of the Ukrainian press to the nationalist Ukrainians and improve the living and working conditions of the *ostarbeiter* (drafted eastern workers) in Germany. However, the Ukrainian leadership soon recognized that Wächter had no power to alter what Himmler had decreed and that bargaining through him was fruitless.

Kubijovyc's ultimate hope was that the Germans and the Russians would fight to mutual exhaustion, to the point where neither of them would have sufficient strength to deny the wishes of a national Ukrainian army. If the scenario played out as he visualized it, the British and Americans would come marching into Lviv following a Balkan invasion. Germans, Russians, British and Americans would be compelled to recognize the Ukrainian Division as the only force capable of maintaining order and would encourage its expansion into a full-scale Ukrainian National Army.[36]

In the end, Kubijovyc's scenario was closer to fairy tale than political reality. When the war ended, the Division, barely able to defend itself, was hastening to surrender in Austria and the Red flag was flying over Lviv.

Incidentally, Kubijovyc's account makes no mention of the agreement supposedly wrested from the Germans guaranteeing that the Ukrainian Division would fight only on the Eastern Front and would never be used against the British and the Americans. No such guarantee is listed by Kubijovyc, nor is it on the list of guarantees expressly desired or sought.[37]

Reunion in Lviv

In 1993, the surviving veterans of the Halychyna Division gathered in Lviv and Kiev to celebrate the newly won independence of Ukraine. Some wore their old uniforms and demonstrated their old German-taught military precision. The Canadian contingent wore the typical Canadian veteran's regalia, the navy-blue blazer, embroidered forage cap and grey slacks. A documentary team working for one of the German television networks filmed their celebration. The TV team's director reports that the aging veterans came from many lands and formed up in national units. Most were quite comfortable being filmed and stared openly at the cameras.[38]

Not all Ukrainians welcomed the veterans' return. In fact, one significant body of Ukrainians bluntly condemned the Division, its OUN genesis and its UPA rival. In 1996, the members of Ukraine's post-Soviet parliament were alarmed by the efforts being made to revive the Organization of Ukrainian Nationalists and to impose its fascist ideology on the newly independent, democratic Ukraine. Streets in Lviv and Lutsk were being renamed after Bandera and Melnyk. Waffen-SS veterans were holding reunions on Ukrainian territory and uniformed youth groups were marching and drilling.

The Ukrainian parliament appointed a parliamentary commission to conduct a legal-political assessment of the OUN, UPA and the Galician Division. The commission's report was supported by ninety-five members of the Ukrainian parliament which issued a statement warning the nations of Europe and the Middle East of the fascist nature of the OUN and its derivatives. In blunt, unequivocal language, the members of parliament, representing the leaders of the major parties on the Ukrainian left, stated: "We...can never forget the hundreds of thousands of innocent victims tortured to death by members of the criminal Organization of Ukrainian Nationalists and its military formations." The statement goes on to cite the "numerous archival materials, court decisions, as well as the testimonies of those who witnessed the criminal activities of the OUN-UPA, the 14th Division SS-Galizien, the Roland and Nachtigall battalions, and numerous works of scholars from various nations confirm their criminal, fascist nature."

The elected members of the Ukrainian parliament, many of whom still retain vivid memories of the bitter days of World War II, recalled "the bestial murder" of at least 100,000 Polish civilians in Volhynia and Galicia alone. "On their conscience lie the massive murders in Babi Yar...and the bloody suppression of the anti-fascist uprisings in Belarus, Poland, Slovakia and Yugoslavia."[39]

The following year, veterans of the Galician SS Division appealed to Ukraine's Attorney General for "rehabilitation," that is the erasure of all criminal charges, the return of seized property and the right to the same pensions and subsidies paid to the veterans who served in the Red Army. The Attorney General replied:

Your appeal concerning the rehabilitation of the soldiers of the "SS-Galicia" Division has been examined. I hereby explain that in accordance with article 2, section 2 of the Law of Ukraine dealing with "The Rehabilitation of Victims of Political Repression in Ukraine" dated 17.04.91, rehabilitation is not considered for those persons for whom there is convincing evidence of responsibility for crimes against humanity and punitive actions against peaceful populations in the form of murder, torture of citizens and aiding the invaders during the Great Patriotic War... [Convicted] persons who during World War II served in the armies of the

SS and other military formations of Germany and her satellites can not be rehabil-
itated. Signed, L. Makoyutyns'ka, Prosecution Section of the Attorney General of
Ukraine.[40]

Apologists for the Division are bound to dismiss the opinion of the Attorney General of
Ukraine and the resolution of the ninety members of Parliament as Communist propaganda and KGB misinformation. However, the Director and General Counsel of the
Crimes Against Humanity and War Crimes Section of Canada's Justice Department cannot be accused of being either a KGB agent or a communist propagandist. In the opinion
of Peter M. Kremer, who directed the unit from 1990 to 1995, "attempts to separate
Waffen-SS units from the SS/Police complex and make them appear 'mere fighting units'
is pure revisionism." "It is a well-accepted historical fact," Kremer wrote in a 1994 letter to
the Canadian Representative of the Simon Wiesenthal Center, "one which is underlined
by various statements of Himmler himself, that the SS was one political identity, guided
entirely by the same ideological principles of anti-Semitism, racism, violence, elitism, and
the rejection of democratic ideas."[41]

Kremer points out that "this ideological creed was the determining factor for every
part of the SS and Police, including the Waffen-SS. Everybody who signed up for the
Waffen-SS—and it is another historical fact that the over-abused excuse of 'having been
forced to join' is not true for the overwhelming majority of members—has by that signed
on to the SS ideology."[42]

It is a travesty, in Kremer's opinion, that some interested groups managed after the
war to create enough disinformation about the true historical facts, to mislead political
authorities into allowing members of the Waffen-SS to immigrate to the west. He regards
it as unfortunate that "the problem of disinformation continues today because the only
detailed histories of Waffen-SS Divisions have been written by former members."[43]

Does this mean that the Halychyna Division veterans who took up residence in Canada, the United Kingdom or the United States are still vulnerable to prosecution? Possibly, although there are no signs that any of these countries intend to act against veterans
of the Division. But if they did decide to act, is prosecution still possible after all these
years? Possibly, given the unit concealed vital information from the Canadian, British
and U.S. authorities. Despite the fact that the British government underwrote their false-
hoods, it may still be possible to muster the evidence to strip them of their citizenship and
deport them to Ukraine—now independent and no longer under Soviet domination.

It would still require a detailed examination of the individual actions of each person
charged. The Nuremberg Tribunal, in its wisdom, rejected the concept of collective guilt,
even for the notorious Waffen-SS. British, Canadian and American courts have high standards and will permit no trifling with due process. They will not strip a man of his valued

citizenship and deport him for some minor flaw in his immigration application, deliberate or otherwise. The prosecution must provide unequivocal proof that his unit participated in atrocities against civilians and that the accused, personally, was there on the day the atrocity was committed and that he, personally, held gun and whip in his hand.

In some case—granted not many—their participation in specific actions can be proven through information residing in Russian and Ukrainian archives. To gather this evidence, it is necessary to determine the individual's pre-war and wartime history, whether he was a member of an auxiliary police unit before joining the Division and in which one. Where did he serve? Who were his comrades in the unit? Under whose command did he serve? When did he join the Division and where did he train? In which actions did he participate?

Given the deliberate destruction of documents and the ailing memories of the handful of surviving witnesses so many years after the war, the evidence would obviously be hard to provide. Nevertheless, whether individuals are prosecuted or not, the history of the Galician Division should be thoroughly and honestly examined. As historian Yury Boshyk states in his introduction to *Ukraine During World War II: History and Its Aftermath*: "...no amount of historical understanding can ever justify the historical fact that, as was true of other peoples during the war, some individuals directly aided and abetted the Nazis in committing crimes against their own people as well as against others."

Notes

1. PRO, FO 371/71663. Zaroubin to Hankey (Translation) June 29, 1948.

2. *Ibid.*

3. *Ibid.*

4. PRO, FO 371/71663.

5. *Ibid.*

6. *Ibid.*

7. *Ibid.*

8. *Ibid.*

9. *Ibid.*

10. PRO, FO 371/64712. Control Commission for Germany (B.S.), Legal Division, Trials of Members of Criminal Organisations, June 5, 1947.

11. Bradley F. Smith, *Reaching Judgment at Nuremberg* (New York: Basic Books, 1977), 18.

12. *Ibid.* 166.

13. PRO, FO 371/64712.

14. PRO, FO 371/71663. Hughes to Rae, July 3, 1948.

15. PRO, FO 371/66712. Memorandum to the British War Office, the Foreign Office, regarding Ukrainian Prisoners of War in Great Britain, June 14, 1947.

16. Simon Wiesenthal, *Justice, Not Vengeance* (London: Weidenfeld and Nicolson, 1989).

17. Commission of Inquiry on War Criminals Report, Part 1: Public,.257.

18. News release issued by Canadian office of the Simon Wiesenthal Center on the heels of the release of the Commission report It should be noted that in those first ten years after receiving the
Deschênes Commission Report, the Special unit on War Crimes appointed to prosecute World
War II war criminals, accused only five persons of war crimes. Of those, it lost its first case before a
jury (Imre Finta); withdrew two cases for lack of sufficient evidence (Michael Pawlowski and Stephen Reistetter); suspended the trial of Radislav Grujisic because of the accused's fragile health
and succeeded in deporting a Vancouver botany instructor (Jacob Luitjens) who had served as a
Nazi auxiliary policeman in his native Holland.

19. Government of Canada news release, July 4, 2001.

20. Arnold Fradkin, "Canada ignored war criminals for 27 years," *The Canadian Jewish News*, January
2, 1997. (Unfortunately, Fradkin died of a heart attack on January 2, 1999.)

21. Commission of Inquiry on War Criminals Report, Part 1: Public, 255.

22. *Ibid.* 261.

23. Alti Rodal, *Nazi War Criminals in Canada: The Historical Setting from the 1940s to the Present*, Prepared for the Commission of Inquiry on War Criminals, printed by Queen's Printer but available
only through Access to Information, 390.

24. Canadian Press, "Canada bent rules to accept German scientists," *The Sault Star*, May 14, 1987.

25. Commission of Inquiry, 254.

26. *Ibid.* 261.

27. See Sol Littman, "In the Wake of Canada's Inquiry on War Criminals: The Deschênes Commission," *Outlook*, Vol. 38. No. 5, September/October 2000.

28. Jules Deschênes, *The Sword and the Scales* (Toronto: Butterworth & Co. (Canada) Ltd., 1979),
182-187.

29. *Ibid.*

30. *Ibid.*

31. Deschênes died in May, 2000.

32. Volodymyr Kubijovyc, "Origins of the Ukrainian Division 'Galicia'," appendix A, English edition, Heike, *The Ukrainian Division 'Galicia' 1943-1945, 141.*

33. *Ibid.* 140.

34. *Ibid.* 140.

35. *Ibid.* 141.

36. *Ibid.* 141.

37. *Ibid.* 143.

38. John Goetz, Berlin, personal telephone conversation, 1997.

39. Deputies of the Ukrainian Parliament, ninety-five signatures, including: S. Dovhan,
V.Ponedilko, K. Samoilyk, Y. Syzonenko, M. Lavrynenko, Y. Marmazov, A. Khrunov, V.
Cherepkov, P. Kuznyetsov and H. Dovzhenko.

40. *Visti Kombatanti*, issue 5-6, 1997.

41. Peter M. Kremer, Q.C. letter of November 14, 1994, to Sol Littman, Friends of the Simon
Wiesenthal Centre for Holocaust Studies.

42. *Ibid.*

43. *Ibid.*

CHAPTER 17

THE OUN, SIS, OSS, AND CIA

COLD WARS MAKE FOR STRANGE BEDFELLOWS!

In 1941, a small, bespectacled man in civilian clothes accompanied the first wave of German troops to storm over the Soviet border. In his pocket he carried a list of Polish intellectuals and political leaders the OUN intended to liquidate. However, in 1984, Yaroslav Stetsko—now a leading member of the Anti-Bolshevik Bloc of Nations (ABN)—was welcomed at the White House by President Ronald Reagan as a noble, anti-Communist freedom-fighter intent on freeing the Captive Nations in Central and Eastern Europe.[1]

Stetsko, one of the prime leaders of OUN/B was appointed Prime Minister of the short-lived independent Ukrainian Republic by Bandera in 1941. Arrested by the Gestapo for his bold nationalism, he shared Bandera's comfortable imprisonment in Sachsenhausen. The arrest served Bandera and Stetsko well since it allowed them to promote the myth that the OUN/B was a victim of German oppression. Mark Aarons, author of *Sanctuary: Nazi Fugitives in Australia,* disagrees with the characterization of the OUN as anti-Nazi: "The truth was that they never broke with the Nazis, and although their Ukrainian Insurgent Army (the UPA) occasionally harried the Germans towards the end of the war, throughout most of the war years it carried out massacres of Jews and Poles and helped the Nazis fight Soviet partisans."[2]

Logically, the OUN should have withered and died with the defeat of Hitlerism, but British covert operations breathed new life into a fundamentally spent political movement. Aarons comments further: "As part of the anti-Communist crusade, the British Secret Service not only shielded OUN members from justice for their wartime involvement with Nazis, but gave a virulently racist group the oxygen, to say nothing of the money, with which to survive and continue its political campaign to this day."[3]

At war's end, when the British secret service (SIS) began to recruit Ukrainian nationalists to serve as anti-Soviet spies, it was Stetsko who selected suitable candidates from the ranks of the Galician Division. British officers stationed in Germany instructed the

OUN recruits in the use of secret codes, radio transmission and photography. Some were flown to Britain for parachute training and later dropped in Ukraine. Two unmarked C-47 airplanes dropped small groups of Ukrainian parachutists near major Soviet airfields in 1949 with orders to radio back information. They disappeared without contacting their home base.

In March 1951, three teams of Galician Division veterans, totaling eighteen men, took off from Cyprus and parachuted into the Lviv-Ternopil region, never to be heard from again. While it is not certain how many OUN spies were actually dropped on Soviet territory, it is clear that few of the missions were successful. In almost every case, the KGB gathered them up soon after they landed. Whether this was due to the penetration of OUN ranks by the KGB or the treachery of Kim Philby, Britain's most notorious spy, is still debated by historians.[4]

Philby was one of several brilliant Cambridge students recruited by the Soviet intelligence service (NKVD) and its successor the KGB, to serve as Soviet agents. After a brief career as a journalist covering the Spanish Civil War, he joined Britain's Secret Intelligence Service (MI6). Charming, highly intelligent and boasting an "old school tie," Philby was appointed head of the counter-espionage section dedicated to counter-acting Soviet advances in the post-war world. Assigned to liaison with the American intelligence apparatus, he was party to both British and American plans to penetrate Soviet defences. The ease with which the KGB rounded up British and American spies parachuted into Albania and the Baltic countries is attributed to Philby's betrayal.[5] It is highly likely that he played a part in betraying the Halychyna veterans recruited by the SIS as well.[6]

As the Cold War chill deepened, the stated determination to bring to justice those responsible for Nazi atrocities enunciated in the Moscow Declaration was first evaded and then ignored.[7] As early as April 1945, while the war was still in progress and the Soviet Union was still an ally, William Donovan, head of the Office of Strategic Services (OSS) secretly ordered his agents to make Soviet intentions in the Balkans a prime intelligence target.[8] In the autumn of 1944, an OSS mission in Romania under the command of former Wall Street lawyer Frank Wisner launched one of the earliest Cold War operations against the Russians. Wisner's agents reported that the Soviets were making strong efforts to dominate local anti-Nazi resistance movements so they could take political control of them in the post-war world.[9] In the opinion of John Ranelagh, author of *The Agency: The Rise and Decline of the CIA*, "It was the start of what was, in effect, a secret foreign policy which found form only when America recognized the Cold War in 1947."[10]

The Americans realized that the Russians were on the march and that they needed better intelligence and more agents to insert behind Soviet lines. By 1946, the Soviet Union was gaining influence throughout Eastern Europe; civil war was raging in Greece, while Turkey and Iran were feeling Soviet pressure. In 1948, the communist coup in Czechoslovakia shocked American policy makers and persuaded them that the Soviets needed to be contained.[11] Consequently, irrevocably committed anti-Communists such as the veterans of the Halychyna Division became a valuable Cold War asset. They spoke the local language, were familiar with the countryside and were past masters at manipulating the inter-ethnic conflicts between Poles, Russians and Ukrainians.

The British, first in the field recruiting east-European collaborators, found they could not stay the course. By 1950, drained by her wartime expenditures, Britain realized she could no longer afford her extensive covert operations and called on the Americans to take up the burden. British links with the OUN and UPA were ceded to the CIA, successor to the OSS. The Americans were more than willing to take on the job and readily adapted to the chicanery, ambiguity and self-interest practiced by British policy makers and intelligence gatherers.[12]

The Gehlen Organization

The employment of former enemy personnel to spy on the Russians became common practice. "Within weeks of the end of the war in Europe, suspicion of Russia secured special privileges for General Reinhard Gehlen, head of the Abwehr's Foreign Armies East section (Fremde Heere Ost—FHO) and responsible for German military intelligence about the Soviet Union."[13]

Two weeks after the German surrender, Gehlen came out of hiding to give himself up to American forces patrolling in Bavaria. Interrogated by U.S. intelligence officers, he impressed them with the information he had gathered on Soviet plans to retain Poland, Czechoslovakia, Bulgaria, Hungary and Romania as satellite states. Gehlen also claimed to have a network of agents in Eastern Europe who were adept at gathering intelligence and engaging the Communists in guerrilla warfare.[14] According to Gehlen a modest infusion of American funds would resurrect a well-trained cadre of saboteurs, espionage agents and strong-arm specialists in eastern bloc countries.[15] With the support and blessings of U.S. General Edwin Sibert, the chief of Army Intelligence in Europe, Gehlen constructed a new intelligence apparatus consisting of German "experts" on the USSR.

Among the "experts" taken on board the newly formed "Organization Gehlen" were a half-dozen former SS and SD officers—men who were not only true believers in the Nazi cause but notorious war criminals as well.[16] Chief among them were senior SS officers Franz Six and Emil Augsburg.[17] Six, a former lecturer at Koenigsberg University, rose to the rank of *SS Brigadeführer* in Himmler's RSHA (*Reichssicherheitshauptamt*, Reich Security Main Office). Tried by a U.S. military tribunal at Nuremberg in 1948 for ordering the

execution of hundreds of civilians while in command of a *Jagdkommando* (pursuit formation) on the Smolensk front in 1941, he was sentenced to twenty years imprisonment.
However, four years later, Six was granted clemency by John J. McCloy, U.S. High Commissioner in Germany, and was free to become a leading executive in the Gehlen Organization.[18]

Dr. Emil Augsburg rose to the rank of *SS Standartenführer* (Colonel) in Adolf
Eichmann's Department S-4 that dealt with the "Jewish Problem." During the war, he
commanded a murder squad in German-occupied Russia and won high praise from his
superiors for achieving "extraordinary results."[19] With the defeat of the German forces,
Augsburg fled to Italy where he was assisted by Vatican circles that gave cover to fleeing
Nazis. Two years later, he returned to Germany as Dr. Althaus and was hired by Gehlen
in key positions in Karlsruhe and Pullach.[20]

In addition to his German experts, Gehlen set about recruiting the displaced and dis-
contented of Europe. He drew in Latvian Legionnaires, Lithuanian and Estonian death
squad members, as well as the Russian NTS *(Naroddnyi Trudovoy Soyuz)*, the monarchist
Brotherhood of St. George (ROND) and the OUN. Indeed, Gehlen established a special
camp for OUN/B spies and saboteurs near Oberursel.[21]

In his negotiations with the American command, Gehlen drove a hard bargain. Although the Americans would finance Organization Gehlen, "his organization would not
be regarded as part of the American intelligence services but as an autonomous apparatus under his exclusive management. Liaison with American Intelligence would be maintained by U.S. officers who would require Gehlen's approval."[22] However, the Americans
would have the exclusive use of the intelligence produced. In the event that German and
American interests should diverge in the future "it was accepted that the organization
would consider the interests of Germany first."[23]

The Gehlen Organization became operational in 1946. When West Germany was established as an independent state in 1949, Gehlen was appointed head of the West German intelligence service, the BND *(Bundesnachrichtensdienst)*, a position he maintained
until his retirement in 1968. It was later learned that many of the networks Gehlen
claimed to be operative, and much of the information he provided, proved to be fanciful.
Nevertheless, it was eagerly received and widely believed by American officials caught in
the throes of Cold War hysteria.[24] Christopher Simpson, in his book *Blowback*, describes
the many misadventures of American intelligence agencies. Simpson claims that
Gehlen's operatives and analysts strongly reinforced the American paranoia about communism and the USSR, thereby contributing significantly to a body of widely believed
misinformation about Soviet behavior.[25]

The "Rat Line"

The Gehlen Organization and its Nazi-tainted personnel was not the only post-war venture to prove embarrassing to the United States when exposed in later years. For example, the U.S. Army's 430 Counter Intelligence Corps (CIC) established an elaborate escape route for former enemies who had become American agents that became known as the Ratline. The 430 CIC unit provided exposed spies, anti-Soviet politicians and Nazi torturers with new personas and false documents. CIC agents shepherded them carefully along a route that led from central Europe to Naples and Genoa. From there, ships carried them to South American ports in Chile, Peru, Brazil and Columbia.

The CIC personnel that operated the Ratline collaborated closely with Msgr. Krunoslav Draganovic, a Croatian priest with strong pro-Nazi connections. Draganovic's ties to the Ustasha regime were well known, as was his participation in the "relocation" of Serbs and Jews by the wartime Croatian regime. Draganovic also maintained extensive contacts with a variety of émigré organizations, especially those that had joined the Nazi cause and were no longer welcome in their homelands. Known to the CIC personnel as the "Good Father," they depended on Draganovic to choose which of the fleeing Ustasha camp commanders, Slovak Hlinka Guardists and Gestapo torturers merited sanctuary in South America. The good priest was regarded by his CIC confederates as "completely corrupt" and the operator of a visa racket that charged $1500 per head "with no questions asked." CIC personnel recognized him as a fascist and war criminal and a person who would be sternly condemned by U.S. State Department officials if they had known of his presence.[26]

Klaus Barbie

Gestapo agent Klaus Barbie, known as "The Butcher of Lyons," was among those who received the Croatian priest's blessings. Draganovic personally greeted Barbie and his CIC escort at the Genoa railway station and conducted the Nazi torturer to his hotel to await his ship. When the ship proved to be overbooked, the "Good Father" bribed the ship's purser to make room for Barbie and his family.[27]

While serving the Gestapo in Holland in 1941, Barbie personally led attacks on the Jewish community of Amsterdam and commanded the firing squad that executed two of Holland's most respected leaders. He set a trap for three hundred Jewish apprentices and shipped them to Mathausen concentration camp where most of them died. The SS used some of the youths as guinea pigs in early gassing experiments.[28]

In 1942, Barbie was posted to France where he served as head of the Gestapo's Section IV in Lyons. Section IV was responsible for tracking down members of the French *resis-*

THE OUN, SIS, OSS, AND CIA / 193

tance as well as Communists and Jews. Ruthless and sly he scored numerous successes against the inexperienced agents parachuted into the Lyons sector by the British. He took cunning advantage of the political differences between the various French *resistance* organizations to infiltrate their ranks and identify their leaders. "His leadership was efficient, dynamic and totally uncompromising," says British writer Tom Bower in his book, *Klaus Barbie: Butcher of Lyons.* His uncompromising interrogation techniques included severe beatings, electric shock, immersion in ice-cold baths, injection of acids and burning with a red-hot poker. He tortured children in the presence of their helpless parents and caressed his mistress while his subordinates tortured a screaming suspect.

Barbie was also instrumental in the deportation to Auschwitz of forty-one Jewish children, aged three to thirteen years of age from a children's shelter in the French village of Izieu, north of Lyons. In a report to his superiors, Barbie boasted, "This morning a stop was put to the activities of the home for Jewish children *'colonie enfant'* Izieu, Ain: Forty-one children aged from three to thirteen years were arrested. In addition, the entire Jewish staff, ten strong including five women, was arrested as well."[29]

Without question, Barbie was a vicious sadist who thoroughly enjoyed other people's suffering. His most prominent victim was Jean Moulin, General de Gaulle's representative to the politically divided resistance movement. Captured on his way to a meeting of resistance leaders in Paris, Moulin refused to give his interrogator any information. Barbie beat him to death.[30]

Barbie's cruelty put him on everyone's war criminals list. The French were eager to arrest him. A permanent military tribunal was appointed to hear witnesses on Barbie's crimes against the *resistance* in the Jura and St. Claude regions. Both the Central Registry of Wanted War Criminals and Security Suspects (CROWCASS) published in Paris and the United Nations War Crimes Commission (UNWCC) compiled in London, listed him as guilty of torture and murder in Lyons. However, operating under a variety of aliases and sheltered by the *Kameradenschaft,* a secret organization of former SS officers, Barbie managed to avoid arrest.

How did it happen then, that the widely sought Gestapo agent came under the CIC's protection?

Again, the Cold War provides the answer. As the American ardor for prosecuting Nazi war criminals diminished in the face of the Communist threat, some of Barbie's old Gestapo confederates persuaded the Americans that they commanded a vast network of informants in Europe stretching from Lisbon to the Soviet border.[31] Peter Grose, author of *Operation Rollback: America's Secret War behind the Iron Curtain,* claims that "Real, and more often, fictitious sources of information [were] dangled before the Americans in return for favorable treatment from war crimes courts."[32] Barbie recognized that he could find safety and a good living by offering his services to his former enemies. In 1947, he was hired by a CIC detachment headquartered in Munich to penetrate a suspected Soviet spy ring in Bavaria.

However, Barbie's presence did not go unnoticed by the CIC detachment in Frankfurt that demanded his immediate arrest. But Munich replied that Barbie was too valuable to dispense with. According to CIC agent Robert Taylor, Barbie had provided the CIC with extensive connections to French Intelligence agencies working uninvited in the U.S. zone of occupation. In addition, he had provided contact to high-ranking German, Romanian and Russian circles. Taylor described Barbie as a Nazi idealist "who believes that he and his beliefs were betrayed by the Nazis in power."[33]

For the next four years, Barbie swaggered about Munich in command of a constantly expanding network of former Gestapo agents. However, by 1951 the Americans had begun to doubt the accuracy and validity of the information he produced. They also began to question whether the network of agents for whom Barbie was submitting expense accounts was real or a figment of his imagination. At the same time there was mounting pressure from Frankfurt to dispense with Barbie's services. The French government, well aware that Barbie was lurking in the U.S. occupation zone, was also applying pressure. The U.S. State Department was also growing curious and addressing inquiries to the Military Government. All in all, Barbie was becoming a serious embarrassment.

Barbie's controllers decided it was time to put Barbie on the Ratline.[34]

The former terror of Lyons chose Bolivia for his exile because "sixty percent of the nation's economy was owned by the German community; German nationals trained and led the national army during the thirties."[35] Barbie grew rich and powerful in Bolivia and served as an advisor to General Hugo Banzer, a right-wing dictator who ruled the country with the aid of a dreaded secret police that specialized in torture and repression.

Meanwhile, much of the world lost interest in the former Gestapo agent and his crimes. That is until Beate Klarsfeld took up the chase in 1972. Audacious and unrelenting, Beate staged protests and lobbied French and German officials to demand Barbie's extradition from Bolivia. Despite threats to her life by Bolivian police, the German-born, Protestant woman—married to a French-born Jewish lawyer—chained herself to a La Paz park bench where she held daily press conferences. However, despite her best efforts, it was not until February 1983, when a new liberal government replaced the Banzer regime that Barbie was returned to France. After a lengthy, emotional trial, the French court sentenced him to life imprisonment.[36]

Criminal Conspiracy or Blatant Discrimination

Barbie and the Gehlen Organization was not the only evidence of the USA's forgiving attitude to the worst of Nazi war criminals. In the opinion of Tom Bower whose several books have won the respect and admiration of academic historians, the shenanigans of the CIA, FBI and the U.S. Immigration Service amounted to a criminal conspiracy:

> In Washington, the U.S. House of Representatives' Judiciary Committee for many
> years has been investigating and publishing disturbing evidence that many east-
> ern Europeans, who had willingly aided the Germans in the extermination of mil-
> lions of Jews and others during the war, had been smuggled illegally into the
> USA, had been granted American citizenship and were leading peaceful, prosper-
> ous lives. Investigation had revealed that their presence in America was the result
> of an extraordinary criminal conspiracy between the CIA, the FBI and the U.S. im-
> migration services.[37]

However, Allan A. Ryan, former Director of the Office of Special Investigations (OSI), the U.S. Justice Department's war crimes prosecution unit, questions whether their actions rose to the level of a criminal conspiracy. Ryan does not deny that the agencies looked the other way when wanted war criminals stole into the country or were deposited in Latin America. He himself cites the case of Andrija Artukovic, the Minister of the Interior in the puppet Croatian government, who oversaw the ethnic cleansing campaign that saw thousands of Jews, Serbs and Gypsies stabbed, tortured and dismembered. Artukovic came to the United States on a visitor's visa. Although ordered deported in 1950, he was still a California resident when Ryan wrote *Quiet Neighbors* in 1984.[38] In Ryan's judgment the Barbie case was an exceptional circumstance not typical of the CIA.[39]

While rejecting the charge of criminal conspiracy, Ryan levels a much more serious allegation at the post-war American government. He insists there is abundant proof that "Nazi war criminals came here by the thousands, through the openly deliberated public policy of this country, formulated by Congress and administered by accountable offi-cials."[40] He claims that the vast majority of Nazi war criminals "came in by the front door" with their papers in order. They were aided, not by corrupt officials, but by a law openly debated and passed by Congress.

The Displaced Persons Act of 1948 made room for 200,000 Europeans displaced by war and shifting national boundaries, to enter the United States. Humanitarian on its face, the law was deliberately crafted to exclude Jewish concentration camp survivors and to encourage German, Ukrainian and Baltic refugees to come to America. The act gave clear preference to farmers, whether Latvian, Lithuanian, Estonian or Volksdeutsche. Ryan claims that the drafters of the new law were fully aware that only a minor percentage of Jews survived the *Einsatzgruppen* slaughter in Eastern Europe and fewer still had been farmers. According to Ryan, "It was no accident that the DP Act excluded the vast majority of the Jews in the Displaced Persons camps and gave preference to the very groups that had been found to be infested with Nazi collaborators." Ryan further asserts that "The House and Senate committees that produced the bill were dominated by isolationists who had no desire to throw open the gates to any European huddled masses, and particularly not Jews."[41]

But weren't the refugees rigorously screened before they were admitted? Wasn't the CIC required under the Act to check their backgrounds to determine if they had been active Nazis? Weren't the CROWCASS and UNWCC records available to the American screeners? In theory, yes! In fact, the screening process was limited and grotesquely inept. Both CROWCASS and UNWCC records dealt primarily with Nazi barbarities in Western Europe and were largely blind to the atrocities inflicted in the east. Neither agency would have had a record of Klaus Barbie's activities if he had operated in Poland or Romania instead of Holland and France. While the Germans were massive, compulsive record keepers, they were little interested in the misdeeds of their Ukrainian, Hungarian and Slovak fellow travelers. As a result, CIC investigations were limited largely to a brief interview in which the applicant could present himself in any guise he wished since personal records were almost universally "lost in the war." So long as a resident of a Displaced Persons camp was anti-Communist, behaved himself reasonably in camp and claimed to be a child of the soil, he had a good chance of being admitted to the United States. As the *New York Times* expounded in a 1948 article, the passage of the Displaced Persons Act "made it easier for a former Nazi to enter the United States than for one of the Nazis' innocent victims."[42]

Cold War Assassins

In more cases than the U.S. cared to admit, the CIA "owed" these former Nazis a refuge for their services as Cold War assassins. Simpson in *Blowback* says: "Covert operations chief [Frank] Wisner estimated in 1951 that some 35,000 Soviet police troops and Communist party cadres had been eliminated by guerrillas connected with the Nazi collaborationist OUN/UPA in Ukraine since the end of the war."[43] A CIA covert operation dubbed Operation Ohio made use of a squad of Ukrainian ex-Nazis to carry out at least twenty murders in Displaced Persons camp at Mittenwald, south of Munich.[44] According to the CIA, the victims were double agents, Soviet spies and other undesirables

The issue here is not the morality of assassinations as a political weapon by the Americans. The Soviets also made considerable use of this tool to strike at Cold War opponents and to settle their own internal quarrels. Stalin's agent Jacques van Dreschd posed as

Leon Trotsky's friend and admirer before dispatching him with an ice-axe in Mexico City in 1940. KGB agent Bogdan Stashinsky dispatched OUN leader Lev Rebet in 1957. Two years later, he murdered Stefan Bandera with a poison gas pellet.[45] The issue raised by Simpson can be stated as follows: Who was recruited to serve as assassins and why were they chosen? Christopher Simpson, a harsh critic of American covert operations, states:

> To put the case bluntly, many American clandestine warfare specialists believed that the most 'productive'—and least compromising—method of killing foreign officials was to underwrite the discontent of indigenous groups and let *them* take the risks... Former Nazi collaborators made excellent executioners...because of both their wartime training and the fact that the U.S. government could plausibly deny any knowledge of their activities.[46]

Intermarium

As World War II closed down and the Soviet Union was perceived as the next imminent threat to the free world, the United States sought to create a vast anti-Soviet movement to help win the ideological battle against Communism. One of the key instruments in the battle was the revival by the CIA of a spent, largely Catholic organization founded in the mid-thirties.

Intermarium (Between the Seas) began its complicated life as an amalgamation of anti-Communist Catholic lay organizations in Eastern Europe. During the war years it served as an instrument of the *Abwehr* to gather information on the numerous refugee communities in Europe. Under CIA sponsorship *Intermarium* sought to draw together the plethora of pre-war nationalist organizations that longed to see the restoration of the authoritarian puppet states formed under German rule in Croatia, Slovakia, Hungary and Serbia.

With the war's close, *Intermarium* leaders such as Draganovic and Buchko, advocated the creation of a volunteer anti-Communist army to recapture the "captive nations" that had fallen under Soviet dominance. They urged the Western Allies to reorganize their forces and launch an immediate attack on the USSR and world communism.[47]

Although no overt invasion of Soviet territory took place, U.S. intelligence did conduct many covert operations. Simpson, who has made full use of numerous declassified documents obtained through the Freedom of Information Act, states:

> In case after case, a clear continuity of personnel can be established, beginning with the Vatican refugee-smuggling networks in 1945, continuing into *Intermarium* and winding up in a variety of CIA financed political warfare projects in the 1950s. A score of *Intermarium* leaders ended up as officials in Radio Free Eu-

rope, Radio Liberation and the Assembly of Captive European Nations (ACEN), each of which the U.S. government has admitted as having been a CIA controlled and financed enterprise. A number of *Intermarium* activists, including some, who were war criminals even by the strictest definition of the term, followed this pipeline into the United States.[48]

Dr. Ferdinand Durcansky, who was listed by the United Nations War Crimes Commission as a "Category A" war criminal, nevertheless became a leading *Intermarium* figure. Durcansky, who served as Foreign Minister of the Nazi-sponsored breakaway Slovak state from 1939-1945, was tried *in absentia* and convicted as a war criminal by the post-war Czechoslovakian government. (It is important to note that that the Czechoslovak government at the time of his trial was fully democratic. It was not until 1948 that it was taken over by the Communists.)[49] Nevertheless, Durcansky became a leading *Intermarium* figure and traveled freely between Europe, Latin America, United States and Canada.

Mykola Lebed

Among the war criminals and Nazi collaborators "piped" into the United States was Mykola Lebed. In 1934, Lebed was among the OUN activists arrested with Bandera for plotting the assassination of Poland's Interior Minister, Bronislaw Pieracki. A 1986 *Village Voice* article by Joe Conason based on a lengthy U.S. General Accounting Office (GOA) investigation, states: "U.S. Army Counterintelligence reports say that Lebed initially escaped from Warsaw but was recaptured in Stettin, Germany, and returned to Poland by the German authorities. Convicted in a mass trial, Bandera and Lebed were condemned to death, but their sentences were commuted to life imprisonment."[50] In the confusion that accompanied the German invasion of Poland, Lebed and Bandera were released from prison in 1939 and allowed to continue their political work.

The *Village Voice* article alleged that Lebed was chief of the OUN's security arm and in that capacity, ordered the murder of many of his countrymen. He also attended a Gestapo training school in Poland where Jews were murdered for practice. Lebed was allowed into the United States because he was regarded as an extremely valuable intelligence asset by the U.S. Central Intelligence Agency, which protected him from prosecution as a war criminal by the Soviets and concealed his true past from the Immigration and Naturalization Service.[51]

The Ukrainian nationalist movement inhabited a fiercely competitive, viciously conspiratorial world of its own. Melnyk's organization repeatedly denounced the Bandera group to the Gestapo.[52] In return, Lebed "consolidated OUN power by murdering the leaders of several rival Ukrainian nationalist groups during the war."[53]

After the war, the OUN/B continued its hard-line political stance. Under the banner of anti-communism, it brought together other Eastern European émigré groups in the Anti-Bolshevik Bloc of Nations, many of whom collaborated with the Nazis during the war. The OUN/B was a founder member of the World Anti-Communist League, an organization that brought together Second World War collaborators, South American death squads, right-wing U.S. senators and right-wing regimes around the world.[54]

The Birth of the CIA

The CIA was born in a flurry of bureaucratic competition and controversy. The United States had entered the war without a civilian intelligence apparatus because Americans did not believe in peacetime spying, considered it ungentlemanly and distasteful. But OSS director William Donovan, having tasted the drama, thrills and perils of covert operations, advocated the creation of a permanent intelligence agency equal in rank and status to the army, navy and airforce. "The control of intelligence in peacetime, he...suggested should be 'under the direction and control of the President' and should be taken away from the military."[55] However, the Joint Chiefs of Staff were bitterly opposed to Donovans's scheme. Congress was reluctant to endorse a peacetime intelligence service; Conservative congressmen viewed OSS as too liberal, too social and too glamour-seeking. (The OSS had recruited bankers, lawyers, professors, writers and film makers—men and women who were little inclined to show the desired respect for the military and its personnel.) The FBI was opposed because its monopoly on Latin American intelligence operations would be threatened.

Donovan, who had done a capable job of penetrating the ranks of two of the most secretive nations in Europe—Nazi Germany and the Soviet Union—was unable to counter the bureaucratic forces arrayed against him at home. On September 20, 1945, President Harry Truman signed an order dissolving the OSS, only to realize that the intensification of the Cold War pointed unerringly at the need for a centralized intelligence service. Truman realized that the end of the shooting war had not brought real peace but an intense intelligence battle throughout Europe. Both the West and the East were avidly recruiting German scientists.[56] Political leaders, informers and double agents were being kidnapped and murdered. Italy, in particular, was in danger of electing a communist government and Greece was in turmoil. Even if gentlemen did not spy on each other, America could not afford the luxury of doing without a strong intelligence arm of its own.

George Kennan, a former American ambassador to the Soviet Union, was the most persuasive of the many post-war bureaucrats pushing for an agency capable of engaging in covert action. On May 4, 1948, Kennan submitted a lengthy brief pointing to the need to roll back Soviet aggression by means of covert political warfare, utilizing every means "short of war."[57] Kennan recommended the immediate creation of a directorate of political warfare operations with complete authority to engage in economic warfare, support of indigenous forces combating communism and preventive direct action measures.[58]

On January 22, 1946, Truman ordered the creation of a Central Intelligence Group jointly funded by the Departments of State, War and Navy. By July 26, 1947, the National Security Act was passed and the Central Intelligence Group metamorphosed into the Central Intelligence Agency. Seven months later, Congress authorized the creation of an even more aggressive agency, the Office of Policy Coordination (OPC), devoted exclusively to covert operations. Once organized, it became the aim of the OPC to roll back the Soviet forces and liberate Eastern Europe. Former OSS officer Frank Wisner, who had successfully divined Soviet intentions in Romania, was chosen to lead the Americans in combating the Soviet Union and its satellites. Under Wisner's dedicated direction, the OPC grew from 300 to 3000 personnel between 1949 and 1952. Its budget ballooned from 5 million to 80 million in the same years.

A full-scale, Cold War warrior, Wisner was committed to a wide repertoire of political, psychological and paramilitary actions. The OPC recruited secret armies of émigré Ukrainian, Polish, Romanian, and Bulgarian exiles in the war of East *versus* West.

As the Red Army advanced westward in 1944, the bulk of the OUN members who had served as mayors, police chiefs and auxiliary policemen, fled with the retreating German army. However, an estimated 40,000 OUN/UPA partisans, under the command of UPA General Taras Chuprynka, remained hidden in the Carpathian Mountains and continued to conduct periodic raids against Soviet forces.[59] Wisner arranged to supply the Ukrainians resisters with explosives and arms in the hope of sparking a wider anti-Soviet conflagration. Since Ukraine was regarded diplomatically as an integral part of the USSR, the American action was tantamount to a declaration of war against the Soviet Union. Ranelagh, author of *The Agency*, comments:

> It demonstrated the determination with which the United States entered the cold war. It also demonstrated a cold ruthlessness: the Ukrainian resistance had no hope of winning unless America was prepared to go to war on its behalf. Since America was not prepared to go to war, America was, in effect, encouraging Ukrainians to go to their death.[60]

The Anti-Communist Bloc of Nations

The first conference of the Subjugated Peoples of Europe and Asia was held secretly on November 21, 1943, in the forests outside Zhytomyr, Ukraine. Organized by the OUN, delegates to the conference included representatives from Poland, Belarus, Lithuania, Latvia, Finland and Ukraine. The conference emphasized "the need for a coordinated strategy among all the imprisoned nations of the Soviet Union with the goal of initiating an entire collapse of the Soviet Union."[61] This first conference provided the groundwork for the organization of yet another OUN/B front group, the Anti-Bolshevik Bloc of Nations (ABN). According to Yaroslav Stetsko who assumed the role of ABN President, the aim of the organization was the "complete annihilation of the Russian empire" through a series of insurrections that would destroy the USSR from within.[62]

Today, the adherents of the ABN claim that Stetsko and his comrades warred simultaneously against both the Nazi and Bolshevik forms of tyranny. In fact, the conference in the woods was inspired by the *Abwehr* and guarded by a Georgian military unit that fought on the German side. Their second meeting a year later, considerably less secret, was held in Krakow while the city was still in German hands.[63]

Once the Nazis were defeated, the ABN was adopted by the cash-short British, who then handed it on to the CIA, which could finance it more generously. The ABN in turn became a founding member of the World Anti-Communist League, which has been described as: "an organization that brought together Second World War collaborators, South American death squads, right-wing U.S. senators and right-wing regimes around the world, including Taiwan, South Korea, and Saudi Arabia."[64] Operating on a global basis, it held annual meetings in Taipei, Saigon, Bangkok, Manila, Tokyo, Mexico, New York, Rome, Malta, Frankfurt, Edinburgh, Escorial, Bolzano, Guatemala, Sydney and Toronto.[65]

Investigative journalists Scott and Jon Lee Anderson, authors of *Inside the League*, describe the ABN as the largest and most important umbrella for Nazi collaborators in the World. "ABN officers constitute a virtual *Who's Who* of those responsible for the massacre of millions of civilians in the bloodiest war in history."[66]

The ABN executive board included a number of well-known Nazi collaborators and its newspaper, *ABN Correspondence*, carried articles of fulsome praise for Ustasha leader Ante Pavelic and Slovak Hlinka Party leader, Msgr. Jozef Tiso. In addition, Alfred Berzins, the Latvian political leader, who sent thousands of Jews to the death camps, and Byelorussian quisling Radislaw Ostrowsky served on ABN's "People's Council."[67] As the ABN evolved under American sponsorship, the list of blatant anti-Semites, war criminals and representatives of repressive military regimes grew exponentially. While the world may have needed an anti-Communist front, it had no need of the ABN. Scott and Jon Lee Anderson put it best:

> Perhaps what is most wrong with the World anti-Communist League is what lays behind it and what it has rejected. In the name of anti-Communism, it has embraced those responsible for death squads, apartheid, torture and the extermination of European Jewry. Along the way it has repudiated democratic government as a viable alternative, either to govern or to combat communism.[68]

The Prometheus League

The origins of the *Prometheus League* are as vague and complicated as those of *Intermarium*. Essentially an amalgam of pre-war, ultra-nationalist, pro-fascist organizations that sprang up in Poland, Byelorussia and the Baltic states, it was another of the organizations initially adopted by the British Secret Service prior to the war which defected to the Nazis when Hitler seized power. After the war, it was revived again by the British and then passed on to the Americans when England found it could no longer financially support its operations. Its members conducted anti-Communist propaganda and trained to carry out terrorism and sabotage.[69]

General Shandruk, whose membership in the organization began years earlier when he was a contract officer in the Polish army, became a leading figure in *Prometheus'* post-war reincarnation.

General Shandruk did not join his men in their captivity. Instead, he changed into civilian clothes and with the aid of loyal friends and sympathizers made his way to Munich in the American zone of occupation where many of his political allies and supporters had taken shelter. In Munich, Shandruk re-established his *Prometheus* connections and made contact with *Prometheus* members in London.

Agents of the U.S. Counter Intelligence Corps investigated Shandruk and his associates in September 1947. The CIC report commented favorably on Shandruk's support of *Prometheus*, interpreting it as a sign of his unfailing, unquenchable anti-Communism.[70] The same report noted that Shandruk, "After serving in the Third (Iron) Division under Petliura, he was employed by the Second Staff Section (Intelligence) in the Polish Army. In this position, and even before the outbreak of the war, he did espionage for the Germans."[71]

Shandruk's double agent role does not seem to have deterred the CIC from singing his virtues. A 1950 CIC report states: "In view of [Shandruk's] well established and consistent anti-Communist attitude, and in view of the Soviet propaganda attacks (radio) on his character…nothing in the information filed at this headquarters which would indicate that [Shandruk's] continued presence in the United States would affect materially the security of this country."[72]

Shandruk's leadership in Prometheus, his continuing contacts with the officers of the Galician Division and his close relationship with Mykola Levytsky, president of the Ukrainian National Committee, made him too valuable to discard despite his checkered career. In a saner time, intelligence officers might hesitate to endorse a man who successively served the Russian Czar, the Ukrainian Nationalists, the Polish army and the German Nazis. But the times were far from sane. By 1950, Shandruk had been admitted to the United States and elevated to the leadership of the *Prometheus League*.[73]

Once he had arrived in the United States, Shandruk kept in loose touch with a variety of Ukrainian veterans associations, especially with the Brotherhood of Veterans of the 1st Division of the Ukrainian National Army.[74]

The Route to America

Shandruk was not alone in America. Several thousand members of the Division also made their way to the United States by various routes between 1948 and 1952. According to Shandruk's memoirs, a column of 1,300 retreating members of the Division found themselves in the American zone. The general does not make clear whether they were a fragment of the 1st Division or a remnant of the reserve regiment that was cut off from their retreating comrades.

His description of yet another body of Ukrainian soldiers is equally vague. Shandruk explains that during his brief stay in Weimar, Germany, he encountered Colonel Dyachenko, "who had a miraculous escape...from death or Soviet imprisonment... His Division, in spite of all his attempts, was drawn into battles with Soviet troops in Czechoslovakia..."[75] He relates that during several days of fierce rearguard battles, the Division held out successfully against overwhelming Soviet tank groups, but anti-tank ammunition ran out and the Division, unsupported by neighboring German units became demoralized and lost sixty percent of it personnel. The survivors, according to Shandruk, managed to break through the encirclement and were "taken over" by American troops.[76] Since Dyachenko was a senior regimental officer in the Galician Division, one must assume that soldiers who escaped the encirclement were members of the Division who found themselves separated from the main body.

Military historian Michael Logusz in his book on the Galicia Division makes reference to yet another body of men who fell into American rather than British hands:

> Proceeding northward, approximately 700 Division soldiers crossed the Austrian border into Southwestern Germany. There in the vicinity of Radstadt, they surrendered to the Americans... In addition to these [700], it is also known that a

number of Divisional soldiers were captured individually, or in small groups, by the Americans. Blending in with other prisoners, it appears the greatest number survived...[77]

International Refugee Organization

Whatever their source and whatever their experience, Division soldiers captured in the American occupation zone were confined initially in typical prisoner-of-war camps. However, the Allied occupation authorities decided in 1947 to release them and allow them to take up life as civilians in Germany.[78] A majority of those released claimed refugee status and gained shelter in Displaced persons camps operated by the International Refugee Organization (IRO).

Sponsored by the United Nations Relief and Rehabilitation Administration, the IRO established camps throughout Germany, Austria and Italy to provide temporary care and maintenance for more than a million refugees wandering post-war Europe. Once basic food, shelter and clothing had been taken care of, the IRO assisted camp residents to return home to their country of origin or to find new homes in countries of their choice. However, the IRO limited its assistance to those it considered "genuine refugees" and excluded "war criminals, quislings and traitors." It also excluded those who had "voluntarily assisted the enemy in operations against the United Nations or in persecution of civilian populations."[79] The IRO manual setting out the rules of eligibility for IRO assistance specifically stated: "Taken as a group [the 14th Galician Waffen-SS Division] are *prima facie* outside the mandate of the IRO.[80]

However, as a humanitarian agency representing the highest ideals of the newly founded United Nations, the IRO sought to be fair and consistent in its treatment of those displaced by the war. It provided, therefore, a generous loophole through which the Division's ex-soldiers could gain entry to Displaced Persons camps. "It will be remembered," states the IRO manual, "that as early as 1943 some Ukrainians were forced into the training base which was located in Lemberg. After the Battle of Brody, Ukrainians were conscripted into the Division."[81]

The difficulty presented by this proviso was the inability of the IRO to determine which members of the Division had been drafted and which had enthusiastically volunteered. The IRO had no apparatus, no body of investigators to check the applicant's stories. In any event, most of them claimed that their papers had been destroyed in one disaster or another since the Division was formed in 1943. There are also numerous reports, including that of Allan A. Ryan, who headed the U.S. Office of Special Investigations, that many ex-Nazis obtained positions of influence in the IRO apparatus and utilized their position to assist their comrades to emigrate:[82]

> Actual practice in IRO screening for war criminals and collaborators was superficial and according to a number of accounts, at times corrupt. One employee of the American DP Commission who worked closely with IRO staff resigned in disgust, calling the IRO's certification process 'a complete racket.' Many of the IRO's clerks, he charged, were former collaborators themselves who coached applicants in the techniques of successful deception or who simply filled out papers on behalf of applicants, submitting them for rubber-stamp approval by unsuspecting IRO officials.[83]

Investigations of Displaced Persons applying for entry to the United States were conducted by the Counter Intelligence Corps "which had no access to the records that would indicate that a Ukrainian, Balt or other Eastern European had been a Nazi collaborator."[84] Ryan reports that by the time the DP Act expired in June 1952, nearly 400,000 immigrants had been admitted to the United States. "Some 337,000 (85%) of those were DPs, the rest were Volksdeutsche. One third of them (including many Ukrainians) listed their country of birth as Poland… Some 18 percent were born in the Baltics, 15 percent in Germany, nearly all the rest from Yugoslavia, Hungary, Czechoslovakia, or other Eastern European countries. Fully three-quarters of them settled in New York, Illinois, Pennsylvania, New Jersey, Michigan, Ohio, California and Massachusetts, in that order."[85]

Obviously, not all of the 400,000 immigrants who gained admission to the United States by virtue of the Displaced Persons Act were war criminals and collaborators. Most had suffered political persecution, displacement from their homes, physical exploitation and hunger. Yet, Ryan estimates that at least two and a half percent probably took part in Nazi crimes, making for approximately 10,000 Nazi persecutors.[86] In Ryan's opinion, the Displaced Persons Act was a peculiar mix of American generosity and racism. On the one hand it sought to relieve the suffering of those rotting in idleness in Displaced Persons camps and on the other hand it hypocritically excluded those who had suffered most. Ryan comments ironically: "In 1948, Congress sought out groups that had much to conceal and encouraged them to apply. It erected barriers against those who had nothing to conceal. The disqualification of Jews by means of the early cutoff date was strong and effective; its disqualification of Nazis by means of legal fiat and cursory background checks was weak."[87]

In answer to the question: "How did the Nazi war criminals come to the United States?" Ryan replies: "We invited them in."

Fascists or Freedom Fighters

Only a remnant of the Galician Division survives today. According to life tables supplied by the Guardian Insurance Company, only 27.1 percent of the Division's members were likely to be alive in the year 2000.[88] Nevertheless, branches of the Brotherhood of Veterans of the 1st Division of the Ukrainian National Army continue to meet regularly is most cities with a sizeable Ukrainian population in the United States, Canada, the United Kingdom, Germany or Argentina. Like the anti-Castro Cubans in Miami, whose intransigence and reputation for violence has cowed much of the American Cuban community, the stubborn insistence of Division veterans that they were pure soldiers whose only sin was to fight for the freedom of Ukraine has silenced alternative Ukrainian voices.

Today, the Division's veterans represent themselves as veteran freedom fighters, advocates of democracy and national self-realization. However, given the ideological history of the Division and its OUN sponsor, its advocacy of democratic freedom rings hollow. Bandera, Melnyk, Lebed, Stetsko and Dontsov remain revered figures in the Nationalist firmament; their fascist ideology barely camouflaged by the "integral nationalist' label. Nationalist Ukrainian scholars and journalists have laboured hard to portray Ukrainian Nationalism as a righteous national liberation movement and to distance it from the fascism of Hitler and Mussolini.[89] Frequently, they elaborate on spurious distinctions without a significant difference. For example, one journalist insisted that fascism was a way of *organizing* an existent state, but since the Ukrainians had not yet achieved independent statehood, they could not be considered fascists.[90]

Such laboured rationalizations fail to disguise the fascist nature of the OUN. Alexander J. Motyl, author of the Columbia University monograph, *The Turn to the Right: The Ideological Origins and Development of Ukrainian Nationalism, 1919-1929,* reports that there were Ukrainian Nationalists who openly called themselves Ukrainian fascists. He cites also Dontsov's reference to "Ukrainian fascism" and the absorption of the League of Ukrainian Fascists into the League of Ukrainian Nationalists as "incontrovertible evidence that Ukrainian fascists…did in fact exist." He adds that "the ideological and philosophical subtleties differentiating Ukrainian nationalism from Fascism did not in practice mean much to Ukrainian fascists."[91]

The period of the Cold War abounds in cynicism and irony. The British and American intelligence networks sought to make use of their old enemies in a silent war against the newly defined 'Evil Empire.' At the same time, the leadership of nationalist movements that had collaborated with the Nazis was happy to change sides to gain CIA financing. CIA funds served to breathe new life into obsolescent nationalist movements that bore no loyalty to their sponsors or to democracy. It also provided them with a respectability they had never enjoyed before. They were now invited to sit at the head table with presidents and cabinet ministers. The votes of their followers were eagerly solicited and their opinions conscientiously sought. Peter Grose, in *Operation Rollback* reports that "Anticommunist zealots running for public office found [their foot soldiers] in the east European ethnic communities in the American Middle West."[92]

But much of the "spook" business is necessarily illusion. The psychological warfare, for which OUN/B and its offshoots were recruited, proved to be no more than a series of dirty card tricks. In the end it had little bearing on the end of the Cold War and nothing to do with the establishment of an independent, democratic Ukraine. Rudgers in his *Journal of Contemporary History* article on the origins of covert actions, holds that "the tottering Soviet Commonwealth imploded on its own accord in 1991, without outside existence," and that its end "raises the question as to whether CIA covert actions contributed to the result, or whether they were sort of a narcotic for policy makers, carried out as an end in itself because they could be."[93]

The very men who forged the American policy of containment, who sought to roll back the Iron Curtain that divided Europe and liberate the captive nations came to realize that they had created an uncontrollable Frankenstein. Over the years, the CIA recruited Nazis to do some of their dirty work, manipulated democratic elections, overthrew governments, supported dictatorships, plotted assassinations and engineered the Bay of Pigs disaster.[94] Through *Prometheus*, *Intermarium* and the ABN, it held out the promise of liberation and national independence to the supporters of the OUN and the veterans of the Ukrainian Division. Was the promise sincere and wisely offered? Was the U.S. government genuinely interested in a free and independent Ukraine anymore than they had been in democratic regimes in Chile or pre-Castro Cuba?

As early as 1956, during the heyday of CIA covert activity, leading American policy makers complained that the conduct of covert action was "in the hands of individuals who were often irresponsible, usually unaccountable, and infatuated with action both for its own sake and to maintain their positions."[95] Much the same could be said regarding the leadership of the OUN and those who formed and led the Ukrainian Division.

Fortunately, the OUN and the Division were negligible factors in the dissolution of the Soviet Empire and the establishment of an independent, democratic Ukraine. In fact, after a decade of independence, Ukraine is still not the happiest, most economically successful country in Eastern Europe. Nevertheless, one shudders to think what might have happened had the OUN and its Ukrainian Division succeeded in capturing power. How many Ukrainians would now be confined in Ukrainian gulags and how would the slogan of "Ukraine for the Ukrainians" have been implemented?

Notes

1. Nick Lowles, "Dangerous Liaisons," *Searchlight* (London), February 2000, No. 296, 18. Also photographs 24 and 25 following page 244 in Mark Aarons and John Loftus, *Ratlines* (London: William Heinemann Ltd., 1991).

2. Mark Aarons, *Sanctuary: Nazi Fugitives in Australia* (Port Melbourne: William Heinemann Australia, 1989), 55.

3. *Ibid.*

4. Aarons and Loftus, *Ratlines*, 217.

5. See Philip Knightley, *The Second Oldest Profession* (London: Andre Deutsch, 1986), 77-78, 105-108.

6. Peter Grose, *Operation Rollback: America's Secret War behind the Iron Curtain* (New York: Houghton Mifflin Company, 2000), 172.

7. The Moscow Declaration warned that those responsible for Nazi atrocities in occupied countries would be punished. The agreement was signed by representatives of the U.K., USA, and USSR at the 1943 three-power conference in Moscow.

8. See: John Ranelagh, *The Agency: The Rise and Decline of the CIA* (New York: Simon and Schuster, 1986), 70.

9. *Ibid.* 70.

10. *Ibid.* 70.

11. David F. Rudgers, "The Origins of Covert Action," *Journal of Contemporary History*, Vol. 35, No.2, 2000. 250.

12. "Dangerous Liaisons," *Searchlight*, February 2000, 21.

13. *Ibid.* 91.

14. *Ibid.* 92.

15. Christopher Simpson, *Blowback* (New York: Weidenfeld & Nicolson, 1988), 4.

16. *Ibid.* 91.

17. *Ibid.* 17.

18. E. H. Cookridge, *Gehlen: Spy of the Century* (London: Corgi Books, 1972), 295.

19. Simpson, *Blowback.* 49.

20. *Ibid.* 295.

21. Cookridge, *Gehlen: Spy of the Century* (London: Transworld Publishers, 1971), 298.

22. *Ibid.* 176.

23. Reinhard Gehlen, *The Service: The Memoirs of General Reinhard Gehlen* (New York: The World Publishing Company, 1972), 122.

24. *Ibid.* 5.

25. Simpson, *Blowback,* 54.

26. Peter Grose, *Operation Rollback,* 29.

27. Tom Bower, *Klaus Barbie: Butcher of Lyon* (London: Michael Joseph, 1984), 180-181.

28. *Ibid.* 24-26.

29. Serge Klarsfeld, *The Children of Izieu: A Human Tragedy* (New York: Harry N. Abrams, Inc., 1984), 98-99.

30. Brendan Murphy, *The Butcher of Lyons; The Story of Infamous Nazi Klaus Barbie* (New York: Empire Books, 1983), 193-196.

31. Bower, *Klaus Barbie*, 139.

32. Peter Grose, *Operation Rollback*, 23.

33. Brendan Murphy, *The Butcher of Lyon*, 228.

34. *Ibid.* 262.

35. Tom Bower, *Klaus Barbie*, 181.

36. Klaus Barbie died of cancer in his French prison on September 28, 1991.

37. Tom Bower, *Klaus Barbie*, 231.

38. Allan A. Ryan, Jr., *Quiet Neighbors: Prosecuting Nazi War Criminals in America* (New York: Harcourt Brace Jovanovich, 1984), 190.

39. *Ibid.* 4-5.

40. *Ibid.* 5.

41. *Ibid.* 17.

42. *New York Times*, August 30, 1948.

43. Simpson, *Blowback*, 149.

44. *Ibid.* 151.

45. *Ibid.* fn, 152.

46. *Ibid.* 148-149.

47. *Ibid.* 181-182.

48. *Ibid.* 184.

49. Jozef Lettrich, *History of Modern Slovakia* (New York: Frederick A. Praeger, 1955), 137-139.

50. Joe Conason, "To catch a Nazi," *Village Voice*, February 11, 1986. Lebed, who was seventy-five years old when the *Village Voice* article appeared, chose to remain silent. However, Lebed's colleagues denounced the article as "scurrilous," "replete with total distortions, deliberate manipulations of facts and half-truths." The GOA report was characterized as a Soviet attempt to discredit the Ukrainian liberation movement. See: *The Ukrainian Weekly*, February 16, 1986, pages 1 and 4.

51. *Ibid.*

52. Mark Aarons and John Loftus, *Ratlines*, 176.

53. *Ibid.* 247.

54. Nick Lowe, "Dangerous Liaisons," *Searchlight*, No. 296, February 2000.

55. John Ranelagh, *The Agency: The Rise and Decline of the CIA* (New York: Simon and Schuster Inc., 1986), 96.

56. Tom Bower, *The Paperclip Conspiracy* (London: Michael Joseph, 1987), 97.

57. Rudgers, *supra*, 253.

58. *Ibid.* 253.

59. Yaroslav Stetsko, "The Light of Freedom from the Forests of Ukraine," *ABN Correspondence*, No. 4-6, Vol. XLIV, August-September 1993, 3-8. Taras Chuprynka was killed in a battle with KGB border guards in March 1950.

60. Ranelagh, *The Agency*, 137.

61. *ABN Correspondence*, August-December 1993. 2.

62. *Ibid.* 4-5.

63. *Ibid.* 4.

64. Nick Lowe, *supra*, 18.

65. *Ibid.* 7.

66. Scott and Jon Lee Anderson, *Inside the League* (New York: Dodd, Mead & Co., 1986), 35.

67. Simpson, *Blowback*, 269.

68. *Ibid.* 266.

69. Mark Aarons, *Sanctuary* (Port Melbourne: William Heinemann Australia, 1980), 73-74.

70. FOI, File D 148204, To: Commanding Officer, 970th CIC Detachment, Headquarters, EUCOM, APO 757, U.S. Army, 3 September 1947.

71. *Ibid.*

72. FOI, Headquarters Region IV, 66th CIC Detachment, Visa Section, APO 407-A, U.S. Army, 9 June 1950.

73. Shandruk, 287.

74. Wasyl Veryha, "General Pavlo Shandruk: An Appraisal," *Ukrainian Quarterly*, 1984, 176.

75. Shandruk, 287-288.

76. *Ibid.* 288.

77. Michael Logusz, *Galicia Division: The Waffen-SS 14th Grenadier Division 1943-1945* (Atglen, PA: Schiffer Military History, 1997), 360-361.

78. Shandruk, 293.

79. International Refugee Organization, *Manual for Eligibility Officers*, 3, 31.

80. *Ibid.* 66.

81. *Ibid.* 66.

82. Ryan, *Quiet Neighbors*, 20-21.

83. *Ibid.* 20.

84. *Ibid.* 20.

85. *Ibid.* 25.

86. *Ibid.* 26.

87. *Ibid.* 28.

88. Telephone conversation with Arthur Emmer, actuary, Guardian Life Insurance, New York, N.Y., April 13, 2000.

89. See Alexander J. Motyl, *The Turn to the Right: The Ideological Origins of Ukrainian Nationalism 1918-1929* (New York: East European Monographs, distributed by Columbia University Press, 1980), 166.

90. *Ibid.* 166.

91. *Ibid.* 168-169.

92. Peter Grose, 199.

93. Rudgers, 261.

94. Frances Stonor Saunders, *Who Paid the Piper? The CIA and the Cultural Cold War* (London: Granta Publications, 1999), 427.

95. Rudgers, 261.

Appendix 'A'

Order of Battle: 14th Waffen Grenadier Division der SS (ukrain.Nr.1)

Appointment	Rank (A) Active (R) Reserve (Leg) Legion	Name	First Name	Seniority	Date of Birth
Kommandeur	Brigfhr.u.Gen. Maj.d.W.-SS	Freitag	Fritz (POLICE)	20.04.44	28.04.94
I a	Stubaf.	Heike	Wolf-Dieter		26.07.13
I b	Hstuf.R.	Schaaf	Herbert	30.01.44	04.03.08
I c	Hstuf.R.	Niermann	Fritz	20.04.44	22.12.15
II a	Stubaf.	Finder	Erich	30.01.45	15.07.08
Pz.Gren.Rgt.29					
(ukrain.Nr.1)	Staf.	Dern	Fritz	01.07.44	05.03.96
I. Btl.	Hstuf.	Blankenhorn	Otto	26.07.44	26.04.12
II. Btl.	Hstuf.	Salzinger	Hans		01.05.10
III. Btl.	Ostubaf.	Wildner	Karl	21.08.44	17.12.97
Pz.Gren.Rgt.30					
(ukrain.Nr.2)	Ostubaf.	Forstreuter	Hans-Otto	17.05.44	01.11.12
I. Btl.	Hstuf.	Klocker	Siegfried	09.11.43	10.11.11
II. Btl.	Stubaf.	Vzermin	Albert	21.08.44	18.04.09
II. Btl.					
Pz.Gren.Rgt.31					
(ukrain.Nr.3)	Staf.	Pannier	Rudolf	09.11.43	10.07.97
I. Btl.	Stubaf.	Kurzbach	Heinz	30.01.45	02.04.16
II. Btl.	Stubaf.	Scholtz	Elemar	21.08.44	06.06.09
II. Btl.					
Füs.-Btl.14	Stubaf.	Dristot	Karl	01.09.44	12.09.15
Waffen.-Art.-Rgt.					
Der - SS 14	Ostubaf.	Beyersdorff	Friedrich	30.01.43	09.08.92
I. Abt.	Hstuf.	Gläss	Kurt	09.11.42	03.07.15
II. Abt.	Hstuf.	Schlesinger	Emil-H.	21.08.44	17.02.16
III. Abt.	Hstuf.	Sparsam	Günter	20.04.44	27.05.16
IV. Abt.	Stubaf.	Beissel	Otto	30.01.44	01.02.93
Pionier-Btl.	Stubaf.	Remberger	Josef	09.11.43	09.06.05
Nachr.-Abt.	Stubaf.	Heinz	Werner	30.01.45	20.09.14
Pz.Jg.-Abt.	Stubaf.	Kaschner	Hèrmann	01.09.44	07.11.14
Nachsch.-Tr.	Ostubaf.	Magill	Franz	20.04.43	22.08.00
Felders.-Btl.	Stubaf.	Kleinow	Johannes	01.09.44	10.02.11

Source: Chancery Office, London, TS 26/903/95198

APPENDIX 'B'

Homily Delivered by Fr. Myron Stasiw on Ukrainian Hour, Ethnic Radio Station, CHIN, Toronto, Ontario, February 24, 1985*

The Ukrainian weekly, Vilne Slova, writes that in the past few years in the United States, and now in Canada, a campaign has come into being under the leadership of Simon Wiesenthal and his associate Sol Littman that spreads hatred and false opinion about Ukrainians. They claim that there were 218 former Ukrainian officers of Hitler's SS (the elite guard) who directed the death camps in eastern Europe, and now live in Canada. Wiesenthal spoke of this in Israel during a radio interview on February 9, and in the following days the Sunday Star and the Toronto Star carried sensational articles on their front pages concerning this. These materials were given in Tel Aviv (Israel). This meant that Wiesenthal is not acting on his own initiative, and this is the greatest issue. All Ukrainians should react against these obscene and calumnious attacks of the Jews. Because they are a total accusation of the entire Ukrainian people, to compromise them in Canada and wherever they live. The laws of Canada prohibit such slanders.

It is a strange commentary that neither Wiesenthal, nor anyone else of the Jewish community, are not hunting out their own blood brothers who were *Judenrath Capos*, who together with the *Gestapo* and the SS killed and destroyed their brother-Jews. On the contrary they are searching out for the so-called Ukrainian war-criminals, who, if such there be, are considerably less numerous than the Jewish war criminals. They should first seek out and bring to justice the Jewish collaborators with the Germans. But of these there is not even a mention.

Wiesenthal is following the Soviet-Communist assertions and so-called witnesses—as it was in the USA against a few Ukrainians, who were supposed to have been guards in the concentration camps. As if these did their work voluntarily and were truly commandants? These did their service under the penalty of death from a German machine gun or automatic pistol. We have in Canada and the USA hundreds of prisoners (Ukrainian) from German concentration camps, and they can vouch for this.

The Jews in their hatred for the Ukrainian people go back 300 years and more, but they do not say what the causes of these Jewish pogroms were—those who had the keys to the Christian churches and would not allow the people to enter to pray. They were the tavern

---

*Fr. Stasiw, a veteran of the Halychyna Division, is Rector of St. Mary's Catholic Church in Toronto. The text and translation from Ukrainian was provided by the CHIN management.

keepers, who robbed the peasants of their land for whiskey and made them their serfs. The Jews likewise do not speak about how Jews poured molten tar and boiling water and stoned the heads of the Ukrainian soldiers, in Berdachev, in 1918, at the time of the Ukrainian State. Nor do they speak of their response to the government of the Ukrainian National Republic, that gave them full cultural autonomy and with their own Jew as minister for Jewish affairs.

What was the action of the Jews in Russia? Who formed the Bolshevik government in St. Petersburg. How many Jews were in the government of Leiba Trotski? Who walled in the captured Ukrainian soldiery (*Sitchovi Strilci*), that had fallen prisoners of the Bolsheviks in Kiev: Consider the achievements of Kaganovich as commissar of the Ukraine in the years of the famine of 1932–33, when more than 7 million Ukrainians perished from the artificial famine? What about the escapades of Beria and many more like him. Wiesenthal and his associates should reflect upon these, and not seek to call the wolf from the forest.

We are decidedly for the punishment of the real war criminals, but we are emphatically against the generalizations of the Jews, and their spreading of hatred against the entire Ukrainian people.

One thing remains, to mobilize against the slanders of the Jews not only the opinion of Ukrainians, scattered throughout the diaspora, but likewise the opinion of Canadians and all peoples, wherever free Ukrainians live. In the first place, the Ukrainian press should raise this issue in rebuttal of the spreading of hatred towards Canadian citizens, so firmly forbidden by Canadian law. This is not an insignificant matter, because the spreading of hatred towards Ukrainians can affect entire generations in Canada, upon people looked on as war criminals.

We must organize planned demonstrations in the entire diaspora with appropriate information for all peace-loving peoples. We must remind them that it is not only they that can demand the punishment of those who slander others. The Canadian law extends to defend all its citizens, and in no way places them in a more favourable position.

Appendix 'C'

Stefan Dshugalo: Soldier, Spymaster, Disillusioned Ukrainian Nationalist[*]

"Our first 'combat mission' after basic training was to guard a group of Jews being sent to the concentration camp."

Stefan Dshugalo, straight-backed, witty, and fully alert at eighty-one, was a veteran of the Ukrainian Waffen-SS Division which fought alongside Hitler's armies. Much of his personal history coincides with the history of the Division he joined soon after it was formed in August 1943. He continued in its ranks until the bulk of the Division surrendered to the British in May 1945.

"A few days after we had completed basic training and taken our oath to Hitler and the German swastika, we were awakened at 2 a.m., equipped with rifles and bayonets and deployed on both sides of the road leading to the railway station," Dshugalo said in an interview in Lviv on June 19, 1989. "Twenty minutes to a half hour later a large group people— women, children and old men, some 200 to 300 of them—were escorted to the railway station. It was our job to prevent any of them from escaping."

"Did you know who they were and where they were going?"

"Of course we knew," he replied. "We all understood that these were Polish Jews being sent to Dachau or some other concentration camp."

Dshugalo, a highly popular teacher of gymnastics and music in the secondary school of Sokol in the Lviv region of Galician Ukraine, felt obligated to join his students in the ranks of the Division.

"There was considerable pressure on the students to join the Division," he said. "The principal addressed them several times. As a result, the whole graduating class marched to the recruiting and signed up. I, as their physical culture teacher, was obliged to join them."

According to Dshugalo, there was no spontaneous rush to join the Division. Although a German broadcast from Krakow boasted that 60,000 Ukrainians had rushed to volunteer as soon as the German occupation authorities announced its formation in March 1943, the former teacher attributed this claim to "German propaganda."

"Few of us were eager to go," he said. "People were pressured in various ways to sign up. For example, I was asked almost daily by the head of the *gymnasium* (secondary school) whether I had joined up yet. As an avowed Ukrainian Nationalist and—what would you call it?—yes, a role model to the younger generation, I was expected to lead the way. German gendarmes visited me twice at home to tell me what a fine contribution I could make to the

---

[*]An account of the Galician Waffen-SS Division as recounted by one of its veterans as told to Sol Littman, Lviv, June 1989.

cause. Finally, I thought it best to accompany my students." Those who could afford to "buy their way out" were able to avoid service, he added ironically.

The Division—formally listed as the *14th Grenadier Volunteer Waffen-SS Division* (Galician No. 1)—assembled for training at Heidelager, a camp near Krakow used exclusively to train Ukrainian SS men. The instructors were Germans and all orders were issued in the German language. The training period lasted five months, from August to December 1943.

Not all of the men received their training at Heidelager. Raised primarily as a police unit to combat partisan activities behind the German lines, sub-units received special training in military camps in France, Czechoslovakia and Germany. One group trained in France and participated in sweeps against the French Resistance which was engaged in the rescue of downed British and American airmen.

His basic training completed, Dshugalo was ordered to Breslau, Germany, for training as a non-commissioned officer. He returned to the Division in May 1944, but two or three months later he was seconded for officers' training at a camp in Czechoslovakia.

During the time he was away, the members of the *Schutzmannschaftbattalion* 201, consisting of former members of the Roland and Nachtigall Battalions, were transferred to the Division. These brigades had been recruited and trained by the *Abwehr*, the German army's secret service, as sabotage and espionage units. Both battalions were in the vanguard of the German forces when Hitler invaded the USSR and participated in the horrible pogrom of Jews and Polish intellectuals that followed on the heels of the German invasion. After their espionage and sabotage services were no longer required by the Germans, they were formed into the 201st Police Battalion that committed numerous atrocities in White Russia in the name of "anti-partisan" warfare. By 1944, the Red Army had advanced so far westward that the 201st could no longer perform as an anti-partisan unit. They were then placed in the ranks of the Ukrainian Waffen-SS Division.

The Division itself was now stationed in the Brody area east of Lviv. Each of the unit's infantry regiments was commanded by a German officer, with at most two Ukrainian officers in subsidiary positions. "Each combat unit was under a German officer," Dshugalo stated. "No unit was commanded by a Ukrainian."

Careful not to say anything that would leave him liable to war crimes charges, Dshugalo stated that he was aware of actions taken by the Division but that fortunately he was away on a training course when they happened. For example, he had heard of the formation of a special anti-partisan strike force under the command of Major Beyersdorff that is reported to have devastated numerous villages. "I heard talk about the formation of the Beyersdorff detachment but I don't know too much about its activities," he said. "I also heard that the Germans gave instructions that a village called Huta Pieniacka should be destroyed. The village was in some contact with the partisans. Some of our combat units surrounded the village and murdered all the villagers."

Before Dshugalo could complete his officers' training course, the Division was badly mauled by the Red Army in a battle near Brody. Two-thirds to three-fifths of the Division was lost. The Division's commander, SS General Fritz Freitag, a former German policeman, was openly critical of the fighting quality of the Ukrainians under his command. "Freitag called the men of the Division traitors, men who didn't have the German fighting spirit and couldn't be counted on to fight for the Reich," Dshugalo recounted.

Dshugalo never did finish his officers' training course. There was a more urgent task for him to perform. He was sent to Neuhammer, Germany, where the remnants of the Division had been gathered after Brody. There he helped train the Division's new recruits. "Many of them were former policemen and German agents who fled from the Russian army," he explained. "Some were deserters from the Red Army who had been captured by the Germans. Most were young Ukrainians who had been sent to Germany as slave laborers and were now given their choice of remaining in the factories and mines or joining the Division." Since the death toll from overwork, hunger and disease was extremely high, many of the young men saw a combat division as a preferable alternative.

A number of the nationalist leaders who had been detained by the Germans were now set free to recruit slave laborers for the Division. They were provided with travel documents that permitted them to travel anywhere in the shrinking German empire. The documents called on all civil and military agencies to provide them with whatever assistance they required to succeed in their mission. Dshugalo met one of these leaders, Osyp Tushka in Austria. Tushka's main task was to arrange transport for those slave laborers who wanted to join the Division.

The nominal commander of the camp at Neuhammer was Yevhen Pobihushchy, former commander of the Roland Battalion and *Schutzmannschaftbattalion* 201. There was a shortage of German officers at the time so that the Division made use of a larger number of Ukrainian officers. "By the way, Pobihushchy is now living in Munich where he is editor of the *Christian Voice*," Dshugalo said. "He was awarded two German medals for his wartime service to the Reich."

The Division was equipped with the regular grey-green, Waffen-SS uniforms. On their collar tabs they wore the runic SS and on their sleeves they carried the symbol of the Galician lion. "There was no sign that we were Ukrainian until the last weeks of the war when General Shandruk ordered that the lion should be replaced with the Tryzub. But we had no means of getting them manufactured so very few were actually worn."

In mid-summer of 1944, the Division was sent to Slovakia to help suppress the Slovak Uprising. Led by officers and men of the regular Slovak army, the people of Slovakia rebelled against the pro-Nazi Slovak government. The back of the rebellion was quickly broken by overwhelming German forces, but small scale partisan warfare continued for a while in the mountainous and wooded areas of Slovakia.

"Our main task was to sweep the traitors—consisting largely of Slovak army men—out of the dense woods," Dshugalo said. "Our unit was stationed in the village of Konski, near Rayeski Teplica. Two or three times a week we sent patrols through the woods to flush out partisans.

"One day, we received word that German forces had surrounded a vast wooded area in order to drive out the last of the partisans, so we spent most of the day beating the bushes. About three o'clock in the afternoon we encountered two partisans who immediately fled.

"Our unit was staffed by two Ukrainian officers; I was the sole non-commissioned officer. The two officers were armed with high velocity, the other ranks with ordinary, rifles.

"Our point men signaled that they had spotted two partisans up ahead. My squad was ordered to proceed straight ahead while the two officers led flanking movements to the right and the left. Before long we heard automatic rifle fire. When we arrived at the scene of the action we discovered that one partisan had fled while the other had been severely wounded by one of the officers. Two of our men were assigned to carry the wounded man on a stretcher and hand him over to the German authorities."

Dshugalo regretted the wounding of the Slovak partisan. "The Slovak people regarded us as fellow Slavs and were very kind to us. They gave us gifts of food and pleaded with us not to shoot their sons. It wasn't necessary to shoot the poor fellow; the partisans were completely out of ammunition."

Dshugalo claims this was the only action he saw in Slovakia. When the "cleanup" in Slovakia was over Dshugalo returned to officers' training school, this time in Posen. But the German need for manpower again prevented him from finishing the course. After only two weeks of training, the officers-in-training were formed into a combat unit and sent to the front along the Varta River. The new unit, which remained an official part of the Galician SS Division, consisted entirely of Ukrainians except for its German officers.

The unit came under heavy fire from Soviet tanks and was forced to withdraw. It continued its retreat until it reached Berlin. Before joining the rest of the Division which was beating a retreat through Yugoslavia towards Austria, the unit rested briefly in the Italian Alps. All too soon they were ordered to rejoin their Ukrainian comrades at the front near Marburg, Austria.

When Dshugalo rejoined the Division, General Freitag was still in command, although nominally the command had been transferred to General Shandruk of the non-existent First Ukrainian Army.

On May 10, 1945, the Division surrendered to the British forces at Graz, Austria, and were immediately transported by the British to a prison camp in northern Italy.

"It was easy to break out of the compound," Dshugalo said. "I left the regiment behind and made my way to Austria where I posed as a D. P. (Displaced Person). Before long, I was working for UNWRA and then for the American-Ukrainian Relief Committee."

In 1956, the OUN (Organization of Ukrainian Nationalists) proposed that he join them in their Munich headquarters to take part in the "so-called" K-3 program.

"This was a department of the American secret service which specialized in training spies," he related. "In order to conceal American participation, the actual training was done by a team of Italians. During the time I worked for K-3, we parachuted two groups of spies into the Soviet Union." Since nothing further was heard from either group once they landed, Dshugalo assumed that they were captured by the Soviet Union.

"For several years I also served as chief paymaster for the OUN," he continued. "All of that organization's financial matters were well known to me."

But how did he come to return to the USSR? "After a time I realized that the main purpose of the OUN leaders was to enrich themselves and not to liberate the Ukraine," he replied. "I wrote a letter to the USSR consul in which I described my whole life, including some facts which testified against me, and asked permission to return to my motherland. Two months later, I received a note inviting me to visit the Soviet consul in Vienna. There I received permission to return.

"When you returned, were you placed under arrest?'

"No."

"Were you interrogated?"

"Yes, thoroughly. But after that I was permitted to become a free citizen again."

Many of Dshugalo's comments were tinged with irony. "We were told that the Division would serve as a model of a Ukrainian National Army. What a model! What an army!"

Dshugalo did not hold a high opinion of Stefan Bandera, the leader of the OUN assassinated by the KGB in Munich in 1956. "He wasn't even a nice man, let alone a heroic figure."

The interview over, Dshugalo shook hands courteously and left the room.

The Dshugalo interview confirms:

- The Division's recruits were not coerced "at the point of a gun." Although there were social pressures and attempts at persuasion, they were not likely to be shot for failing to volunteer.

- The Division was involved in the transportation of Jewish victims to death camps and atrocities against Polish villages such as Huta Pieniacka.

- The Division fought not only against the Russians but assisted the Germans in putting down the revolt in Slovakia and opposing Yugoslav partisans.

- Division members took an oath to Hitler and the Greater German Reich rather than to a nationalist Ukraine.

SELECTIVE BIBLIOGRAPHY

Aarons, Mark, *Sanctuary*, (Port Melbourne, AU: William Heinemann Australia, 1989).

Aarons, Mark, and John Loftus, *Ratlines*, (London, UK: William Heinemann, 1991).

Abella, Irving and Harold Troper, *None is too Many*, (Toronto, ON: Lester and Orpen Dennys, 1982).

Ainsztein, Reuben, "Final Solution of the Slav Problem: Colonization with Assassination," *The Wiener Library Bulletin*, March 20, 1950: 36-38.

———. *Jewish Resistance in Nazi-Occupied Europe*, (London, UK: Paul Elek Publishers, 1964).

———. "The Myth about the Fatalistic and Helpless Galician Jew," in *Jewish Resistance in Nazi Occupied Europe*, 252, (New York, NY: Barnes and Noble, 1974).

Anderson, Scott, and Jon Lee Anderson, *Inside the League*, Dodd, Mead & Co., 1986.

Army, The Magazine of Landpower, June 6, 1990.

Apenszlak, Jacob, ed., *The Black Book of Polish Jewry under Nazi Occupation*, (New York,NY: The American Federation of Polish Jews, 1982).

Armstrong, John A., *Ukrainian Nationalism, 3rd ed.*, (Englewood, CO: Ukrainian Academic Press, 1990).

Baker, Thomas M., *Social Revolutionaries and Secret Agents: The Corinthian Slovene Partisans and Britain's Special Operations Executive*, East European Monographs, (New York, NY: Columbia University Press, 1990).

Barnett, Correlli, ed., *Hitler's Generals*, (London, UK: George Weidenfeld & Nicholson Ltd, 1990).

Bartov, Omer, *Hitler's Army*, (Oxford, UK: Oxford University Press, 1991).

Belgion, Montgomery, *Victors Justice*, (Hinsdale, IL: Henry Regnery Co., 1949).

Bender, Roger, and Hugh Page Taylor, *Uniforms, Organizations and History of the Waffen-SS.* Vol. 4. (San Jose, CA: R. James Bender Publishing, 1982).

Betcherman, Lita-Rose, *The Swastika and the Maple Leaf; Fascist Movements in Canada in the 30s*, (Toronto: Fitzhenry & Whiteside, 1975).

Bormann, Martin, *Hitler's Table Talk*, (Oxford, UK: Oxford University Press, 1953).

Boshyk, Yuri, ed., *Ukraine During World War II: History and Aftermath*, Edmonton, AB: Canadian Institute of Ukrainian Studies, 1986).

Bower, Tom, *Klaus Barbie, Butcher of Lyons*, (London, UK: Michael Joseph, 1984).

———. "How the SS Came to Britain." *The Times*, August 20, 1987.

———. *Blind Eye to Murder*, (London, UK: Grenada, 1983).

The Brown Book: War and Nazi War Criminals in West Germany, (Berlin: Verlag Zeit im Bild, 1956).

Brotherhood of Veterans of 1st UD UNA, *Bii pid Brodamy*, New York, 1974 (Ukrainian language).

———. *Ukrainska Dyvizia Halychyna*, Toronto, 1990, (Ukrainian language).

Browning, Christopher R., *Ordinary Men: Reserve Battalion 101 and the Final Solution in Poland*, (New York, NY: Harper Collins Publishers, 199)2

Burleigh, Michael, *The Third Reich; A New History*, (New York, NY: Hill & Wang, 2000).

Butler, Rupert, *Legions of Death: The Nazi Enslavement of Eastern Europe*, (London, UK: Hamlyn Paperbacks, 1983).

Calvocoressi, Peter, and Guy Wint, *Total War*, (Middlesex, UK: Penguin Books, 1972).

Canot, Robert, *Justice at Nuremberg*, (New York, NY: Harper and Row, 1983).

Cesarani, David, *Report on the Entry of War Criminals and Collaborators into the UK, 1945-1950*, (London, UK: All Parliamentary War Crimes Group, House of Commons, 1988).

——. *Justice Delayed: How Britain Became a Refuge for Nazi War Criminals*, (London, UK: Heinemann, 1992).

Chopyk, Dan B., "The Origin and Activities of the Nightingale Legion—DUN." *The Ukrainian Quarterly*. XLII, No. 1-2, Spring-Summer (1986): 69-80.

Chornovil, Vyacheslav, *The Chornovil Papers*, (Toronto, ON: McGraw-Hill, 1968).

Clark, Alan, *Barbarossa: The Russian-German Conflict, 1941-45*, (New York, NY: Quill, 1945).

Conason, Joe, "To Catch a Nazi," *Village Voice*, February 11, 1986.

Cookridge, E.H., *Gehlen: Spy of the Century*, (London, UK: Corgi Books, 1972).

Cornwell, John, *Hitler's Pope: The Secret History of Pius XII*, (New York, NY: Penguin Books, 1999).

Cowell, Alan, "Files Suggest British Knew Early of Nazi Atrocities Against Jews," *New York Times*, November 19, 1996.

Cowgill, Anthony, Thomas Brimelow and Christopher Booker, *The Reparations from Austria in 1945: The Cowgill Inquiry*, (London, UK: Sinclair Stevenson Ltd., 1990).

Dallin, Alexander, *German Rule in Russia, 1941-1945: A Case Study of Occupation Policies*, (London, UK: Macmillan & Co., 1957).

Dallin, David J., *Soviet Espionage*, (New Haven, CT: Yale University Press, 1955).

Davidson, Eugene, *The Trial of the Germans*,(New York, NY: Macmillan Co. 1966).

Davies, Raymond Arthur, *This is our Land: Ukrainian Canadians Against Hitler*, (Toronto, ON: Progress Books, 1943).

Dawidowicz, Lucy, *The War Against the Jews 1939-1945*, 7th printing ed., (New York, NY: Bantam Books, 1961).

Deschênes, Jules, *The Sword and the Scales*, English ed., (Toronto, ON: Butterworth & Co., 1979).

——. *Commission of Inquiry on War Criminals, Part I*, (Ottawa, ON: Government of Canada, 1986).

Dobroszycki, Lucjan and Jeffrey S. Gurock, *The Holocaust in the Soviet Union: Studies and Sources on the Destruction of the Jews in the Nazi-Occupied Territories of the USSR, 1941-1945*, (Armonk, NY: M.E. Sharpe, 1993).

Dmytryshyn, Basil, "The Nazis and the SS Volunteer Division 'Galicia'," *The American Slavic and East European Review.* 15 (1956): 1-10.

Dorril, Stephen, *MI6: Inside the Covert World of Her Majesty's Secret Intelligence Service,* (London, UK: The Free Press, 2000).

Einstein-Keshev, Betty, "The Story of Independent Ukraine," in *Fun Noenten Oiver (Out of the Recent Past),* (New York, NY: Central Yiddish Cultural Association, 1957).

Fleming, Gerald, *Hitler and the Final Solution,* (Berkeley, CA: University of California Press, 1982).

Fradkin, Arnold, "Canada Ignored War Criminals for 27 Years," *The Canadian Jewish News,* January 2, 1997.

Friedman, Philip, *Their Brothers Keepers,* (New York, NY: Holocaust Library, 1978).

Friedman, Saul S., *Pogromchik: The Assassination of Simon Petlura,* (New York, NY: Hart Publishing Co., 1976).

Gehlen, Richard, *The Service: The Memoirs of General Richard Gehlen,* (New York, NY: The World Publishing Company, 1972).

Gitelman, Zvi, *Bitter Legacy: Confronting the Holocaust in the USSR,* (Bloomington, IN: Indiana University Press, 1997).

Grose, Peter, *Operation Rollback: America's Secret War behind the Iron Curtain,* (New York, NY: Houghton Mifflin Company, 2000).

Hanson, Joanna K.M., *The Civilian Population and the Warsaw Uprising of 1944,* (Cambridge, MA: Cambridge University Press, 1982).

Headland, Ronald, *Messages of Murder,* (Toronto, ON: Fairleigh Dickinson University Press, 1992).

Heike, Wolf-Dietrich, *The Ukrainian Division 'Galicia' 1943-1945: A Memoir,* (Toronto, ON: Schevchenko Scientific Society, 1988). Some may prefer the original German version, *Sie Wollten die Freiheit: Die Geschichte der Ukrainischen Division 1943-1945,* Dorheim: Podzun, Vig., 1973.

Hilberg, Raul, *The Destruction of the European Jews, 1st ed.,* (New York, NY: Harper and Row, 1961).
———. *Perpetrators, Victims, Bystanders: The Jewish Catastrophe 1933-1945,* (New York, NY: Harper Collins, 1992).

Hills, Dennis, *Tyrants and Mountains,* (London, UK: John Murray Publishers, 1982).

Himka, J-P, "World Wars," in *Encyclopedia of Ukraine,* ed., Danylo Husar Struk, V, 722-728, (Toronto, ON: University of Toronto Press, 1993).

Hohne, Heinz, *Canaris,* (London, UK: Secker and Warburg, 1979).
———. *The Order of the Death's Head: The Story of Hitler's SS,* (London, UK: Pan Books, 1972).

Horbatsch, O., "Ukrainians in Foreign Armies during World War II," in *Ukraine: A Concise Encyclopaedia,* ed,. Volodymyr Kubijovyc, II, 1086-1089, (Toronto, ON: University of Toronto Press. 1963-1971).

Hunchak, T., *U Mundyrakh Voroha,* Chas Ukrainy, Kiev 1993 (Ukrainian language).

Hunczak, Taras, "Ukrainian-Jewish Relations during the Soviet and Nazi Occupations," in *Ukraine During World War II: History and Aftermath*, ed., Yuri Boshyk, (Edmonton, AB: Canadian Institute of Ukrainian Studies,1986).

International Refugee Organization, *Manual for Eligibility Officers*.

Jaeger, H., "Anti-Bolshevist Bloc of Nations," *Wiener Library Bulletin* XVI, No.2, April 1962.

Kahane, David, *Lvov Ghetto Diary*, (Amherst, MA: University of Massachusetts Press, 1990).

Kaufman, Max, "The War Years in Latvia Revisited," in *The Jews in Latvia*, ed., M. Bobe and S. Levenberg, (Tel Aviv, Israel: Association of Latvian and Estonian Jews in Israel, 1971).

Keegan, John, *The Second World War*, (New York, NY: Penguin Books, 1989).

Kirkconnell, Watson, *Canada, Europe and Hitler*, (Toronto, ON: University of Toronto Press, 1939).

Kershaw, Ian, *Hitler, 1936-1945: Nemesis*, (New York, NY: W.W. Norton & Company, 2000).

Kirby, Dianne, "Divinely Sanctioned: The Anglo-American Cold War Alliance and the Defence of Western Civilization and Christianity, 1945-48," *Journal of Contemporary History*, Vol.35, No.3, July 2000.

Klarsfeld, Serge, *The Children of Izieu: A Human Tragedy*, (New York, NY: Harry N. Abrams, Inc., 1984).

Klee, Ernst, Willi Dressen and Volkeriess, *"The Good Old Days" The Holocaust as seen by its Perpetrators and Bystanders*, (New York, NY: The Free Press, 1988).

Knightley, Philip, *The Second Oldest Profession*, (London, UK: Andre Deutsch, 1986).

Kolisnyk, R., *Viiskova Uprava ta Ukr. Dyvizia Halychyna*, Shevchenko Scientific Society of Canada, Vol. 30, Toronto, 1990 (Ukrainian language).

Kozak, V. and L. Shanovsky, "Ukrainians in Foreign Armies from 1918," in *Ukraine: A Concise Encyclopaedia*, ed., Volodymyr Kubijovyc, II, 1080-1084, (Toronto, ON: University of Toronto Press. 1963-1971).

Kosyk, Wolodymyr, *The Third Reich and the Ukraine*, Irene Levins Rudnytzky (transl.), (New York, NY: Peter Lang, 1993).

Krausnick, Helmut, and Martin Broszat, *The Anatomy of the SS State*, (London, UK: Granada, 1968).

Krausnick, Helmut and Hans-Heinrich Wilhelm, *Die Truppe des Weltanschauungskieges; Die Einsatzgruppen der Sicherheitspolizei und der SD 1938-1942*, (Stuttgart, GR: Deutsche Verlags-Anstatlt, 1981).

Krannhals, Hanns von, *Der Warschauer Aufstand 1944*, (Frankfurt am Main, GR: Bernard & Graefe Verlag für Wehrwesen, 1964).

Krokhmaliuk, R., "Division Galizien," in *Encyclopedia of Ukraine*, ed., Volodymyr Kubijovic, 1, 680-681, (Toronto, ON: University of Toronto Press, 1993).

——. *Zahrava na Skhodi,*, Brotherhood of Veterans1st UD UNA, Vol. 1, (Toronto, ON, and New York, NY, 1978, Ukrainian language).

Kubijovic, Volodymyr, "The Ukrainians in German-Occupied Territory," in *Ukraine: A Concise Encyclopaedia*, ed., Volodymyr Kubijovic, 1, 874-876, (Toronto, ON: University of Toronto Press, 1963-1971).

——. "Ukraine During World War II," in *Ukraine: A Concise Encyclopaedia*, ed., Volodymyr Kubijovic, 1, (Toronto, ON: University of Toronto Press, 1963-1971).

——. *Encyclopedia of Ukraine*, (Toronto, ON: University of Toronto Press, 1985), Vol. 1 p. 680.

Laloy, Jean, *Yalta: hier, aujourd'hui, demain*, (Paris, France: Robert Laffont, 1988).

Landwehr, Richard, *Fighting for Freedom: The Ukrainian Volunteer Division of the Waffen-SS*, (Silver Spring, MD: Bibliophile Legion Books, 1985).

Laqueur, Walter, *The Terrible Secret: Suppression of Truth about Hitler's "Final Solution,"* (Middlesex, UK: Penguin Books, 1980).

Lettrich, Jozef, *History of Modern Slovakia*, 2nd ed., (Toronto, ON: Slovak Research and Study Centre, 1985).

Lichten, Joseph L., "A Study of Ukrainian-Jewish Relations," *The Annals of the Ukrainian Academy of Arts and Sciences in the U.S.*, Vol. V, No. 2-3, 1160-1177.

Lincoln, W. Bruce, *Red Victory: A History of the Russian Civil War*, (New York, NY: Simon and Schuster, 1989).

Litman, Jacob, *The Economic Role of Jews in Medieval Poland*, (Lanham: University Press of America, 1984).

Littlejohn, David, *The Patriotic Traitors: A History of Collaboration in German-Occupied Europe 1940-1945*, (London, UK: Heinemann, 1972).

——. *Foreign Legions of the Third Reich*, Vol. 4, (San Jose, CA: R. James Bender Publishing, 1987).

Logusz, Michael O., *The Waffen-SS 14th Grenadier Division 1943-1945*, (Atglen, PA: Schiffer Publishing Ltd. 1997).

——. *Battle of Brody*, *Veterans' News*, Toronto, 1994.

——. *Galicia Division*, Atglen Military History, (Altgrn, PA: Shiffer Publishing, Ltd., 1997).

Lowles, Nick, "Dangerous Liaisons," *Searchlight"* (London) February 2000, No 296

Luciuk, Lubomyr and Stella Hryniuk, editors, *Canada's Ukrainians; Negotiating an Identity*, (Toronto, ON: University of Toronto Press, 1991).

Luciuk, Lubomyr, "Ukraine's wartime unit never linked to war crimes," *The Globe and Mail*, March 26, 1985.

——. "Selective Justice," *New Statesman and Society*, August 19, 1985.

Markevitch, Jerzy, *Nie dali ziemi skad ich rod*, (Lublin: Wydawnictwo Lubelskie, 1965).

Markus, V., "Ukrainian Military Formations in 1938-43," in *Ukraine: A Concise Encyclopeadia*, ed., Volodymyr Kubijovic, II, 1085-1086, (Toronto, ON: University of Toronto Press, 1963-1971).

Marrus, Michael, *Unwanted: European Refugees in the Twentieth Century*, (New York, NY and Toronto, ON: Oxford University Press, 1985).

Martin, David, *The Web of Disinformation: Churchill's Yugoslav Blunder*, (New York, NY: Harcourt Brace Jovanovich, 1990).

Martin, Gilbert, *The Holocaust: A History of the Jews of Europe During the Second World War*, (New York, NY: Holt, Rhinehart and Winston, 1986).

Martynowych, Orest T., *Ukrainians in Canada*, (Edmonton, AB: Canadian Institute of Ukrainian Studies Press, 1991).

Matas, David, *Justice Delayed*, (Toronto, ON: Summerhill Press Ltd., 1987).

McCauley, Martin, *Octoberists to Bolsheviks: Imperial Russia 1905-1917*, (London, UK: Edward Arnold Publishers, 1984).

Melnycky, Peter, "Political Reaction to Ukrainian Immigrants: The 1899 Election in Manitoba," in *New Soil—Old Roots*, ed., Jaroslav Rozumnyj, (Winnipeg, MB: Ukrainian Academy of Arts and Sciences in Canada, 1983).

Motyl, Alexander J., *The Turn to the Right: The Ideological Origins and Development of Ukrainian Nationalism, 1919-1929*, (New York, NY: Columbia University, East European Monographs, 1980).

Murphy, Brendan, *The Butcher of Lyons: The Story of the Infamous Nazi Klaus Barbie*, (New York, NY: Empire Books, 1983).

Padfield, Peter, *Himmler, Reichsführer SS*, (London, UK: Papermac, 1990).

Panchuk, Bohdan, *Heroes of their Day: The Reminiscences of Bohdan Panchuk*, (Toronto, ON: The Multicultural History Society, 1983).

Pankivskyi, K., *Roky Nimetskoi Okupatsii*, Zhyttia i Mysli, Vol. 7, (New York, NY and Toronto, ON, 1965 (Ukrainian language).

Pohl, Dieter, *Nationalsozialistische Juden Verfolgung in Ostgalizien 1941-1944: Organisation und Durchführung eines staatlichen Massenverbrechens*, (Munich, GR: R. Oldenbourg Verlag, 1996)

Porter, David Haldane, "Refugee Screening Commission Report on Ukrainians in Surrendered Enemy Personnel (SEP) Camp No.347 Italy," (Rome, IT: Refugee Screening Commission, 1947, unpublished). Listed in London Public Record Office as Military, LACAB/RSC/RIC.

Possony, Stefan T., "The Ukrainian-Jewish Problem: A Historical Retrospect," *The Ukrainian Quarterly* XXXI, No. 2 (Summer) 1975.

Prokop, M., "The Ukrainian Insurgent Army," in *Ukraine: A Concise Encyclopaedia*, ed., Volodymyr Kubijovic, 2, 1089-1092, (Toronto, ON: University of Toronto Press, 1963-1971).

Prus, Edward, *Herosi spod znaku tryzuba*, (Warsaw, Polland: Institut Wydawniczy Zwiaskow Zawadowych, 1985).

Ranelagh, John, *The Agency: The Rise and Decline of the CIA*, (New York, NY: Simon and Schuster, 1986).

Reitlinger, Gerald, *The SS: Alibi of a Nation*, (London, UK: Heinemann, 1956).

Reitlinger, Gerald, *The Final Solution: The Attempt to Exterminate the Jews of Europe 1939-1945*, (New York, NY: Perpetua, 1961).

——. *A House Built on Sand*, (New York, NY: Viking, 1960).

Reshetar, John S., *The Ukrainian Revolution, 1917-1920: A Study in Nationalism*, (Princeton, NJ: Princeton University Press, 1952).

Revutsky, Abraham, (trans.), *Wrenching Times in Ukraine: Memoir of a Jewish Minister*, (St. John's, NFD: Yksuver Publishing, 1998) Originally published as *In di shvere teg oyf ukraine: zikhroynes fun a yidishn ministr* by Yiddiishe Literarisher Verlag, Berlin, 1924.

Rings, Werner, *Life with the Enemy: Collaboration and Resistance in Hitler's Europe 1939-1945*, (New York, NY: Doubleday & Co., 1982).

Rodal, Alti, *Nazi War Criminals in Canada: The Historical and Policy Setting from the 1940s to the Present*, (Ottawa, ON: Commission of Inquiry on War Criminals, 1986, unpublished manuscript).

Rückerl, Adalbert, *The Investigation of Nazi War Crimes 1945-1978: A Documentation*, Derek Rutter, (transl.), (Karlsruhe, GR: C.F. Müller, 1979).

Rudgers, David F., "The Origins of Covert Action," *Journal of Contemporary History*, Vol. 35, No.2, 2000.

Ryan, Allan A. Jr., *Quiet Neighbors: Prosecuting Nazi War Criminals in America*, (New York, NY: Harcourt Brace Jovanovich, 1984).

Saunders, Frances Stoner, *Who Paid the Piper? The CIA and the Cultural Cold War*, (London, UK: Granta Publications, 1999).

Saunders, Ronald, *Shores of Refuge: A Hundred Years of Jewish Immigration*, (New York, NY: Henry Holt & Co., 1988).

Schellenberg, Walter, *The Schellenberg Memoirs*, (London, UK: Andre Deutsch. 1956).

Schoenfeld, Joachim, *Holocaust Memories*, (Hoboken: KATV Publishing House, 1985).

Serbyn, Roman, "Alleged War Criminals, the Canadian Media and the Ukrainian Community," in *Ukraine during World War II: History and its Aftermath: A Symposium*, ed., Yuri Boshyk, (Edmonton, AB: Canadian Institute of Ukrainian Studies, 1986).

Shandruk, Pavlo, *Arms of Valor*, Roman Olesnicki, (transl.), (New York: NY: Robert Speller and Sons, 1959).

Shtul, O. and Ye. Stakhiv, "OUN Expeditionary Groups," in *Encyclopedia of Ukraine*, ed., Danylo Husar Struk, III, 740-741, (Toronto, ON: University of Toronto Press, 1993).

Simpson, Christopher, *Blowback*, (New York, NY: Weidenfeld and Nicholson, 1968).

Special Subcommittee on the Judiciary, House of Representatives, H. Res. *Displaced Persons in Europe and their Resettlement in the United States*, Washington, DC, 1950.

Spector, Shmuel, *The Holocaust of Volhynian Jews 1941-1944*, (Jerusalem: Yad Vashem, 1990).

Stein, George S., *The Waffen SS: Hitler's Elite Guard at War,1939-1945*, (Ithaca, NY: Cornell University Press, 1966).

Stetsko, Yaroslav, "The Light of Freedom from the Forests of Ukraine," *ABN Correspondence*, No. 4-6, Vol. XLIV, August-September, 1993.

Subtelny, O., *Ukraine: A History*, (Toronto, ON: University of Toronto Press, 1988), pp.472, 477, 555, 566-7.

Sudoplatov, Pavel and Anatoli Sudoplatov. *Special Tasks: The Memoirs of an Unwanted Witness: A Soviet Spymaster*, (Boston, MA: Little Brown and Company, 1994).

Syndor, Charles W., *Soldiers of Destruction: The SS Death's Head Division, 1933-1945*, (Princeton, NJ: Princeton University Press, 1977).

Tessin, Georg, *Verbände und Truppen der Deutschen Wehrmacht und Waffen-SS im Zweiten Weltkrieg 1939-1945*, (Osnabruck: Biblio-Verlag, 1978).

Time Out, "Queer of the Realm," London, June 19, 1997.

Toland, John, *Adolph Hitler*, (Garden City, NJ: Doubleday & Company, Inc., 1976).

Tolstoy, Nikolai, *Victims of Yalta*, (London, UK: Corgi Books, 1977).

Tomasevich, Jozo, *The Chetniks: War and Revolution in Yugoslavia, 1941-1945*, (Palo Alto, CA: Stanford University Press, 1975).

Trevor-Roper, Hugh R., eds., *Hitler's War Directives 1939-1945*, (London, UK: Pan Books, 1964).

Trials of War Criminals before the Nuremberg Military Tribunal Under Control Law No. 10, "The Einsatzgruppen Case" and "The RuShA Case," Vol. IV, Nuremberg: U.S. Government Printing Office, 1949.

Uustala, Evald, *The History of the Estonian People*, (London, UK: Boreas Publishing Co. Ltd., 1952).

Veryha, Wasyl, "The 'Galicia' Ukrainian Division in Polish and Soviet Literature," *The Ukrainian Quarterly*, XXXVI, No.3, Autumn, 1980: 252- 270.

——. *Along the Roads of World War II*, (Toronto, ON: New Pathway Publishers, 1980).

——. *Dorohamy Druhoi Svitovoi Viiny*, Shevchenko Scientific Society of Canada, Vol. 21, Toronto, 1981, Ukrainian language.

Wachs, Philipp-Christian, *Der Fall Theodor Oberländer (1905-1998): Ein Lehrstück deutscher Geschichte*, (Frankfurt, GR: Campus Verlag, 2000).

Wegner, Bernd, *The Waffen-SS: Organization, Ideology and Function*, Ronald Webster (transl.), (Oxford, UK: Basil Blackwell Ltd, 1990).

Wheeler, Mark, "Yugoslavia," in *The Oxford Companion to World War II*, ed., I.C.B. Dear, 1295, (Oxford, UK: Oxford University Press, 1985).

Weisberger, Bernard A., *Cold War, Cold Peace*, (New York, NY: American Heritage Publishing Co., 1984).

Wells, Leon Weliczker, *The Janowska Road*, Washington, DC, Holocaust Library, 1999.

Wistrich, Robert, *Who's Who in Nazi Germany*, (London, UK: Weidenfeld and Nicholson, 1982).

Wrangel, Petr Nikolaevich, *Memoirs of General Wrangel*, (New York, NY: R. Speller, 1957).

Yaremko, Michael, *From Separation to Unity*, Shevchenko Scientific Society, 1967.

Yurkevich, M., "Organization of Ukrainian Nationalists," in *Encyclopedia of Ukraine*, ed., Danylo Husar Struk, III, 708-710, (Toronto, ON: University of Toronto Press, 1993).

Yuzyk, Paul, "The Political Achievements of Ukrainians in Canada," In *New Soil—Old Roots: The Ukrainian Experience in Canada*, ed., Jaroslav Rozumnyj, (Winnipeg, MB: Ukrainian Academy of Arts and Sciences in Canada, 1983).

ARCHIVAL DOCUMENTS CITED

U.S. National Archives (Washington, DC)

U.S. National Archives, Microfilm Publications, Call No. T-175, Roll No. 74, "Records of the Reich Leader of the SS and the Chief of German Police" (Himmler's papers)

U.S. National Archives, Microfilm, Call No. T-175, Roll No. 94, "Himmler's Speech to the Division."

U.S. National Archives, Microfilm, Call No. T-175, Folder 332

U.S. National Archives, Microfilm, Call No. T-175, Folder 263

U.S. National Archives, Microfilm, Call No. T-175, Folder 74

U.S. National Archives, Microfilm, Call No. T-580, Folder 89. "Governor of the District of Galicia to the *Kreishauptleute, Stadthauptman, Lemberg Stadt und Landkommissare,*" Lemberg, April 28, 1943

The following U.S. National Archives microfilm rolls provided additional background information but were not specifically cited:

T-715, 74

T-313, 400, 401, 413

T-313, 401, 413

T-580, 89

State Archives of Ukrainian SSR

State Archives of Ukrainian SSR (Lviv) "Statement of Witness" (ACT), May 24, 1944

State Archives of Ukrainian SSR (Lviv), "Statement of Witness Herasym Myktovych Makukh."

State Archives of Ukrainian SSR (Kiev), "Telegram from Dr. Hasse, Governor of Lublin District to Dr. O. Losacker, Minister of Interior, General Government." February 6, 1943

State Archives of Ukrainian SSR, (Kiev), "Chronicles of the SS Halychyna Division."

Centralle Stelle der Landesjustizverwaltungen (Ludwigsburg)

Centralle Stelle der Landjustizverwaltungen, "Die Waffen-SS; einem Auszug über die SS-Division Galizien."

United Nations War Crimes Commission

UNWCC, 4645/FR/G/1880, "Correspondence of the High Commissioner for Germany," July 1, 1953 to Commander-in-Chief, U.S. Army Europe.

UNWCC, 214/P/G/26

UNWCC, 215/P/G/21

UNWCC, 79/P/G/16, April 24, 1944

UNWCC, 4889/P/G

U.S. Freedom of Information

U.S. Freedom of Information, CIC Agent Report, dossier number ZF10016, Volume 1, "Shandruk, General commanding 1st Ukrainian Army," submitted November 2, 1948.

U.S. Freedom of Information, declassified Secret CIC, dated May 19, 1950

London Public Record Office
PRO, TS 26/903

PRO, FO 371/48815

PRO, FO 1020/42

PRO, FO 371/15679. "Disposal of Ukrainians in Italy."

PRO, FO 371/64722

PRO, FO 371/67370

PRO, FO 371/67370

PRO, FO 371/66604, "Refugee Defense Committee to His Excellency Lord Inverchapel," February 19, 1947

PRO, FO 371/66710, "Hector McNeil to Refugee Department," April 2, 1947

PRO, FO 371/56791

PRO, FO 371/66605

PRO, FO 371/66712, "Felix Wirth to Tom Driberg," June 7, 1947.

PRO, FO 371/66712, Carruthers, letter. Date indistinct.

PRO, FO 371/66712, "Letter to Carruthers signed by P. Gore-Booth," July 9, 1947; "M.L. Hyam to R.H.S. Crossman," June 12, 1947; "Memorandum, Wilkinson to Crossman"; "Unsigned to L.W. Carruthers," July 9, 1947; Extract from *Manchester Guardian*, "Ukrainians in England," June 12, 1947

PRO, FO 371/3362

PRO, 371/72039, "Wilkinson's discussion with Coal Board."

PRO, FO 371/166590/136950, "Draft Recommendation by United Nations War Crimes Commission," April 21, 1947

PRO, WO 32/13749

PRO, WR, February 24, 1947

PRO, WO 204/1044, "LACAB from Refugee Screening Commission," February 8, 1947

PRO, HO 213/1881

Public Archives of Canada
PAC, RG 25, Vol. 1896, File 165, pt.1

PAC, RG 25, Vol. 1896, File 165, Part II

PAC, MG 30, E350, vol. 1

PAC, RG 25, GI, Vol. 1896, File 165, Part III

PAC, RG 18, Vol. 120, Privy Council of Canada, Subject: War Criminals

PAC, RG 25, Vol. 2108 AR 405/4

PAC, RG 76, Vol. 656, File 53802, Part 2

PAC, RG 26, Vol. 115, File I-20-20, June 28, 1949

RG 76, Vol. 656, File B53802, part 2, Laval Fortier to C.E.S. Smith, June 6, 1950

Security Panel Document SP-119, "Immigration Security Policy, Nazis, Fascists and Collaborators"

Security Panel, 42nd Meeting, May 15, 1952

INDEX

CHILE AND THE NAZIS FROM HITLER TO PINOCHET

Graeme S. Mount

Based on documentary evidence from the archives of the Chilean Foreign Office, and from U.S., British, German, and, intercepted, Japanese documents, Mount is one of the first authors to provide evidence of the events and circumstances surrounding Chile's reluctance to sever diplomatic ties with Nazi Germany allowing it to maximize its opportunities there, influencing Chilean politicians, military operations, and the popular media.

> Mount reveals the conflict, the espionage, and the difficulty with policy which resulted from widespread Nazi influence...all issues that continue to be of importance even now, after the return of democracy to Chile. —Professor Florentino Rodao, President of the Asóciacion de Estudios del Pacífico

> A most impressive book, based on a variety of archival and oral historical sources from three continents...about a hitherto little-known, but fascinating aspect of twentieth-century history. —Stan Hordes, Latin American and Iberian Institute, University of New Mexico

GRAEME S. MOUNT teaches history at Laurentian University in Sudbury, Ontario.

204 pages
Paperback ISBN: 1-55164-192-5 $19.99
Hardcover ISBN: 1-55164-193-3 $48.99

HOW THE FIRST WORLD WAR BEGAN THE TRIPLE ENTENTE AND THE COMING OF THE GREAT WAR OF 1914-1918

Edward E. McCullough

By reviewing the events of the pre-1914 period, the responsibility of Germany for the outbreak of the war is reconsidered. The book begins with a short account of the situation after the Franco-Prussian War, when France was isolated and Germany secure in the friendship of all the other Great Powers, and proceeds to describe how France created an anti-German coalition. The account of the estrangement of England from Germany attempts to correct the usual pro-British prejudice and to explain the real causes of this development.

> Historian Edward McCullough pulls no punches in this controversial book. He offers new insights into the Great War. —*St. Catharine Standard*

For 32 years, EDWARD E. MCCULLOUGH taught as a university teacher at Concordia University in Montrèal.

368 pages, bibliography, index
Paperback ISBN: 1-55164-140-2 $28.99
Hardcover ISBN: 1-55164-141-0 $57.99

THE GERMAN HISTORIANS

Hitler's Willing Executioners and Daniel Goldhagen
Fred Kautz

In 1997, Daniel Goldhagen published his ground-breaking international bestseller entitled *Hitler's Willing Executioners*. Drawing on a wealth of unused archival materials, principally the testimony of the killers themselves, Goldhagen took his readers into the killing fields where Germans voluntarily hunted Jews like animals, tortured them, and then posed cheerfully for snapshots with their victims.

An explosive work, exhaustively documented, and richly researched, it offered irrefutable proof that should have forced a fundamental revision in our thinking and recording of events, but instead of seeing this work as a chance to seriously re-evaluate what happened in Germany, the influential German historians angrily rejected it with accusations of a lack of scholarship, to a reaction against its popularity. This investigative work deals with that historical bias and the resulting complicity.

Fred Kautz, himself an historian, could not understand why leading, professional, German historians refused to take up the gauntlet thrown by Goldhagen. *The German Historians* is the result of his attempt to get to the bottom of this mystery. First he presents an overview of Goldhagen's work, then he subjects the public, and private, utterances, and the written reviews of three prominent German historians—Hans Mommsen, Hans-Ulrich Wehler, and Eberhard Jackel—to a very close examination, and finally he draws some conclusions, and warnings, about how we record history.

> Kautz points out that all the major German Holocaust historians were trained by the earlier generation of historians, all of whom were in one way or another involved with the Nazi regime, and he exposes just how restrictive and punitive the German academic system is of anyone who adopts an approach not favoured by those in authority. —Harry Redner, *The Australia/Israel Review*

FRED KAUTZ, a Canadian of German origin, received his BA from Brock University, St. Catharines, his MA from Carleton University, Ottawa. He is currently a freelance historical researcher working and living in Darmstadt, Germany.

216 pages, photographs, bibliography, index
Paperback ISBN: 1-55164-212-3 $24.99
Hardcover ISBN: 1-55164-213-1 $53.99
History / Military History

GERMANY EAST DISSENT AND OPPOSITION

Bruce Allen

This work on the scope of dissent in East Germany integrates the post World War II uprising and the birth of the opposition forces with the 1980s social change movements, as well as developments since the destruction of the Berlin Wall.

> Thoroughly documented, but readable enough to allow readers to see dissent for what it is: the inevitable uprising of a suffering people.—*Books in Canada*

BRUCE ALLEN, an autoworker and trade-union activist, is author of numerous articles on development in Central and Eastern Europe.

191 pages, biography
Paperback ISBN: 0-921689-96-9 $18.99
Hardcover ISBN: 0-921689-97-7 $47.99

EUROPE CENTRAL AND EAST

Marguerite Mendell, Klaus Nielsen, editors

This volume of essays examine changes in the former USSR and the eastern bloc thereby placing them in a larger historical and sociological perspective. Contributors include: Mihailo Crnobrnja, Jerzy Hausner, Bob Jessop, Tadeusz Kowalik, Domenico Mario Nuti, Birgit Muller, Hilary Wainwright, Claire Wallace.

> The list of participants is impressive.—*Canadian Book Review Annual*

MARGUERITE MENDELL and KLAUS NIELSEN are associated with the Karl Polanyi Institute in Canada, and internationally. Part of the series *Critical Perspectives on Historic Issues*.

298 pages
Paperback ISBN: 1-895431-90-5 $19.99
Hardcover ISBN: 1-895431-91-3 $48.99

LOOKING EAST LEFTWARDS FORMER "STATE SOCIALIST" WORLD

David Mandel

This collection, covering Russia, the Ukraine, Belarus, Hungary, Poland, China, and Cuba combines a unique variety of genres, interviews, diaries, and essays, that provide both analytical insight and a concrete sense of the complex socio-political and cultural processes at work in these societies. Key, in this account of the "post-Communist" regime, is an essay by the editor, entitled "Travels Through Russia, Belarus and the Ukraine: Diaries, Summer—Fall 1996".

DAVID MANDEL teaches political science at the University of Quebec, in Montreal.

250 pages, index
Paperback ISBN: 1-55164-098-8 $24.99
Hardcover ISBN: 1-55164-099-6 $53.99

THE PEOPLE AS ENEMY

The Leaders' Hidden Agenda in World War II
John Spritzler

More than forty-six million soldiers and civilians perished in World War II, not counting more than five million Jews killed in the Holocaust. Whole cities were bombed for the express purpose of killing civilians by the hundreds of thousands.

And yet this war is known as "the good war" on the grounds that the aim of the Allied nations of Great Britain, the United States, the Soviet Union and China, and the outcome of the war, was to save the world from being enslaved by the Axis (Fascist) nations of Germany, Italy and Japan who intended to establish a "master race" tyranny worse than anything the world had ever seen.

That is the official view of the war—the one we have all been taught—but presented here in *The People As Enemy*, is a very different, and disturbing view. This alternative view argues that the aims of the national leaders were not democracy and self-determination, but were, as wars generally are, opportunities to suppress class rebellion—to intimidate working people everywhere from rising up against elite power.

Spritzler maintains that our understanding of World War II is especially important today because the myths of World War II are the same myths that are being used in the "war against terrorism" by government and corporate leaders to control people and pursue ends that have nothing to do with protecting us from terrorism.

> The research is impressive. You do an excellent job unearthing the instances of class conflict, and internal opposition during the "good war." You make a strong argument, well-documented…your point of view needs to be considered seriously. —Howard Zinn, *A People's History of the United States*

JOHN SPRITZLER holds a Doctor of Science degree (in Biostatistics) from the Harvard School of Public Health where he is employed as a Research Scientist engaged in AIDS clinical trials.

216 pages, photographs, bibliography, index
Paperback ISBN: 1-55164-216-6 $24.99
Hardcover ISBN: 1-55164-217-4 $53.99
History / Cultural Studies